The

# VINEYARD

at the

# END OF

# THE WORLD

The

# VINEYARD

at the

# END OF

# THE WORLD

Maverick Winemakers and
the Rebirth of Malbec

# IAN MOUNT

W. W. NORTON & COMPANY

NEW YORK   LONDON

M(50)

For information about permission to reproduce selections
from this book, write to Permissions,
W. W. Norton & Company, Inc.,
500 Fifth Avenue, New York, NY 10110

JUL . . 2012

For information about special discounts for bulk purchases,
please contact W. W. Norton Special Sales at
specialsales@wwnorton.com or 800-233-4830

Manufacturing by Courier/Westford
Book design by Ellen Cipriano Design
Production manager: Julia Druskin

ISBN: 978-0-393-08019-3

W. W. Norton & Company, Inc.
500 Fifth Avenue, New York, N.Y. 10110
www.wwnorton.com

W. W. Norton & Company Ltd.
Castle House, 75/76 Wells Street, London W1T 3QT

1 2 3 4 5 6 7 8 9 0

*For Robert Henry Mount (1930–1995),*
*who always appreciated a good story,*
*and a good wine.*

# CONTENTS

# Contents

# PREFACE

*The Vineyard at the End of the World* tells the remarkable story of how an economically, geographically, and politically isolated country became one of the world's great wine powers. The story is set in an era in which an increasingly broad part of humanity started buying wine, a beverage whose consumption had previously been limited to international elites and more humble natives of traditional wine cultures. Argentina had the luck to appear on the international scene just as this mass of neophyte drinkers was being seduced by the romance and history—the *Tao*—that makes wine different from vodka or beer. But Argentina's success did not result from mere circumstance or luck; this nation on the far curve of the globe would not have enjoyed such success without its four centuries of winemaking experience, or without a series of political and economic events that, at the end of the twentieth century, brought it back into the international fold after decades as a deeply troubled state. This book travels on two rails then: wine and Argentina. Why does a simple drink of fermented grapes fascinate us so? And what is it about Argentina that inspired such captivating wines?

To illustrate those questions, I'll start with two anecdotes that brought me to this book.

...

During March 2008, in the middle of a new vineyard on the outskirts of Vista Flores, a tiny Argentine town in the Andes rain shadow, Brian Gillespie squatted next to a row of fragile young vines. Gillespie was grasping a sprig of tiny grapes that had just been handed to him, the first fruit from his vineyard. He rubbed his free hand over the smooth dome of his shaved pate. He was a bit choked up; his eyes were damp. "It sounds cheesy," he said to me, "but it's like a dream beginning to come true." By day the creative director of a San Francisco marketing agency, Gillespie was on a month-long winemaking internship in Mendoza, where he and his wife had purchased 5 acres—for $125,000—at a private vineyard development called the Vines of Mendoza.

I was intrigued that two thirty-something professionals like Gillespie and his wife were willing to invest such a tidy sum of money in a vineyard, especially one that they didn't expect to return a big profit: "If we don't sell one bottle of wine, that's not the point. We're creating something and it's something we're doing together," Gillespie told me. "It's like going to Vegas in a really big way. I'm going to have a good time, and if it doesn't work out it was a great experience." I was even more intrigued to learn that two of the three founders of the Vines of Mendoza were American, that they had raised $3.4 million in seed capital, and that they had bought or optioned 1,500 acres for their turnkey vineyard project, in which armchair Mondavis buy parcels of land and pay the Vines of Mendoza an annual fee to care for the vineyard and make the wine. The two friendly, laid-back American founders were Michael Evans, a forty-six-year-old political campaign worker with straw-tinged hair and a farmer's perpetual sunburn; and his friend David Garrett, forty-two, a six-foot four-inch serial entrepreneur with a prep-schooler's easy slouch. They had visited Argentina after John Kerry's loss in the 2004 presidential campaign left Evans out of a job, and they had fallen in love with the country and its wine. Neither they nor their investors were naïve, and their buyers seemed to understand the risks. There was something in these mountain vineyards that impassioned people, I realized, and there was money to be made in that.

A year after Gillespie caressed his first grapes, I had a minor operation that demanded I spend a night in a Buenos Aires hospital. My room filled me with nostalgia for the *Rockford Files* 1970s of my youth: chipped iron bed, flickering fluorescent ceiling lamp, and floor tiled in a gray with aspirations to purple. My doctor was an Argentine classic: well educated in a book sense and also well trained in improvisation by the country's topsy-turvy economy. She was a petite, hilarious Corsican with skin tanned to a leathery nut brown and a pack of Marlboro reds peeking from the hip pocket of her frayed lab coat.

Like doctors everywhere, she was an expert in insurance plan arcana, and she pointed out that my insurance gave its members a hundred-peso allowance for incidental expenses. I would be in the hospital only twelve hours, my doctor noted, but still, it would be a shame to waste a hundred pesos (about thirty dollars at the time). What I should do, she said, was get the hospital's café menu and order the best bottle of wine on it. But, she warned, I had to remember to tell the nurse's aide who delivered the wine to leave the bottle corked.

I already knew that wine ran like water in Argentina. As Familia Zuccardi winery owner José Alberto Zuccardi had told me, "We incorporate wine into the family table as children. Wine with soda is typical for kids of five or six years of age. For us it's not alcohol; it's nourishment." But my doctor's advice made a deeper point about wine's central importance to Argentine culture: not only was wine so prevalent in Argentina that even hospitals had wine lists; it was also valuable enough to be worth engaging in gimmickery to get.

...

One of the wine industry's common jokes is this: "How do you make a small fortune in wine?" The punch line, of course, is "Start with a large one." While the world's top wineries do well economically, many others regularly stumble and are put on the auction block, in part because their products are not needed. One of the trade secrets of the wine industry is that it churns out far more wine than its customers want to drink. In recent years, EU officials have tried to introduce measures to stabilize the industry's untenable economics by pulling vines and marketing European wine overseas. As of 2007, Europe was producing about 1.7 billion bottles more than it sold annually—enough for every Parisian to have two bottles a day for a year—and the European Union was spending almost $680 million a year distilling surplus wine into industrial alcohol.

Yet there is an almost endless supply of aspiring vintners who are willing to pay to join the game. Of course, some of the buyers have reason to believe they will turn a profit. The Chinese buyers who picked up five Bordeaux châteaux in the last three years were no doubt encouraged by the fact that, in 2010, Bordeaux wine exports to Hong Kong and China doubled. But for many, the romance of being a winery owner outweighs all economic reality.

To aspiring winemakers, wine epitomizes the undeniable lure of aristocracy, righteousness, and art. The classic image of a winery owner's retreat—a castlelike château, full of slightly threadbare antiques, that is nestled among the rolling vineyards of Bordeaux—practically screams of nobility. But it is not a sloppy, dissipative gentility; there is something honest, true, and joyful about the work (or at least about our image of it). A winemaker is an aristocratic farmer who dirties his hands while trying to coax great fruit from capricious vines. And what he creates from that fruit is not merely a product. It is thought to express history, passion, and national identity. Like Picassos and Matisses—and unlike beer—the world's top vintages are stored for decades and sold at auction; a 2010 Hong Kong auction set a new record when a buyer spent almost $700,000 for three bottles of Châteaux Lafite Rothschild 1869. "One bottle is worth $15,000, and it's called wine. Another is worth $3, and it's called wine," says Argentine viticulturist Pedro Marchevsky. "That doesn't happen in other industries. You buy bread and there is no $1,000 bread and $3 bread. Even in cars it's not a thousand to one in the price."

From the points of view of both winery owners and the drinkers they sell to, what is important to remember is that wine is more than a drink: it's a story. To command top prices, a winery owner has to make a delicious liquid and get high scores from the usual magazines, of course, but he also has to market the story—the aristocratic righteousness, the art, the uniqueness of his winery—that brought him into the business in the first place. Having a good wine is great, but it's only the cost of entry. "These days, making good wine is not enough. A lot of people are making good wine. It's difficult to sell wine if you have to show you're so much better than the next guy," Donald Hess, the Swiss owner of Argentina's high-altitude Bodega Colomé winery and the Napa Valley's Hess Collection, explained to *Departures* magazine. "You have to have a good story, a true story. In Napa we are known as the winery with the art collection. Here in Argentina we have the highest vineyard in the world."

Selling image is part of the marketing for any beverage, of course. But wine plays in a different league than beer or vodka, because it is so much more expensive and so much more fraught with intimidating connoisseurship. With its multiple price levels and social class gradations, wine is also an intrinsically aspirational drink. Those who drink it are forever looking up at the next step on the wine ladder. Wine is also unique in that it is a communal product. The kind of wine we buy says something about our knowledge of history, agriculture, chemistry, present, and past. After making our choice, we display the bottle on the table like some sort of hunting trophy, even, or especially, in the most expensive restaurants. *"How will drinking this in public make me look good?"* is the question that the winemaker must answer. To reach the pinnacle of the contemporary industry and charge a hundred dollars for a bottle of fermented grape juice, a winemaker has to convince today's clientele that they will look both aristocratic and savvy by wrapping themselves in his winery's story.

The wine world comprises five basic levels: the winery owner and his technical staff, the importer and/or distributor, the reviewer, the retail store or restaurant, and the consumer. Until a point in the not-so-distant past—the 1980s—this was a fairly fossilized chain. Wealthy international wine drinkers drank French wines, largely from Bordeaux wineries that had been ranked in a famous 1855 classification that Napoléon III had requested in preparation for that year's Exposition Universelle in Paris, and they paid prices set by the local *negociants* wine merchants. More humble drinkers in wine cultures like Italy, France, and Spain bought what they knew and could afford, usually from their region. In this system, reviewers had little power; and the consumers, even less. There was almost no way, either commercially or culturally, for a new wine to break into such a world.

But then Americans got into wine drinking beginning in the 1970s and '80s. In fact, they did so with such enthusiasm that in 2010 the United States passed France to be the biggest consumer of wine on the planet. Because most Americans were ignorant of and largely uninterested in traditional French château rankings—they just wanted a good amount of quality for their money—their naïveté forced the industry to design new ways of marketing and selling. Thus, one saw the rising power of American review publications, like the *Wine Spectator* and Robert Parker Jr.'s *Wine Advocate*, which used plain language to advise these novice drinkers on what was worth their money. Soon the world witnessed an explosion of wine from previously unsung countries, as meritocratic Americans sought out good deals, the more unusual the better. In a society where consumers are more interested in the relationship between a wine's price and quality than in the fame of its name, France slipped, and Australia, Chile, New Zealand, and South Africa rose.

But there was something unique about Argentina. While Australia, Chile, and other New World countries make great wines, Argentina is the only one with an Old World wine culture, a multicentury history in which wine played as important a role as meat or pasta or milk. But it is still very much a part of the New World and has been wrought by immigration in a very New World way.

The more time one spends in Argentina, the easier it is to see how this country produced the writer Jorge Luis Borges, who often explores the idea of the palimpsest—a slate written upon and wiped clean, only to be written on again. It is a country with a culture reimagined multiple times, each version inscribed upon the ruins of the last, and consequently as fascinating and confusing as a Gordian knot.

Simultaneously Italian, Spanish, Syrian, Jewish, German, indigenous, and English, Argentina is a Byzantine mix of often contradictory cultural currents. Whereas the queues at stores and government offices are strictly ordered via a numbered chit system, the roads are a high-speed free-for-all where lane markers and stop signs are largely ornamental. Or, while it is rude to state what one wants at a business meeting, at least not before spending several hours over coffee, it is more or less acceptable to beat the living crap out of a fan of the opposing team at a *fútbol* match. The populace's representatives have installed an elaborate web of laws and rules, many of them quite reasonable, which the populace then spends its considerable intellectual and creative resources evading (a mentality known as *viveza criolla*). The country is rich in resources and educated people, yet it has suffered so many financial crises that the most respected business talent is the ability to improvise with the paltry tools at hand, a skill known as *atalo con alambre*, or "tie it with wire." It is a *machista* culture, yet men kiss on meeting and parting. And while many adults drink at every dinner, it is wildly uncouth to get drunk.

Because of this convoluted and fascinating culture, Argentina intoxicates many of its visitors. With its gauchos, open plains, wine, and tango, Argentine culture is redolent with the freedom of the frontier. At the same time, Argentina's old Italian winemaking families have histories that anchor their industry in tradition. When the most recent wave of foreign winemakers began coming to Argentina's western wine regions in the late 1980s and early 1990s, they were faced with the country's mix of old and new. Argentines had been making wine for four hundred years, and as of 1970, Buenos Aires was third only to Paris and Rome in world wine-consuming capitals. Vineyards were spread along the Andean range from Salta, San Juan, and Mendoza in the desert north to the Patagonian provinces of Río Negro and Neuquén in the south. Not only was the geography diverse, but the varied vine varietals ran from well-known Cabernet Sauvignon and Merlot to what would soon become Argentina's gems: the inky Malbec, the citrus-tinged Torrontés, and the fruity Bonarda. And the vineyard land was beautiful. The Andean west's towering mountain range and wide-open vistas are both postcard perfect and monumentally intimidating—a place where Old World charm and elegance meets the New World's Wild West. It was hard to see Mendoza after one of its winter dustings of snow, its vineyards' silent rows of virginal white backdropped by mountains, and not want a piece of it.

I was lucky enough to arrive in Argentina in 2005, when it was truly beginning to bloom after the 2002 financial collapse and peso devaluation destroyed its economy. Argentina has been party to many disasters, its history a long chain of near greatness ruined by economic mismanagement, military coups, and natural disasters, but the collapse of 2002 was a necessary clearing of the pipes. It served as the second half of the country's two-part reinsertion into a globalized world. The first step was President Carlos Menem's 1990s regime, which, while corrupt, opened the economy to foreign investment that renewed many industries, wine-making included. The second part was the 2002 devaluation, which made Argentina and its products, especially the newly great wine from refurbished wineries, tantalizingly cheap for foreigners bearing dollars and euros (not to mention profitable for its producers).

And so, Argentina's west became a magnet for any foreign or local vintner who had money to spend. Winemakers were so enchanted by Argentina's physical and cultural *terroir*—that elusive mix of soil, climate, and history—that in the 1990s they invested some $1.5 billion in the Argentine wine industry, with $1 billion of that coming from overseas. As late as 2008, when an acre of good vineyard land in California's Napa Valley could go for up to $300,000, an acre in Mendoza could still be found for as little as $4,000. With an investment of $200,000—or less—one could, at least in a minor way, join the winemaking aristocracy. With its homegrown talent, beautiful land, and cheap prices, Argentina seemed to be, in the wine industry, the world's last wide-open space, an oenophile's slightly threadbare Shangri-la, the vineyard at the end of the world.

City of Mendoza

•Escorihuela •Godoy Cruz

Potrerillos

Maipú
•Zuccardi

•Chacras de Coria •La Rural
•Trapiche

Alta Vista Enrique Foster •Lopez
Nieto Senetiner •Trivento
Vistalba• •Luigi Bosca •Luján de Cuyo
Renacer•
Terrazas de los Andes •Mendel
•Benegas

•Domaine St. Diego •Esmeralda
Achaval• Perdriel Altos las Hormigas
Ferrer• •Norton Junín•
Ruca Malen•
Viña Cobos• Angelica
Dominio del Plata• •Agrelo Vineyard
Chandon• Rivadavia•
Catena Zapata•
La Pirámide Vineyard
Pulenta Estate•

86 •Ugarteche
•Domingo Vineyard
Adrianna •Tupungato
Vineyard
Sophenia•
•Azul
Salentein•
MENDOZA
89 40

Vines of
94 Mendoza Lurton •Tunuyán
•
•Vista Flores
Clos de los Siete• 92
Nicasia Vineyard •Altocedro
La Consulta• •San Carlos
•Finca La Celia
•O. Fournier
40

# SALTA

City of Salta

Cerrillos

La Merced

El Carril

Payogasta

Cachi

Cuesta del Obispo

Chicoana

33

Valle
Encantado

42

Parque Nacional
Los Cardones

Cnel Moldes

Seclantás

Molinos

• Colomé

La Viña

68

40

Garganta del Diablo
El Anfiteatro

San Carlos

Corralito

El Sapo

Los Castillos

San Pedro
de Yacochuya •

El Esteco

Finca Quara • Cafayate

José L. Mounier •

Etchart •

# PATAGONIA:
# NEUQUÉN and
# RÍO NEGRO

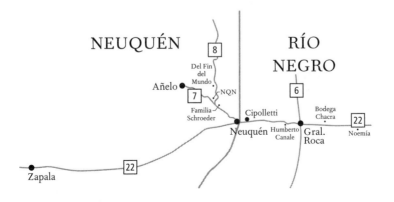

NEUQUÉN

RÍO
NEGRO

8

Del Fin
del
Mundo

Añelo

7

NQN

Familia
Schroeder

6

Cipolletti

Bodega
Chacra

22

Neuquén

Humberto
Canale

Gral.
Roca

Noemía

22

Zapala

# A BOTTLE OF WINE
# AT LUNCH

I T'S A LATE-SUMMER DAY in 1823 in the Andean foothills of the western Argentine province of Mendoza. Grape pickers are harvesting vineyards planted alongside improvised manmade canals. In defense against the pummeling high-altitude sun, the pickers wear hats or wrap their heads in scarves. Just to the west, the perpetually snowcapped Andes contrast with the land's aridity. The region's indigenous name, Cuyo, means "country of sand." As they pick, the farmers nervously flit their eyes to the occasional clouds that pop over from Chile on the other side of the cordillera. Would this cloud drop one of the ferocious sheets of hail that strip one farmer's vineyard of leaves and grapes while leaving his neighbor's untouched? The farmers in these foothill valleys receive a mere eight inches of precipitation per year, and much of that miserly blessing comes in the form of crop-killing hail—as if the farmers need any reminder that despite all their attempts, Mother Nature remains in control.

On this summer day, not far from the harvesting farmers, a young soldier named Manuel de Olazábal steps into the private rooms of his commanding officer, General José de San Martín.

...

Born in 1778 on the banks of the Uruguay River in the subtropical Argentine province of Corrientes, San Martín had striking black eyes, thick arched eyebrows, a large aquiline beak, and a boundless reserve of patriotism. The Argentine-born son of a Spanish colonial lieutenant governor, San Martín personified the clash between Old World and New. Shortly before his sixth birthday, his parents took San Martín back to their native Spain, where he began the military career expected for someone of his lineage. He fought against the Moors in North Africa and helped push back Napoléon's invasion of the Iberian Peninsula, reaching the rank of lieutenant colonel. During these battles he met James Duff, a Scottish noble who introduced him to fellow New World–born soldiers who dreamt of liberating their birthplace. Soon, San Martín turned against Spain, and in 1811 he traveled to London, where he joined the Gran Reunión Americana, a secret anticolonial society founded by Venezuelan independence leader Francisco de Miranda. The next year San Martín embarked on a ship to Buenos Aires, and after a fifty-day voyage he was commissioned as an officer by the fledgling country's independence-minded government. As a comment on his dark coloring and hinterland birthplace, the South American elite referred to San Martín as "The Mulatto" and "The Paraguayan." Despite this snobbish treatment, San Martín spent the next decade fighting to free Argentina, Chile, and Peru from Spanish colonial rule. For that, he was awarded a new nickname: *El Libertador* ("The Liberator"). Argentina's very own George Washington.

The Liberator was distracted when the twenty-three-year-old Olazábal entered his office. Several months earlier, San Martín had resigned his position as *Protector del Perú*—a kind of military viceroy—and returned to Mendoza, where he had once been governor of Cuyo. His resignation had brought him somewhat closer to his young wife, María de los Remedios de Escalada—twenty years his junior—who was still six hundred miles to the east, in Buenos Aires. Escalada was gravely ill, but San Martín's efforts to visit her had been thwarted. A government minister—Argentina's future first president, Bernardino Rivadavia—had denied his request to visit on the grounds that it wouldn't be safe for San Martín, a partisan of Argentina's interior provinces who had sided with regional leaders against those who had wanted to centralize power in Buenos Aires. In reality, Rivadavia was one of the sore centralists, and he worried that San Martín's presence might inspire his political enemies to action.

On this day, the Liberator's mind was occupied by a less urgent problem. On the desk in front of him sat four bottles of wine and a small printing press. The general fiddled with several labels. San Martín was obviously up to something. "Why don't you guess what I'm doing?" he said. "No sir," said Olazábal. "Look here then: when we invaded Chile in 1817, I left about 50 bottles of muscatel at my farm," San Martín said. "Of course I'd totally forgotten about it, but a few days ago the man who watches the farm, Pedro Alvíncula Moyano, brought me a dozen of the bottles."

Olazábal waited in silence. San Martín was known for his Spartan tastes; he always took lunch alone in his room—a bit of soup, a piece of meat, and a small dessert, all eaten with the same utensil. But he was also an oenophile who liked to compare the wines of Europe, especially those from Spain, and discuss the soil, flavors, and origin of each. On this day he was going to dine with Olazábal, a Colombian named Mosquera, and Antonio Arcos, the former head of the Corps of Engineers of San Martín's army.

"Today I have Mosquera, Arcos, and you at my table, and with dessert I'm going to ask for these bottles," he told the young soldier. "But I'm going to swap the labels so the Spanish wines from Málaga read 'Mendoza' and the Mendoza wines say 'Málaga.' You'll see how we Americans are, how we always prefer imports."

Arcos and Mosquera arrived, and over lunch they reminisced with San Martín. As the men finished their plates and the time for dessert arrived, San Martín turned to Olazábal and asked him for the bottles he had previously prepared.

"We'll see if you are all in agreement with me about the superiority of Mendozan wines," San Martín said. It was an absurd claim. People like Mosquera and Arcos—men well educated in the oenological superiority of Old World wine—would never agree.

San Martín poured the Spanish wine that had been labeled "Mendoza" and tasted it alongside his guests. "And?" he said with a smile. "Yes . . . it's good," Mosquera said with little conviction as he studied the play of light through the wine swirling in his glass. "Nonetheless," Arcos said, with a touch of smugness, "I'd say that for it to be truly complete it needs a little aroma."

"Fine," San Martín said as he poured the wine labeled "Málaga" into new glasses. "Let's see what you think of this one." His guests carefully inhaled the scent of the supposed Spanish wine and slowly let it flow over their tongues. "Ah!" exclaimed Arcos. "There's a *huge* difference." "This is *exquisite*," Mosquera said. "There's no comparison." San Martín burst into laughter. "You're just a bunch of scoundrels dazzled by a label," he exclaimed, explaining to his guests the trick he had played on them.

From their facile, piffling critiques, San Martín knew his companions had no idea which was the better of the wines, or why. Their words were the empty expression of the universal prejudice for Old World over New. Worse, if even these men, soldiers who had risked death to free the New World from its European masters, held such prejudices, what hope did Argentina have of surviving?

That question would have to wait for another day. Or another century. When San Martín sat down with Arcos, Mosquera, and Olazábal, Argentine wine already had a two-and-a-half century history of being dismissed, suppressed, and ignored. It would suffer another 170 years before foreigners and Argentines would come around to San Martín's opinion.

San Martín, however, was not disposed to wait. After he had finished the friendly rebuke of his comrades, the general turned to the young Olazábal. "Serve me some of the Mendozan wine, son," San Martín said, laughing. "And save the Málaga for my guests."

As San Martín realized back in 1823, the story of Argentine wine is a tale of greatness emerging despite cultural prejudices, missed opportunities, institutional inertia, and rampant corruption. It's also an immigrant's tale of man breaking desert and turning it to his wishes, an entrepreneur's tale of generations of hardworking Argentines who risked everything in the name of progress, and a winemaker's tale of coaxing sublime taste from fruit on the frontier of civilization. Most important, it's a story of a unique and beautiful place, one that these men could not have conquered or invented alone. Not without exquisite luck. Not without the perfect land. And not without an unloved grape with an unlovely name: Malbec.

# CHAPTER 1

# PLANTING THE
# NEW WORLD

*La fundación de Mendoza por Don Pedro del Castillo* ("The Founding of Mendoza by Don Pedro del Castillo"), by Rafael Cubillos, oil, 1936.

I N THE WINEMAKING MECCA on Argentina's western edge, the landscape is harshly photogenic. A desert slope pressed into the rain shadow of the Andes, Mendoza and its fellow Argentine wine capitals of Salta and San Juan look like the set of a Sergio Leone spaghetti western. These oases beneath the cordillera are happy accidents, precarious outposts that, save for the lucky nutrition provided by Andean snow runoff, would be little more than places where dirt goes to die.

Like the western frontier of the United States, Argentina's Andean desert was a place where pioneers struggled against an unforgiving and brutal landscape. Even today, you won't hear *Mendocinos* speak of "conquering" their land, for fear of tempting whatever fates cause the earth to tremble and the sky to unleash hailstones. "To survive in the desert we must nourish ourselves from and pay tribute to the oasis, with her myths and legends, with her iron rules," says Jaime Correas, the editor of the Mendoza newspaper *Diario UNO*. "We all must respect her, under pain of disappearance—not her disappearance, but our own. In this sense, the oasis, besides being indestructible, is cruel."

In Argentina's west, such natural miserliness did more than just humble these self-reliant frontiersmen. For those who had settled in the

Andean high desert, being forced to fight the unforgiving land and draw from it sustaining life made its inhabitants strong, resilient, and *good*. The brutality of the land demands community and cooperation of its inhabitants; if a farmer takes more than his allotment of water from the irrigation system's finite supply, his neighbor's fields may dehydrate and die. To this day, residents in Mendoza and throughout the west think of themselves as more honest, hardworking, and respectful than the glib sharks in the raucous capital of Buenos Aires.

"Nature has been stingy with spontaneous gifts in this part of the Argentine territory," Domingo Faustino Sarmiento, the future Argentine president who was born in the western wine province of San Juan, wrote in 1851. "Its population would have degenerated by now into brutishness, had not the need to exercise man's physical and moral strengths been born from that very scarcity of natural resources."

Appropriately, like these stress-tempered men, the best wine is supposed to come from grapes born of vines that have been challenged to greatness with a diet of intense sun, near-drought conditions, and rocky, nutrient-poor soil. That is, born of places just like Mendoza.


During the first days of 1561, a bearded forty-year-old Spanish conquistador named Pedro Ruiz del Castillo, along with forty-seven soldiers, crossed the Andes from Chile into Argentina. After picking their way down the mountain range's precarious footpaths, they informed the local Huarpe Indians that they were now subjects of the Spanish King Felipe. The platoon then marched to the Huarpe's riverside settlement. There, on March 2, 1561, Captain Castillo declared the founding of a colony named for his *patrón*, Chilean Governor García Hurtado de Mendoza. Castillo plotted a road grid and split the area into farm plots for his soldiers, including a tract destined for a vineyard, and for good measure he parceled out the local population of Huarpe Indians to the new owners as well.

Seven months after Castillo founded the colony, Governor Mendoza of Chile was replaced by Francisco de Villagra, who wore a goatee that, with his combed-forward hair, gave him the look of an aristocratic Robin Hood. Villagra immediately installed a new staff. Castillo fled to Peru before his replacement, Juan Jufré, arrived. Eager to make a contribution, Jufré moved the colony "two shots of a musket"—about two hundred yards—and renamed it Resurrección.

The colony moved, but its awkward new name did not help it thrive in the new soil. Mendoza—or Resurrección—offered a hard life, and the colonial Spaniards who had been expected to move to Argentina and pour their resources into the new colony chose instead to stay in Chile, nearer to civilization, and have agents manage their Argentine holdings. In 1567, the town's lawyer complained that there were only a dozen residents. Worse, because so many of the local Huarpe tribe were forced to trek to Chile to work in its mines, there was almost no one (or at least no slaves) left to labor in the fields. The colony managed to survive—and then just barely—in large part because of the pacifist benevolence of the remaining natives, who, despite the cruelty with which they were treated, did not rise up against the colonists.

Less than a century before the Spanish arrived, the Huarpe had been conquered by the Inca Empire. Having already been subjugated once, they offered little resistance the second time around. They had also gained access to Inca technology: around 1480, either Túpac Inca Yupanqui, the tenth emperor of the Inca dynasty, or his son and successor Huayna Capac, had sent engineers to the valley of Huentata, as Mendoza was then known, to build a gravity-fed irrigation system. The canals they built channeled water from mountain rivers to the valley, where the water was shunted into a series of branches and then to a web of capillary-like ditches that ran beside each arable field. A farmer breached the ditches when he needed to irrigate, allowing water to flow across the dry soil. It was a circulatory system with the Andes as its heart, the careful tending of which enabled the Huarpe to turn a corner of the hardscrabble desert into crop-yielding farmland. Later, the system would serve as the basis for the more sophisticated irrigation network that the European invaders used to turn arid Mendoza into an agricultural oasis.

The Huarpe were a tribe of tall, slender, hunter-gatherers. The men shaved, sometimes daily, and after a tribe member had been dead for a year, his bones were dug up, stripped of flesh, and brightly painted. The Huarpe hunted with brilliant trickery. On a pond where ducks were gathered, they would toss gourds onto the surface to accustom the birds to the presence of the floating shells. Once the gourds had faded into the background, a Huarpe hunter would put a gourd with eyeholes over his head and slip into the water up to his chin. After sneaking up to a duck, he would grab it by its feet and pull it under until it drowned. He would then move on to the next one, his quiet kill unnoticed. The hunting technique the Huarpe used on the guanaco, a cousin of the llama, was equally ingenious: They would trot behind the animal at a distance that would neither scare it to sprint off nor allow it pause for food and drink. Eventually, the animal would collapse in exhaustion.

This ingenuity did little to save the tribe from the Spanish conquistadores. To work in the mines that the Spaniards kept in Chile, Huarpes were frog-marched over the Andes with African slaves as their overseers. Their hands were bound in chains. When a Huarpe slave lost consciousness or died, he was amputated from the chain at the hand so that the caravan could continue, his body left for carrion birds. During a century of such mistreatment, their numbers fell from a hundred thousand to less than a thousand.

Fortunately for Mendoza, Jufré was a better vintner than city planner. An avid grape farmer who had planted large vineyards in Chile, he brought men along on his 1562 city-moving expedition who immediately began planting wine grapes with cuttings that had originally come from Europe. Within a few years, the vines produced grapes suitable to make wine.

By the time those cuttings made their way to Argentina, wine had already had a multimillennial history. In the Bible's Old Testament the world's first vintner, Noah, was famously mocked by his son Ham for passing out naked, drunk on his own rotgut. The world's oldest known winery, found in a cave in Armenia in early 2011, dates back to 4100 BC. The Egyptians had grown wine grapes alongside the Nile as far back as 3000 BC. In Egyptian society, anyone could drink wine, while in Rome women and anyone under thirty was prohibited from imbibing except for religious purposes. And it was the Greeks who invented conservation, adding tar, resin, and spices to preserve wine that they cooked down over a fire until it had the consistency of honey. Later, it was diluted with water when served.

Wine boasts such a long history in part because the process of winemaking is so simple. In the early years, one simply grew grapes, stomped them into juicy mush, allowed naturally present yeast to convert the grape juice's sugar into alcohol, and aged the fermented wine to smooth the flavor. There were basic winemaking choices to be made—to include dark grape skins in the fermentation would produce red wine, to ferment juice alone would make white—but beyond that, for centuries the caliber of the wine depended largely on the variety of the grape and the location in which it was grown. Later, technical innovations like commercial yeast, electric pumps, and steel tanks improved sanitation and quality. But the basic process remains the same.

After Columbus, Spanish conquistadores expanded winemaking to the New World. Because grapes have nutritional value—raisins were easily preserved calories on arduous voyages—and for Catholic ceremonial reasons, on his second voyage Columbus brought vine cuttings packed in open, dirt-filled barrels that were stored on the ship's deck. Though the vines didn't thrive in the sweaty heat of the Caribbean, they did in Mexico, Peru, and Chile. At each new outpost, the Spaniards planted a vineyard. Indeed, in Mexico, Hernán Cortés was said to have ordered his men to plant ten vines for every native in their domain. When the Spaniards arrived in western Argentina, the Huarpe showed them bitter local grapes that were useful only for clothing dye. But it didn't matter; the Spaniards had come packing their own.

To understand how Argentina's west became the outlaw epicenter of wine, one has to understand the country's place in Spain's colonial tapestry. Just as the Incas had done, the Spanish planted their capital in Peru and appointed a viceroy to oversee taxation and the flow of commerce. The New World would ship raw materials to the old country, and in turn the Old Country would have monopoly access to a new market for its manufactured goods. Theoretically. And everything would go through the Peruvian port capital of Lima, where the viceroy could make sure no one cheated.

But those who had settled in the largely forgotten colony of what would later be known as Argentina didn't see any reason to ship their goods through Peru—which was fifteen hundred miles from Mendoza, two and a half times as far as Buenos Aires—or to pay taxes to the Spanish king. Argentines avoided the viceroy's eyes and taxes by building a thriving contraband trade through the port of Buenos Aires, where they sold cowhides to English merchant smugglers in exchange for slaves and manufactured goods. Argentina's economy and identity leaned heavily on smuggling and cheating, which goes a long way toward explaining the lawbreaking that blossomed in the Argentine wine industry soon after the first grapes were harvested, stomped, and left to ferment.

By the early 1600s, Mendoza, with its now eighty inhabitants, was little more than a frontier post on the way to Santiago, Chile. But Argentina's wine industry had already become a problem for Spain. The dry climate and alluvial soil of Mendoza turned out to be perfect for grape growing, and the irrigation network inherited from the Huarpe enabled farmers to regularly water their vines. The vines yielded higher production than winemakers in Europe could ever hope for, and the wines they produced were so hardy that in 1646, Padre Alonso de Ovalle wrote, "[Mendozan wines] are so tough that they can be taken overland more than 300 leagues, through the immense heat of the plains of Tucumán and Buenos Aires, on the back of an ox, on a trip that can last several months, and arrive without having suffered any damage. And with this abundance they can supply all the provinces and make it to Paraguay and even further."

This was a problem: Argentina was supposed to supply Spain with customers for the Spanish wine industry, not enter into competition by producing and selling its own swill. In 1595, King Felipe II prohibited the production of grapes or wines in the New World except by religious orders—a rule that Felipe III felt the need to reaffirm in 1620, 1628, and 1631. Far from the king's reach at the foot of the Andes, however, Argentina's grape growers and winemakers were disinclined to submit to this oenological fatwa, at least not until the king offered a better way to scratch out a living on the frontier. Argentine vintners ignored the law so thoroughly that the colonial government eventually agreed to look the other way, as long as vineyard owners paid the crown 2 percent of their harvest and pledged not to plant any more vineyards. By the mid-seventeenth century, Argentina's winemaking zone—the whole country, in fact—was becoming an outlaw region.

Appropriately, then, during Argentina's ne'er-do-well colonial years, the country's Andean edge hosted a rogues' gallery of frontiersmen, con artists, and nuts that would do David Lynch proud. It was a border town far from the government's prying eyes, where one could make a fortune with hard work and a touch of guile, and its notable characters were rebels and eccentrics. Take Juan de Puebla y Reinoso. Born in Mendoza around

1610—when only two of the town's thirty-two houses had tile roofs as opposed to straw—de Puebla came from one of the richest families of the local Spanish elite. Juan's sister was married to Mendoza sheriff Pedro Gómez; Juan's father, Captain Gregorio de Puebla, had arrived in 1601 as part of an army sent by the Spanish king. For his services to the king, Captain de Puebla had been given five hundred *cuadras*—about 2,000 acres—sixty miles south of Mendoza in what is now Argentina's prime winemaking region, the Uco Valley. As a child of privilege, Juan found his way into a job at town hall. There, in 1630, he met Pedro Bustos and, through him, Pedro's sister Juana. Pedro and Juana were the children of a powerful local landowner and slaveholder named Captain Agustín de Bustos and his wife Doña Teodora Castañeda.

One night in 1633, the widowed Doña Castañeda returned to her house and caught her daughter Juana and Juan de Puebla *in flagrante delicto*. As Juan fled from Doña Castañeda's angry screams, a petrified Juana told her mother that she had consented only after Juan promised to marry her, a common lothario's scheme during the era. Knowing that he would soon be the subject of a massive manhunt—his crime carried a potential death sentence—Juan gathered together a group of horses and friends (curiously, this group included the local lawman, Sheriff Gómez) and fled over the Andes to Santiago, Chile.

The angry widow Castañeda sensed economic opportunity. As a longtime owner of indigenous laborers, she knew that the decimation of the local Huarpe population had vastly increased the value of the remaining few. So Doña Castañeda not only requested the death penalty for de Puebla on the argument that what he had done with Juana amounted to the rape of a minor based on a lie—a harsh accusation in Catholic colonial Spain, where the violation of a virgin body was considered an act of sacrilege—but she also sued for half his worldly possessions, specifically the Huarpes he controlled.

The punishment that Castañeda suggested was a stretch even for the strict Spanish colonial penal code, which generally saved capital punishment for the crimes of murder and treason. That ultimate sentence was applied far less frequently in cases of money counterfeiting, "rape of an honest woman," heresy, and the odd case of bestiality. But if Doña Castañeda could convince the judge that the young man had abused the close relationship between the Bustos and de Puebla families, she might have it declared an aggravating circumstance and win her case.

The royal court agreed with her and sentenced de Puebla to a fine of 10,000 pesos—a hefty sum considering that a century later the richest businessman in Mendoza owned goods worth only 32,000 pesos—and death by hanging. Juan de Puebla was taken into custody and in due course sent to the gallows. But for reasons never fully explained, de Puebla didn't die on those gallows. The machine might have failed, or maybe the rope broke (helped, perhaps, by his friend the sheriff). No matter the cause, the condemned de Puebla was set free. Mechanical failures during an execution were considered acts of God.

The providentially freed de Puebla returned to Mendoza high society, his reputation scrubbed clean. He married, had nine children, and found himself in great demand as an appraiser and executor of wills. For money, he built Mendoza's largest shipping company, which, in the 1640s, ran ten cargo carriages—there were only forty-five to fifty such carriages in the area—to Buenos Aires and other cities.

Juan de Puebla also opened a *bodega* (winery) and turned himself into one of South America's first and biggest fine-wine *bodegueros*. His winery produced at least 25,000 liters a year, some of which he shipped in carefully tar-sealed and wicker-wrapped earthenware barrels on his carts to Buenos Aires. It's not entirely clear why de Puebla emphasized the quality of his wines when other winemakers didn't, but it appears that he was insecure about his soul's destiny. At the time, local winemakers donated their best wine to the church to get the friars to pray for them. De Puebla was no exception: in the final will and testament read after his 1678 death, the *bodeguero* bequeathed to the local Santo Domingo convent eighteen hundred liters of wine.

Not all early wild-west *bodegueros* were such endearing characters. Born in the 1670s, the French Basque Michel Harizmendi captained a coast guard frigate along the French coastline before immigrating to Argentina around 1716. Moving to Mendoza, he learned Spanish, changed his name to Miguel de Arizmendi, bought land downtown, and launched a business making wine and liquor and shipping it to Buenos Aires. In 1718, he married his fifteen-year-old society neighbor Tomasa Ponce de León.

Arizmendi's entrepreneurial ventures triumphed. By 1739, he was among the five richest men in the city. His 32,000-liter winery and a winery owned by Juan de Puebla's grandson Santiago de Puebla were the largest non-church-owned *bodegas* in the region.

But although he was a business success, Arizmendi's personal life was a study in the bizarre. A religious ascetic, Arizmendi flagellated himself and wore hair shirts. He was in perpetual conflict with the exuberant Tomasa. A conservative man such as Arizmendi expected his young wife to dedicate herself to domestic chores and tend to him when he returned from his business trips. Tomasa, however, was passionate and proud; during his long trips, she took over the wine business, making decisions, paying bills, and managing the winery.

Influenced by friends among the Inquisition authorities, in 1746 Arizmendi built a private prison at his farm and took to locking his wife inside when he went on his trips. This "War of the Roses" period was short-lived, however: Arizmendi died in Buenos Aires in January 1748. Tomasa didn't bother to let Arizmendi's body cool before marrying a younger man. Two weeks after news of Arizmendi's death reached Mendoza, Tomasa and a Spaniard named José Miguel Rodríguez de Arellano y Esclava were wed in borrowed clothes. The smooth Spaniard, educated and broke, had been hunting for a rich widow for some time. But by July, when it became clear that Tomasa would not be able to claim Arizmendi's estate from the Inquisition priest who was executing the will, Rodríguez was gone.

The success achieved by early wine merchants like de Puebla and Arizmendi shouldn't blind one to the fact that the future wine meccas in Argentina's desert west were tiny dust bowls perched on the southern edge of the Spanish Empire. Mendoza had barely a thousand residents in 1650; by 1720 it had only grown to three thousand. However, with little government intervention standing in the way, a startlingly large number of these residents had become involved in the production and sale of wine. In 1739, Mendoza had more than 110 vineyards and at least ten wineries, producing 800,000 liters of wine. By 1757, Mendoza and San Juan were each producing 2.9 million liters a year. And plenty of it got to Buenos Aires, where a major street of merchants selling goods from the province was named for Mendoza. For Buenos Aires, Andean wine was a good thing: wine taxes were one of its top moneymakers, and the city used the income from its liquor sales to build a cathedral and upgrade its fort.

How that wine was made was not always pretty, however. Compared to the high-tech labs one finds inside a contemporary winery—a celebration of stainless steel tanks, sterile piping, chemical meters, and eight-hundred-dollar French oak barrels stacked with Zen garden perfection—the primitive winemaking of Argentina's colonial era came straight out of *The Flintstones*. Whereas the modern winemaker needs chemists, botanists, and marketers on the payroll, the colonial *bodeguero* made their products with mules, Indians, and slaves.

The winemaking season begins in March—late summer in Argentina—when the grapes have aged to sugar-packed maturity. African slaves and local indigenous people were sent into the vineyards, where they would load the grapes into huge, mule-mounted leather baskets known as *arganas*. After taking the fruit back to a *bodega*, usually a jury-rigged lean-to made of adobe with a cane roof, they dumped it into a *lagar*, a bull skin that had been stretched over wooden stakes pounded into the ground. Climbing into the *lagar* itself or standing above the grapes while hanging in harnesses from nearby trees, they pressed the grapes with their feet until the juice ran out the hollowed-out bull's tail and into waiting leather buckets. The juice was fermented in ceramic tanks stored inside the *bodega* and then, after fermentation had finished, poured through a leather strainer into earthenware storage containers that were buried in the ground to guard against sudden changes in temperature. After the wine was aged, the winemakers cooked it into syrup to toughen it for the journey—the technique invented by the Greeks several thousand years earlier—and packed it into skins or earthenware jugs lashed to the back of a mule. The mules then spent weeks hauling the wine through the strength-sapping desert heat and unfriendly indigenous tribes of the pampas to Buenos Aires, Paraguay, and beyond.

Argentine winemakers prospered for the next century, despite great upheaval in the Spanish Empire. In 1700, Philip of Anjou, of the French House of Bourbon, had ascended to the Spanish throne after the death of the childless and tragically inbred Charles "The Hexed," who was mentally disabled and physically disfigured and had a tongue so large he drooled and had difficulty speaking. Once they had consolidated their power, the Bourbons began to apply enlightenment thought to an empire that had fallen into decadence under the Hapsburgs. One of those modern beliefs was laissez-faire capitalism—that is, "free trade"—and in 1778 Charles III declared that ports in Spain and Spanish America could trade among themselves without limitation.

Argentina's wine regions suddenly found themselves staring at the business end of this colonial free-trade agreement. Buenos Aires was flooded with cheap, tax-free imports from Europe. Local wine couldn't hold its own against the deluge of competition. Perversely, wine shipped to Buenos Aires by boat from the Iberian Peninsula was cheaper than that sent by land from Argentina's west: besides paying shipping costs that amounted to 80 percent of the price of the wine, winemakers had to deal with provincial governments along the trail that charged commerce tolls, as well as protection taxes to keep the route safe from hostile Indians. In Buenos Aires, imported wine went for ten pesos a barrel, while the same amount from western Argentina could cost thirty-six pesos. That was great for the *Porteños*, as Buenos Aires residents are known, but devastating for producers in the interior, whose wines were priced beyond the reach of drinkers. "For no price can you find someone to buy wine. There are amazing wines for sale, but one can't sell a thing," *Mendocino* Juan A. Videla wrote to a friend in 1779.


Colonial free trade turned Argentina's west away from wine. By the beginning of the nineteenth century, Mendoza was home to some eighteen thousand inhabitants. It was still an agricultural flyspeck, run by a handful of large landowning families who grew rich fattening cattle that traveled from ranches in the eastern pampas to market on the other side of the Andes in Chile. These *latifundistas* planted thousands of acres of alfalfa for the cattle, and to a lesser extent cultivated wheat, olives, fruit, and grapes. Since the launch of free trade, the wine business had been hit-or-miss for Argentine vintners; the industry was saved by an almost continual string of European wars, as Argentine wines could compete only during periods when no ships had recently docked in the port of Buenos Aires. But business concerns soon took a backseat to much bigger issues: Argentina became its own country—and plunged into civil war.

After pillaging much of Europe, in 1808 Napoléon Bonaparte invaded Spain and replaced King Fernando VII with his jovial and not terribly ambitious older brother Giuseppe (Giuseppe asked Napoléon if he could return to his previous and less-demanding gig as king of Naples—a request that Napoléon denied). The Spaniards rewarded Giuseppe with a constant guerrilla war until he returned the throne to Fernando VII in 1813 and not long after moved to a large white manor house in Bordentown, New Jersey.

Besides throwing Europe into an uproar, Giuseppe's brief rule forced

Spain's South American colonies into an existential crisis: If your king is deposed, who's in charge? Like other Latin American states, Argentina answered that question by forming its own government in 1810.

It was during this febrile era that the independence-minded José de San Martín sailed for Buenos Aires. The war was hard on South America's budding economy, and after being named governor of the Cuyo region in August 1814, San Martín tried to help Cuyo's vintners by asking the government to end the war taxes they were charging on wines. The taxes were absurd, but the vintners continued to give more than they received: When anti-independence forces took over Chile, San Martín turned for help to Cuyo's winemakers. The vintners offered funds to support San Martín's army, and local society women sold their jewels to finance his campaign against Spanish rule.

The end of the independence wars helped Argentine wine sales, but the bump was only a brief respite in a long, slow decline. After its independence, Argentina found itself with no real central government. Soon it was mired in a simmering, decades-long civil war. With no dependable markets for its ample food and wine, the isolated west settled into a long economic depression.

In 1825, a traveler named Francis Bond Head passed through Argentina to set up a mining company. What he found in Mendoza was a small, neat backwater of whitewashed mud houses, a lazy desert oasis peopled by idle shopkeepers who took five-hour siestas and women who washed themselves naked in the shallow river that ran alongside the town's main promenade. "In the mornings and in the evenings they really bathe without any clothes in the Rio de Mendoza, the water of which is seldom up to their knees, the men and women all together; and certainly, of all the scenes which in my life I have witnessed, I never beheld one so indescribable," the scandalized Head wrote in 1826.

In the end, however, it was the *Mendocino* indolence that most impressed Head. "Provisions are cheap, and the people who bring them, quiet and civil; the climate is exhausting, and the whole population indolent," he wrote, thinking back to the lazy evenings he had spent eating flavored ices on the promenade while listening to the sound of thunder rumbling against the distant cordillera. "Their situation dooms them to inactivity; they are bounded by the Andes and the Pampas, and, with such formidable and relentless boundaries around them, what have they to do with the history, or the improvements, or the notions of the rest of the world? Their wants are few and nature readily supplies them—the day is long, and therefore as soon as they have had their breakfasts, and have made a few arrangements for their supper, it is so very hot that they go to sleep, and what could be better?"

A decade later, on March 27, 1835, Charles Darwin arrived in Mendoza on one of the many side trips he took during his famous voyage on the HMS *Beagle*. He came to a similar conclusion about this stagnant desert Shangri-la: "The country was beautifully cultivated and resembled Chile. The neighborhood is celebrated for its fruit; and certainly nothing could appear more flourishing than its vineyards and the orchards of figs, peaches, and olives. We bought water-melons nearly twice as large as a man's head . . . for a halfpenny apiece," he wrote in his diary. The city, however, did not impress. "The prosperity of the place has much declined in late years. The inhabitants say, 'It is good to live in, but very bad to grow rich in.' The lower orders have the lounging, reckless manners of the Gauchos of the Pampas . . . To my mind, the town has a stupid, forlorn aspect," he wrote. "I agree with Sir F. Head: the happy doom of the Mendozinos [*sic*] is to eat, sleep and be idle."


But then, just as Napoléon I's invasion of Spain in 1808 had set Argentina on the path to independence, another Napoléon unwittingly catalyzed Argentina's wine revolution. Elected by a landslide as France's first president in 1848, Napoléon I's nephew Louis-Napoléon Bonaparte was a profligate womanizer and heavy smoker whose pointed goatee lent him an eerie resemblance to one of Alexandre Dumas's seventeenth-century mustachioed musketeers. In December 1851, frustrated by legislators who would not amend the constitution to allow him to run for a second term, he staged a coup d'état and a year later declared himself Napoléon III, Emperor of the French.

Supporters of France's nascent republic were horrified, and many fled into self-exile. One of those was the thirty-one-year-old Michel Aimé Pouget, an up-and-coming agronomist from Tours who had been awarded a prize for his work with potato seeds. Armed with bags of seeds and plant cuttings, Pouget sailed for Chile, where he was hired by José Patricio Larrain Gandarillas, a science-minded landowner who regularly traveled to Europe to learn the latest agriculture techniques. At Gandarillas's *estancia* near Santiago, Pouget put in place French agronomy's most recent advances. He sent samples of Chile's New World flora to his colleagues back home and, in return, received the European plants he needed.

At the time, Argentina's two bitterly opposed camps were mired in civil war. The Unitarians, European in outlook, wanted to concentrate power in Buenos Aires. The Federalists, whose partisans were drawn mostly from the rural leaders and their poor subjects, favored greater autonomy for the interior ranching provinces. From 1829 to 1852, the tyrannical Federalist *caudillo* (strongman) Juan Manuel de Rosas had run Argentina from the Buenos Aires provincial governor's chair, terrorizing Unitarian leaders, many of whom had fled to neighboring Chile. One of those was Domingo Faustino Sarmiento, a forty-one-year-old public intellectual who had been born to a near-destitute family in the western province of San Juan (nine of his fourteen siblings died) and imagined a future in which Argentina would become a progressive European country. In 1852, as an army journalist with the rank of lieutenant colonel, Sarmiento rode with the troops that defeated Rosas and drove him into exile.

But Sarmiento soon fell out with the winning general, a former Rosas ally and future president named Justo José de Urquiza, and returned to Chile. There, Sarmiento heard rumors of the brilliant French farmer who had been performing miracles. Believing that for his native western Argentina to succeed it needed to launch an investigative model farm—a Quinta Normal—like the one Chile had founded in 1842, Sarmiento began to talk to Mendoza governor Pascual Pedro Segura about how they might steal Pouget—and his plants—for Argentina. "We secretly conspired to launch a Quinta Normal in Mendoza in order to bring in the trees we lacked, improve the vines and bring back the olive and fig trees we'd lost," Sarmiento said in 1884, years after he himself had risen to become Argentina's president (1868–1874). Sarmiento and Segura convinced the legislature to requisition a farm used by the St. Augustine religious order, as well as 2,000 pesos to launch a Quinta Normal, and they offered Pouget the job to run it. With this carrot, Mendoza's government seduced Pouget into coming to Argentina in 1853.

Drinkers of Argentine wine are lucky that Pouget hadn't visited Mendoza before accepting the offer. The city that met him was defined by thin dirt streets devoid of shading trees, churches in deep decay, and canals that flooded when it rained and turned the streets into "avenues of water." There were bars on every corner, and a small bickering aristocracy that governed according to whim. After decades of decline, only some 1,000 acres of vineyards were planted. Worse, the experimental farm Pouget was given—the Quinta Normal—was little more than a 120-acre spread of dry and rocky land full of snakes and huge spiders.

Pouget was not given adequate funds or employees to plant the Quinta Normal correctly, and with scant support from both the government and Mother Nature, even Pouget couldn't turn the water-deprived patch into a thriving farm. After he had suffered a drought, a flood, and a plague of locusts, impatient provincial legislators accused him of embezzlement and cut his salary in half in 1855. He left the government job not long after. But the frustrated Pouget did not abandon the land. He had already fallen in love with Mendoza, and after marrying an Argentine named Petrona Solís, he stayed until his 1875 death. It was in this period after departing the Quinta that he made his impact: both on the fertile farm of a friend where he created a "double" of the Quinta, and on a spread of good land he bought for himself not far from the government plot, Pouget planted his cuttings and revealed the secrets of modern horticulture to a generation of Argentine agronomists.

Before Pouget's arrival, top French grape varietals had not been planted in Argentina. Most of the vines grown in Mendoza were descendants of the plants brought by the conquistadores—cheap *criolla* grapes originally from the Canary Islands, that had mutated and crossbred over three centuries in the New World. Their grapes were plentiful but insipid in flavor, and they made for sweet, often unpleasant, yellowish-pink rosés. Dropped into a desert environment of such botanical limitations, the luggage Pouget shipped from Chile served as a kind of Noah's ark of immigrant flora. The Frenchman brought European beehives and seeds for some 120 new plants and trees. He also packed vine cuttings of Cabernet, Merlot, Sauvignon, Chardonnay, and the grape that, 150 years later, would make Argentine wine famous around the world: Malbec. Pouget's grapes soon spread throughout Argentina's west. In San Juan, one of the province's pioneers, Justo Castro, planted five hundred of Pouget's Malbec plants in 1876.

With this wealth of new plants and European knowledge, Pouget surrounded himself with disciples and taught Argentina how to farm. Pouget was an eccentric with a bawdy sense of humor. Slender and short of stature, he had swept-back black hair and a bushy pirate's beard that gave him the air of genial insanity. Nothing he did dispelled this mad-scientist reputation. Pouget often experimented with grafting plants together, doing it with such frequency and creativity that among those who knew him it became known as "Pouget's Secret." On a block of Mendoza's main avenue, Pouget grafted acacia trees with wisteria flowers. The surreal beauty of trees with the violet flower bunches hanging to the ground stunned passersby. But Pouget went much further. The amazing and unique fruits this agricultural guru invented on his farm so inspired his students that they took to playing hooky from their studies to commix pears, plums, strawberries, and grapes. Several owners of orchards near Pouget's were baffled by cheap pear trees on their properties that suddenly started bearing delicious water pears, at least until they learned that the mischievous Pouget, eager to spice up traditional agriculture, had been sneaking into their land and grafting his own cuttings onto their plants.

Pouget soon developed a witch's notoriety for everything from his habit of eating snake meat (after removing the head and tip of the tail, of course) to botanical inventions that ran from bonsai pears that bore full-sized *muslo de damas* ("lady's thigh") fruit to peaches that tasted of strawberry. This image of a giddy trickster was not lessened by Pouget's sense of humor. On one occasion, while walking with a government minister along the Tulumaya Creek, he succumbed to impish temptation, shoved the public official into the water, and began tossing fallen leaves on the man's head. On another stroll through town with his dogs, he sneaked past workers at the town's main church and climbed to the top of its bell tower. From there he called to the hunting dogs he had left in the main square below, which caused an unholy racket as they sprinted through the church toward him. When cornered for his peccadilloes, Pouget squirmed free the old-fashioned way: with gifts. To the priests he gave beeswax for candles, and the politicians received trays of strawberries and good French wine.

Before Pouget's arrival, Argentina's winemakers were not only short of the raw material for good wines—good French grapes—they also made what they had into a rustic, bitter swill that appealed to few save the roughneck gauchos who roamed the pampas. "One rarely finds good wines," wrote a German scientist named Hermann Burmeister who passed through the region in 1856. "Pressed and dumped into brick lined pits and then stored in large earthenware jugs or wooden tanks that aren't always very clean, the juice soon begins to go bad, either for lack of hygiene or air leaks. Soon it begins to taste like vinegar, until the wine becomes intolerable."

The mischievous Frenchman, however, would not allow his new grapes to be so mistreated. Pouget founded the country's first model *bodega* and taught vintners winemaking tricks such as using sulfur to conserve wines for long voyages. As Pouget's techniques spread, the right attention to quality began to be paid. In 1867, Pouget took an Argentine Bordeaux imitation that he had made to the Paris Expo and won a bronze medal.

In the last decades of the nineteenth century and the first years of the twentieth, Argentina would become a wine powerhouse, its sleepy west transformed into a New World behemoth. But first, the earth would have to move. Literally.

# CHAPTER 2

# THE IMMIGRANTS

Grape harvesters, early twentieth century. Courtesy of *Los Andes*.

ON MARCH 20, 1861, at 8:36 p.m., the ground beneath the tiny colonial city of Mendoza began to snap and shake. At the Hotel Tessier, a waiter had just delivered coffee to twenty-two-year-old Pompeyo Lemos and a young engineer friend when Lemos felt "the earth fainting like the ground was moving over water, and immediately there was a terrifying sound like thousands of carriages full of stones were being dragged over the city." When the earth shuddered to a halt, Lemos heard the hotel owner begging for help from the ruins beneath his feet. Try as he might, Lemos could not free him. The owner was trapped under a fallen wall, his leg completely destroyed. "He asked me to look in the hotel for his wife and daughter, but I only found dead bodies and one nearly blind old lady who by a miracle had been saved," Lemos said. A few moments later Lemos ran north to the main square and found the San Francisco church tilting like some kind of wobbly Jenga tower, "its towers about to fall down, unhinged, like the eastern wall of the cloister, which was listing and about to fall over the length of a block." He watched a crowd of people, including several friends, pick their way, frantically, toward the plaza. Just then, an aftershock collapsed the cloister wall upon them, sending more than sixty *Mendocinos* to their death.

The temblor was estimated to have lasted from two seconds to two-and-a-half minutes, but all accounts agree on one thing: Mendoza's 1861 earthquake (about 7.2 on the Richter scale) and the subsequent four-day fire destroyed all of the region's structures except for one: a winery on the grounds of the Panquehua *estancia*. There, just north of the city, thirty-one-year-old Carlos González Pinto rushed toward his house as the first seismic convulsion jerked the earth under his feet. Inside, he ran to his sons' room and threw himself over their cribs as a wall collapsed atop him and crushed his legs. One of the boys died soon after when a rescuer threw a bucket of cold water on him to snap him out of shock; the icy water instead induced cardiac arrest. González Pinto's other son survived and, although the winery owner found himself temporarily paralyzed and wheelchair bound for weeks, he nonetheless worked alongside his family clearing away the winery's collapsed fermentation tanks so that the building could serve as a field hospital and refuge. In this outpost of adobe houses with cane roofs, the winery at Panquehua was the only building left standing.

About a third of the city's 12,500 residents died in the earthquake. And despite the best efforts of González Pinto and other civic-minded residents, the city went feral. Looting began almost immediately; local newspapers reported on overwhelming terror, hunger, and desolation made worse by the arrival of groups of marauding *campesinos* (farmers/peasants) armed with tools. Looters dug into the ruins; as described by one A. Clereaux, they ignored the injured and dying as they stole "rings and pendants from the virgin and watches and money from the rich landowner." Less than a week after the earthquake, the death penalty was imposed for those caught looting; on March 26, six so accused were put before a firing squad, without trial. The city fell sway to rumor, superstition, and fear. There were tales of a Jesuit priest who just an hour beforehand had given a sermon in the main plaza claiming that Mendoza was split in two and its sinful side would need to perish, and stories of a bride dressed in white who had died at the altar. Residents desperate for an explanation went in search of August Bravard, a visiting French scientist who supposedly had been predicting a seismic event on the basis of his barometric readings—only to find his corpse in his room at the Hotel de Cactus, buried in a pile of ruins. He had been planning to travel to Chile the next day.

Argentina's west would have to be built anew.

As Mendoza dug out from its horrific destruction, wrenching change was marching toward the Andes in another form. In 1806, Great Britain had attempted to expand into South America. In June of that year, a squadron of 1,635 English soldiers led by Brigadier General William Beresford seized Buenos Aires from the Spanish. The easy victory caused much celebration back home: In September, London's *Times* triumphantly announced "our success in La Plata, where a small British detachment has taken one of the greatest and richest of the Spanish colonies." And Sir Home Popham, the admiral of the fleet that had ferried the troops from Cape Town to Buenos Aires, wrote to merchants in London enticing them with tales of a large new market that would shortly be open for business.

Unfortunately for Popham, the citizens of Buenos Aires recaptured their city forty-six days after Beresford's invasion. Comically, because news traveled so slowly between the New World and Old, the retaking of Buenos Aires happened a month and a day before the *Times* published its triumphant article.

Unable to let Argentina go, England invaded again the next year, this time with a more organized force. In July 1807, General John Whitelocke led seven thousand British soldiers into a city that had been expecting exactly that recurrence. Within weeks, a ragtag army of colonists, slaves, and indigenous people drawn from the city's forty-five thousand residents killed or captured more than a third of Whitelocke's men, dragging many through the city's rainy winter streets. It was demoralizing to be routed by an army that, to a pink-cheeked professional British soldier, looked no better than a mob. "Nothing could be more mortifying than our passage through the streets amidst the rabble who had conquered us," Colonel Lancelot Holland wrote in his diary. "They were very dark-skinned people, short and ill-made, covered with rags, armed with long muskets and some a sword. There was neither order nor uniformity among them."

Whitelocke was quickly declared unworthy to serve and cashiered from his office, and England was forced to give up its dream of owning a piece of South America. But even before Whitelocke's loss, Britain's leaders had begun to reconsider their South American strategy. In May 1807, the British secretary of state for war and the colonies, Lord Castlereagh, wrote a memorandum to the cabinet: "The question for the Cabinet to decide . . . is, whether the value of such an occupancy and such a connexion, either during war, or upon a peace, is such as to compensate for the drain and incumbrance it must prove upon our other military operations and our population," he wrote, "and if not, whether some principle of acting more consonant to the sentiments and interests of the people of South America cannot be taken up, which . . . may relieve us from the hopeless task of conquering this extensive country, against the temper of its population." Wouldn't it be easier to end Spain's commercial monopoly of South America by helping its colonies gain independence (Britain's invasions pushed Argentina in that direction; Spain's lack of aid against the invasions had not gone unnoticed) and then just take the colonies' money and resources through trade?

England's shift put into motion events that, seventy-five years later, would bring thousands of winemaking Italian immigrants to the Andean foothills of Argentina's west. To sell goods to Argentines and extract Argentina's resources, the British realized that they had to find a way into the country's forbiddingly vast territories. And that meant laying railways—thousands and thousands of miles of iron.

During the inauspicious 1857 inaugural run of Argentina's first train, the railway's directors—dubious of the safety of their own creation—

decided not to ride inside the coach and instead chose to accompany the train on horseback along its eight-mile track; after the train derailed, they begged the passengers to stay quiet so the railway would not get a bad reputation. Soon, though, London-based rail companies like the Central Argentine Railway Ltd. and the Buenos Ayres Great Southern Railway Co. Ltd. were financing, engineering, and building railways at a rapid clip. In 1880, Argentina had about fifteen hundred miles of track, a number that shot up to ten thousand miles over the next twenty years; by 1890, some 80 percent of those railways belonged to foreign investors, mostly British. To this day, Argentine railways travel on the British left, while that New World invention—the automobile—drives on the American right.

In April 1885, Mendoza saw the arrival of cross-country train service by the state-run Ferrocarril Andino (it would be bought two years later by the British-owned Argentine Great Western Railway); two weeks later, San Juan was added to the route. A journey that, twenty-five years before, had taken two weeks and cost more than a workman's monthly salary could now be done for reasonable cost in a little over a day. Thousands of working-class Argentines and immigrants who could never have considered testing their fortunes in the west suddenly found it within reach. When they arrived, the colossal Andes cordillera must have inspired awe in these new arrivals. In the dim sunlight just after dawn, the range's sepia foothills match the sky, creating a heart-stopping mirage: the snowcaps of the larger mountains behind appear to float above the earth, like magic kingdoms of the air. Above them all looms the massive pyramidal peak of the "Sentinel of Stone," Aconcagua, the highest mountain in the Americas. So imposing is the deadly Aconcagua—it claims the lives of several mountain climbers each year—that it was cast as the villain in *Pedro*, a 1943 Disney cartoon about a family of airplanes. As the family's son Pedro makes an airmail run over the Andes, he nearly meets his end in an encounter with the anthropomorphic face of the fierce, storm-breathing Aconcagua.

People in the west watched the oncoming railway with a mix of excitement and dread. For the smart and entrepreneurial, it promised new opportunities. But for the aristocracy it meant the end of a comfortable way of life. Until then, the west had been a slow backwater run by a lazy oligarchy. The province of Mendoza was controlled by thirty-five elite families whose children spent their copious free time frolicking in Paris. The top 1 percent of Mendoza's landowners controlled 26 percent of the land.

Uninterested in doing the hard work involved in coaxing grapevines from the soil, pressing fruit into wine, and then shipping it east to sell, the aristocracy invested in beef. Indeed, there were only fifty-six primitive *bodegas* at the end of the 1860s, whereas over 90 percent of the area's cultivated land was planted with alfalfa for cattle. Fattening cattle bought in the pampas to the east and then selling them to Chile in the west was easy money. But in the 1870s cattle prices hit a trough, something made worse by the progression of trains across Argentina. The rails, in a sense, eliminated the whole raison d'être of the fattening industry: with cattle cars, animals would no longer need to be fattened after a long walk west; they would *arrive* fat.

The number of cattle exported from Mendoza plummeted from sixty-eight thousand in 1871 to nine thousand in 1879, undermining the pastoral life of Mendoza's elite and highlighting the need for change. The leaders who came to power during this period looked abroad for inspiration, knowing that a comfortable aristocracy would never lead the country to greatness. Like Sarmiento, who had traveled extensively in Europe and the United States before serving as president—during an 1847 US trip he met Horace Mann, Ralph Waldo Emerson, and Henry Wadsworth Longfellow—they saw that Argentina's industry, agriculture, and education would have to be modernized if the country were going to compete on the world stage. Through their patriotic zeal, they also saw that there was plenty of money to be made in the process.

...

General Rufino Ortega was one of the complex and often contradictory men who pushed the west toward modernity. A hard-faced soldier with slicked-back hair, nearly rimless oval glasses, and a long, bushy, black goatee, Ortega had almost been killed in an 1874 battle against the last remnants of Rosas's Federalist forces. Later he served under future Argentine president General Julio Argentino Roca, a man whose craftiness earned him the nickname of *El Zorro* ("The Fox"). Fighting under Roca in the "Conquest of the Desert," the murderous 1879 campaign to exterminate native groups who were inconveniently in the way of Argentina's southern expansion, Ortega massacred "Indians" and took some two thousand prisoners. Some of these prisoners he gifted as domestic help to his politically connected friends, but the vast majority he kept to work on three vineyard-planted farms he owned. Several years later, a judge, David Orrego, wrote to the local newspaper *Los Andes* to denounce their conditions; the prisoners were "hungry, enslaved, exploited and suffering corporal punishment," he said. For years Ortega paid them pennies, and according to another critic he kept "dungeons where he locks up and punishes dozens of his 'servants,'" even into the twentieth century.

Ortega had an equally ruthless sense of humor. According to one account, during the Conquest of the Desert, shortages from one of his food purveyors left Ortega's men hungry during battle. One day, as the delinquent supplier passed through, Ortega served the man a juicy steak for lunch and then invited him on a walk through the camp. At one point, Ortega stopped and pulled back a blanket to expose a dead indigenous woman whose corpse was missing part of its thigh. "Did you like the barbecue?" Ortega asked the nauseated purveyor.

Yet despite his image as a frontier strongman, Ortega promoted progressive policies aimed at modernizing Mendoza. With the support of his friend Julio Argentino Roca, who had been elected president in 1880, Ortega became governor of the province of Mendoza in 1884. The year he came to office, he signed a law organizing and regulating the irrigation system, as well as a decree to pay an agent in Buenos Aires a one-peso commission for each immigrant he could ship west. He told the agent to send men from fourteen to forty-five and women from thirteen to forty who were "experienced in agricultural labor, with a specialization in cultivating vines or making wine." Within a year, the agent sent over a thousand immigrants from Buenos Aires. In another scheme that Ortega put forth in 1884, a man named Santiago Saglieri was commissioned to bring in four hundred European immigrants specialized in vine growing. Ortega saw that immigrants would introduce desire, muscle, and ideas into Mendoza's society. But Ortega's enthusiasm for winegrowing immigrants did not simply arise from a progressive's civic-minded desire to modernize; Ortega was a huge landowner himself, and from personal experience he knew how important it was to have an ample supply of skilled workers. In other words, attracting immigrants would increase his profits. "Everything suffers in labor shortages. The lack of workers, especially in agriculture, makes production costs rise," he told the Mendoza legislature in 1885.

Not all western leaders were as Machiavellian as Ortega. His successor as governor, Tiburcio Benegas, was a plump, bald aristocrat from Argentina's eastern breadbasket who saw that progress was a stool not only built of muscle; it also required legs of science and finance to stand. Benegas would last only two years in office before Ortega had him overthrown, but in those two years Benegas changed the west in immeasurable ways.

Like Ortega, Benegas was friendly with "The Fox," Julio Argentino Roca—they had gone to school together at the famous Colegio del Uruguay—and he was in good standing with the country's oligarchy. In 1870 he married Lubina Blanco, a woman from Mendoza whose father Eusebio wrote the first Argentine winemaking manual, *Manual del viñatero en Mendoza*, by translating a book by the French oenologist Henri Machard and adding his own observations of the local market. Inspired by his father-in-law, Benegas grew increasingly interested in modernizing Argentina's wine industry, and in 1881 he quit his job as the head of his hometown branch of the Banco Nacional to move his family to his wife's native Mendoza. There, the progressive aristocrat bought a 625-acre *estancia* known as *El Trapiche* ("The Mill") because it was in an area where farmers had ground flour when wheat was still a big business. At *El Trapiche* Benegas founded what would soon become the most technically advanced vineyard and winery in the west.

In his short term in office, from 1887 to 1889, Benegas addressed two of the greatest conundrums of Argentina's west. First, he saw that without a bank to lend them money, frontier entrepreneurs would never prosper. Solving this problem was fairly easy. A former banker, Benegas raised 5 million pesos from a Parisian company, Cahen d'Anvers and Co., by putting up enormous swaths of provincial land as collateral. Benegas spent four-fifths of the money founding the Banco de la Provincia de Mendoza. The last 1 million pesos he used to pay for education and to address the second problem: irrigation. Benegas knew that it would be hard to attract immigrants to farm a high-desert oasis unless the state could guarantee them water, something that up to then had been almost impossible. In the early 1870s, only about 200,000 acres in Mendoza had reliable access to water. (Even today, barely 3 percent of Mendoza is irrigated.) Most of that water went to the alfalfa fields, leaving hardly enough to provide more than basic sustenance for the sixty-five thousand people who lived in the province.

Benegas envisioned a pharaonic irrigation project. At the time, the irrigation network was a mess—an improvised web of canals that had been tacked onto the original Huarpe Indian system by landowners whenever they wanted to open new fields. "The canals and ditches that currently exist have been made without knowing the natural slope of the land they're supposed to irrigate," an engineer named Bror Bergman told the provincial government in 1874. "For this reason they're in fairly poor shape."

But Benegas also knew that no one in Argentina had the technical expertise to address the issue, so he turned to Mendoza's representative in Europe, Guillermo Villanueva, to track down the best hydraulic engineer he could, preferably one from Italy, France, or Spain, where "the land has similar problems to that in Mendoza." The man Villanueva found was Cesare Cipolletti, a forty-four-year-old engineer from Rome's Tiber Island, an islet supposedly formed when Roman citizens expelled the last of the Tarquin kings (Lucius Tarquinius Superbus, or "Tarquin the Proud") and in anger dumped the king's wheat into the river.

An orphan at seven years old, Cipolletti had helped to construct aqueducts in Padua, Vicenza, and Milan; to design distribution networks in Egypt's northern Nile; to modernize Swiss irrigation canals that dated from the Middle Ages; and to build a drinking-water plant in Florence. A progressive engineer who, like Benegas, saw that societal progress was closely tied to technological advances, he was an early proponent of hydroelectric generation and the "substitution of natural hydraulic power for coal."

Described by contemporaries as being as robust as an enormous tree, Cipolletti was a self-confident and intellectually curious man with swept-back gray hair and a flowing gray beard split in the middle. Diabetic but otherwise healthy, he lived in an austere style and gave off an air of slight melancholy. Known for speaking calmly but with great insistence, Cipolletti had an Italian accent that lent his Spanish a touch of pomposity.

Learning of Cipolletti's fame, Villanueva began to lobby the Italian engineer to visit Argentina; in April 1888 he offered Cipolletti a job. But wooing him was not easy. At the time of Villanueva's overtures, Cipolletti was in contact with Emilio Rosetti, an Italian engineer who taught at the University of Buenos Aires and knew of Mendoza from his

brother, Nicolás Rosetti, who had lived there while designing and building a prison. Apparently Rosetti's description of a dusty city at the end of
the earth hadn't sounded too appealing. "He'd done us the poor service
of scaring Cipolletti," Villanueva wrote to Benegas, "telling him that life
in America is very hard and expensive, that nothing will get better with
the project we're planning. Because of this, it's been hard to convince
the man that he's been ill informed and that the contract we're offering
is good for him."

Villanueva's pleas and economic enticements finally swayed Cipolletti in October, however, and the imposing engineer arrived several
months later. Over the next few years he led a feverish hydraulic constructing boom, building what would be known as the Cipolletti and
Benegas dikes; installing hydroelectric turbines; expanding and modernizing the irrigation canal network; planning the drinking-water system
for the city of Mendoza; and designing levee, irrigation, and drinking-
water systems for the western desert zones of San Juan, San Luis, and
Tucumán. His work opened up 325,000 acres for agriculture in the province of Mendoza alone, more than doubling the arable land that had been
available just twenty-five years before.

During his short stint as governor, Benegas corresponded regularly
with his future son-in-law, Mendoza aristocrat Emilio Civit, who in later
years would gain fame as an autocratic governor with a penchant for
huge public works. At the time, Civit was traveling through the Médoc
area of Bordeaux, home to many of the world's best wines, and the attention to detail he saw aroused in him a passion to modernize the way his
country grew vines. Because there was so much more money in cattle
fattening than in winemaking, vines in Argentina had traditionally been
planted as afterthoughts amid alfalfa fields in what was known as the *de
cabeza*, or "headed," style. Instead of being packed in the modern order
one sees today—in rows with each plant about three feet from the next,

the vines trained on wires—each plant stood alone, about eight to nine feet from the next vine, and was trained around a wooden pole called a *tutor* so that it grew in the form of a tree. Barely four hundred vines were planted per acre, and they were poorly pruned by inexperienced farmhands. In his letters from France, the excited Civit painted vivid word pictures of Bordeaux vineyards with a thousand vines per acre, trained on a double-wire system.

Even more inspiring, Civit noted, was the beauty of the French wineries, especially compared to those of Argentina, where grapes were still pressed by foot in leather *lagares* and fermented in buildings that were little more than huts. Argentina was working in the dark, Civit said. "Now it's time to get out of this situation, considering the development of the industry," he wrote. "It's all a question of building good *bodegas* and putting in charge people who can run them, not sophisticates or shameless forgers or ignorant savages." For Civit, laws that brought in immigrant vineyard laborers and promoted grape growing were great, but the state had to do more: it had to bring in top scientists and modern technology and teach people how to make wine.

What moved Civit, like Ortega before him, to write Benegas so forcefully was not just wide-eyed progressivism, but rather visions of economic opportunity. Civit saw wine for what it was: an increasingly globalized product in which France held price and quality advantages. But, Civit realized, Argentine *bodegueros* were about to have a unique opportunity to steal a piece of the market. As Civit traveled through France, a vine blight was sweeping the country. The supply of European wine was about to fall dramatically, Civit saw, which meant that less imported wine would flow into Argentina's capital city. There would be no better time for local *bodegueros* to slide in. If Argentina put together a nucleus of capable growers and winemakers schooled in Médoc's best practices, Civit told Benegas, the country could become self-sufficient in terms of wine within a decade and, "completely close the markets of Buenos Aires not only to Bordeaux, but to Italy and Spain as well."

...

Several decades before Civit's letters, in the spring of 1862, a sealed box addressed to a local wine merchant named Monsieur Borty had arrived in the small French town of Roquemaure on the right bank of the Rhône River. While visiting from America the previous fall, a friend of Borty's named Carle had promised to send Borty some of the native grapevines, even though Carle said their grapes didn't produce European-quality wine. Borty put the vines out of his mind, however, because he hadn't expected Carle to follow through. But with the recent advent of transatlantic steamboat service lowering the cost of cargo, Carle had apparently decided to send his friend a botanical present. Inside the case, Borty found rooted vines bearing very American monikers: Clinton, Post-Oak, and Emily.

Borty planted his shipment of New World vines in his walled garden and watched them flourish. Nearby, however, vinegrowers started to notice something odd: Early the next summer, at a vineyard a few miles southwest, the leaves on the vines turned yellow and red and then, by August, desiccated and fell. When farmers uprooted the dead vines, however, there was no obvious disease, save some blackened decay that farmers attributed to fungus. The story started to repeat itself with frightening regularity as the blight spread like a cancerous inkblot. As Christy Campbell vividly recounts in his book *The Botanist and the Vintner*, mysterious vine death spread through Borty's lower Rhône valley, to the Mediterranean Sea, and beyond.

Tales of this silent killer moved from farmer to farmer and then into the press. In fall 1867, Paris's *Journal d'agriculture pratique* reported that the terrifying affliction saw "no difference between young and old vines . . . no distinction between types of soil." Desperation bloomed as local clergy blamed man's choice of science over God; in 1868, a Roquemaure dignitary named Maximilian Richard purchased the relics of Saint Valentine in Rome and enshrined them in Roquemaure's church of Saint-Jean-l'Evangéliste in the hope that the saint would intervene on behalf of local farmers.

And then, on July 15, 1868, a member of a local commission investigating the blight, Montpellier botanist Jules-Émile Planchon, was examining an afflicted vineyard when the roots of a supposedly "healthy" vine were unearthed by an accidental pickax blow. There, barely visible to the naked eye, Planchon saw touches of yellow. Looking closer with a magnifying glass, he was faced with a horrible discovery: clumps of insects feasting happily on the roots. On August 3, 1868, Planchon announced to France's Academy of Sciences that he had identified the cause of France's vineyard devastation: a new insect that would come to bear the villainous name of *Phylloxera vastatrix*, the "dry-leaf devastator."

What Planchon had found was a sap-sucking aphid that had reverse-emigrated from America to the Old World on Borty's vines—the advent of faster steamships had probably allowed it to survive the ocean crossing—and it was acting like the worst kind of guest. The insect's path through a multigeneration sex life is mind-numbingly complex, but the outline is simple and terrifying: the tiny parasites crawl down to the roots from their leaftop birthplaces; there, they perforate the surface to feed on the sap; to keep the root open for return meals, they secrete a poison that prevents the root from healing; and they gorge until their host is sucked dry. And then the cycle repeats again and again: within seven months, a single female can produce a legion of 25.6 billion murderous descendants.

Knowing the problem gave France's vintners hope, but bringing phylloxera into the light didn't stop its destructive spread. In 1870 France's Ministry of Agriculture offered a 20,000-franc prize for anyone who could design a practical remedy—a prize it upped to a then astonishing 300,000 francs in 1874. By 1877, almost seven hundred possible treatments had been submitted, coming from as far away as Brazil and Singapore. But despite the ministry's best intentions, the inventions ran from the bad to the ridiculous. The remedies included living toads (buried under the vine to draw out the poison), white-wine irrigation, cow urine, powdered tobacco, walnut leaves, crushed bone dissolved in sulfuric acid, a blend of whale oil and gasoline, potassium sulfide dissolved in piss, volcanic ash from Pompeii, marching bands, and baths of elder-leaf tea. Carbon disulfide, a volatile chemical used as an industrial solvent, was poured liberally into trenches around the infected vines. The bugs died, but so did half the vines. It was various takes on urine, however, that most caught the public's imagination: in Beaujolais, schoolboys were taken twice a day from their classes to pee in the vineyards.

Nothing worked; panic spread. Phylloxera destroyed 40 percent of France's vineyards inside of thirty years. By 1884, 2.5 million acres of France's vineyards had been killed, and another 1.5 million acres were dying. French peasants abandoned their ruined vineyards and headed for Algeria and the Americas. A favorite of American presidents— Washington had opened a consulate there and Jefferson had toured the area—the top Bordeaux wine region saw consumption of its products plummet. In England, regimental officers' dining halls switched to whiskey and soda. The French wine business nearly died: wine production fell by almost 75 percent, from a peak of 8.5 billion liters in 1875 to 2.3 billion in 1889.

It was only after French winemakers overcame their prejudices toward the New World that the phylloxera blight was stopped. As early as 1869, Bordeaux grape grower Léo Laliman had reported that unlike European *Vitis vinifera* vines, American vine roots were resistant to phylloxera. He suggested that the cure might be found in grafting European vines onto American roots. But French winemakers, worried that their wines would take on the flavor of New World plonk, wasted years searching for a chemical cure to avoid using America's brutish botany. In 1878, a correspondent in *Le Temps* proclaimed that, "Any recourse to America should be forsworn until, should it come, the very day of defeat." The widespread replanting of French vineyards, grafted on American rootstock imported from the most un-French state of Texas, didn't begin until the late 1880s.

By delaying the replacement of its vineyards with American roots, France allowed the parasite to travel to Portugal, Austria, and Switzerland, and then, by the end of the 1870s, to Italy and Spain. In a November 8, 1895, article in the *New York Times*, the US consul in Palermo, William Seymour, noted that twenty-six Italian provinces had been struck, causing the loss of 286,000 vineyard acres, with another 188,000 infected. Sicily was especially hard hit, Consul Seymour said, with 240,000 acres destroyed and $30–$40 million in damage done over three years. "The infection," the consul said, "is spreading." Within thirty years, Italy lost 1.5 million acres of vineyards.

The panicked response in Italy was as ridiculous as the French one: in Lecco, on Lake Como, director of agriculture Nicòla Miraglia and his assistants burned every plant in sight. In the end, the phylloxera vine blight not only helped Argentina take back its own wine market, as Civit had expected, but it also had an unexpected second effect: just as fleeing French peasants had decamped for Algeria and America, taking their winemaking skills with them, thousands of Italian and Spanish vine-growing peasants looked at their withered fields, packed their bags, and took to the seas. They were men like José Gregorio López Rivas, an eighteen-year-old from the small town of Algarrobo in the Spanish province of Málaga. His family of grape and olive growers had had a bad few years: a dip in foreign demand, an 1884 earthquake, and a cholera epidemic the following year. But it was phylloxera that pushed him over the edge. In 1886 he boarded a boat. To Argentina.

Modern Argentina was created by a tidal wave of immigration. It's almost impossible to imagine the scale of change the country experienced; between 1847 and 1939, seven million immigrants came to Argentina. At the beginning of World War I, almost three in every ten Argentines had been born abroad—including almost six of every ten people who lived in the cities. In the wine province of San Juan, the immigrant percentage of the population rose from 4 percent to 14 percent between 1869 and 1914. In Mendoza the number soared from 9 percent to 32 percent; the 1914 census found that 88,354 of the 277,535 residents were foreign born. And among this flood of immigrant *campesinos* who made it to the Andean west were most of the future big names of Argentine wine: Pulenta, Rutini, Furlotti, López, Tomba, Toso, Giol, Gargantini, and Arizu. Many wineries, like the López Rivas–founded powerhouse Bodegas López, still carry their names.

As the names suggest, a great many of the immigrants came from Italy. Between 1861 and the beginning of World War I in 1914, some sixteen million Italians fled poverty, overpopulation, and political unrest in their homeland. A good percentage of those came to Argentina. Among the seven million immigrants who arrived in the South American country, 250,000 came from France, two million from Spain, and three million from the Italian peninsula. After stepping onto soil in Buenos Aires, they poured into neighborhoods like La Boca, remade Argentine cuisine, and created the Spanish-Italian dialect known as *cocoliche*. And thousands of those who had come from Italy's rural winegrowing regions continued their migration west until they reached the Andean foothills. "We were colonized by Spain and conquered by Italy," says Nora Favelukes, an Argentine wine consultant based in New York. "We inherited the worst of both countries," she jokes. "The arrogance of the Spanish and the chaos of the Italians."

Arrogance and chaos aside, the immigrants who came around the turn of the century found in Argentina a land ripe for development, especially on the western winegrowing edge. The wide-open country was almost unpopulated; with only about four million residents, or just under four per square mile, Argentina in 1895 would make contemporary North Dakota look like an urban slum.

Giovanni Giol was born in 1867 to a family of farmers in Vigonovo, a small town in the northeastern Italian region of Friuli. Italy was in the midst of an economic crisis, and Giol's family—his whole town, really—was poor. At the age of eighteen the adventuresome teen left the vineyards and olive groves of Vigonovo and traveled to Greece to work on the four-mile-long Corinth Canal, whose ground breaking Roman Emperor Nero had performed in AD 67. Back in Vigonovo several years later, Giol again caught a case of wanderlust when he heard that the soil of western Argentina was perfect for grapes—that it was even as good as Friuli land. Giol decided to put his agricultural skills to work, and in 1887 he lit out for the New World. After working in Mendoza for three years as a *contratista* (a "contractor," or vineyard sharecropper), Giol scraped together enough money to rent a small vineyard and try his hand at making his own wine. During the first year he did so in three wooden tanks shaded by a grove of walnut trees.

Now known as Juan, the Spanish version of "Giovanni," Giol married Margarita Bondino. Through Margarita he met Bautista Gerónimo Gargantini, a Swiss immigrant who was married to her sister Oliva. Like Giol, Gargantini had left his poor family farm to work in construction—masonry and housepainting in his case—before taking a chance on Argentina in 1883. In Mendoza, he built up a small nest egg working as a mason and then started a delicatessen in the nascent city's central market. There he met an Italian immigrant named Pascual Toso, and in 1890 they started a winery. Giol joined them soon after.

In 1896 the instinctual Giol and the tireless Gargantini purchased 120 acres for vineyards and launched their own winery. It would be called *La Colina de Oro* ("The Hill of Gold"). The growth of *La Colina de Oro* was inexorable. During its first year of existence, the partners built two warehouses; eventually they would build twenty more, each of which they would fill with huge wooden wine casks that sat either on their sides (*toneles*) or on their ends (*cubos*). Their production exploded from 4 million liters of wine in 1898, to 7 million in 1902, 22 million in 1907, and 42 million in 1911, making *La Colina de Oro* the biggest *bodega* in the world. The work of getting the wine from the winery to the train station for shipping was such a large undertaking—they had 350 carriages and 1,400 mules in their stables—that Giol and Gargantini built their own streetcar line. They had four hundred full-time employees, and some three hundred more during harvest. Pictures from the era show a huge carpentry workshop where the winery's eighty stone-faced *toneleros*— Old World coopers in mustaches and long aprons—assembled wine barrels. At their height, Giol and Gargantini owned some 22,000 acres, of which more than 4,000 were planted with vines.

The sheer size and audacity of the operation shocked the winemaking world. A traveling Italian professor named Enrique Ferri compared seeing the winery to visiting the Roman Colosseum; and in the 1906 Milan Exposition, Italy's king gave Juan Giol—who had begun to carry the nickname *El Rey del Vino* ("The King of Wine")—a gold medal honoring the accomplishments of Italians abroad. Just yards apart on the winery grounds, the two owners built sumptuous mansions similar to the Palladian Villas of the Veneto and constructed in the Italian art nouveau style known as Liberty. The palaces had heating systems imported from France, polychromatic lime ceilings and floors from Italy, stained-glass windows featuring Bacchus (the Roman god of wine), and hand-painted toilets. And during the celebrations of Argentina's centennial in 1910, when Giol and Gargantini exhibited an 80,000-liter Slovenian oak tank decorated with a bronze shield that portrayed a panoramic view of the *bodega*, Argentine president-elect Roque Saenz Peña paid tribute to the immigrant winemakers at a lunch at Giol's house where he gave a speech over dessert.

Nothing seemed impossible: when Giol and Gargantini bought a second *bodega* near the train station some one and a quarter miles away, they conceived and built the world's first *vinoducto*, an elevated pipeline, built of steel pipes from Germany's Mannesmann, that joined the building where the wine was crushed, stored, and fermented to the new *bodega* whence it was shipped. Still visible today in the Mendozan town of Maipú, the pipeline could carry twenty-six thousand gallons of wine per hour. It was a poorly kept secret among local alcoholics that one could tap a nail into the pipe and siphon a bit of free booze.

Emigrating to the New World and building the world's largest winery out of nothing demanded hard work and intelligence, hunger, and luck. It also required a touch of mania. Later in his life Giol would join the Italian fascism movement. And Gargantini, a bald man with a thick, gray goatee and a head like a bullet, was famous for his hard hand. When his wife Oliva became pregnant in 1891 after bearing him two daughters, he threatened to kill her if she bore him another girl. Happily for everyone concerned, Oliva gave birth to Bautista Jr., who was sent to school in Switzerland at age ten by a Gargantini frightened that his son would be stricken in one of the epidemics of cholera—thought to have been brought by the new train from Buenos Aires—that regularly swept through Mendoza. Three of his seven other children, including his only other son, died young.

On another occasion, Gargantini and his wife gave their daughter Nora a beautiful doll as a gift during one of their biannual trips to Italy to visit her and her sister at boarding school. Later on that trip, as Gargantini and Nora walked to a doctor's appointment, Gargantini warned his daughter that if she cried he would give the doll to the first girl he saw on the street. The visits were difficult on the girls, who rarely got to see their parents and found them very harsh when they did, and when the sad Nora could not contain her tears, Gargantini fulfilled his threat. "From that I understand why the children of immigrants are so short on affection. The priority for their parents was to educate their children as best as they could and with a very strict hand. I don't think the parents ever got over the Italian independence wars and the hunger they caused," says Nora's granddaughter Alejandra.

In the years leading up to the First World War, the two now wealthy ex-*campesinos* moved back to their native countries. Like many immigrants, they came to "do America" (*hacer la América*), and once they had made their mark they were ready to go. Portly and respectable in waxed mustaches, black suits, tuxedo-collared shirts, and black bow ties, Gargantini returned to Switzerland in 1911; Giol headed to Italy four years later.

For Gargantini it was a tragic time: his father Pietro died the year before his return, and his beloved son Bautista Jr. informed him that he planned to make his own way in Argentina and would not return to the old country. But this bitter pill did not slow down Gargantini, who promptly launched a construction spree. He bought a meadow facing the lake in his southern Swiss birthplace of Lugano and built five palaces. For his part, Giol returned to Italy in the perfect rags-to-riches fantasy. In March 1919 he paid Earl Nicolò Papadopoli about 4 million lire for 2,500 acres of land that included three wineries, as well as Villa Papadopoli, an enormous neo-Gothic castle built in the mid-1800s in San Polo di Piave. Giol repaired the extensive damage the castle had suffered during the war, when it had been used as a barracks for the Austrians and had been bombed by Italian mortars. Over the next decade, Giol bought another 5,000 acres, which were home to forty-three hundred peasants—people much like the one he had once been—and was given the honorary title of *Commendatore* ("Knight Commander"). He died in 1936, a year before Gargantini.

Hungry-immigrant stories like those of Giol and Gargantini were repeated scores of times in Argentina's west. Through thrift, hard work,

Old World vineyard knowledge and a willingness to employ new techniques, humble immigrants saved their meager *contratista* salaries until they could buy their own land. Sometimes, in thanks for their toil, their aristocratic *criollo* overseers would give them a parcel of land at the end of their contract. From such modest beginnings the immigrants made great fortunes and then, like kudzu or nutria or Asian carp, these non-native species pushed aside the defenseless *criolla* aristocracy: In 1895, native-born Argentines owned more than three-fifths of the Mendoza wine business, and Argentine-born Benegas's *El Trapiche* was the biggest winery in the province. By 1910, immigrants controlled 80 percent of the industry and Benegas had fallen to seventh place, with five of the spots above him filled by immigrant-owned *bodegas*.

The new arrivals did not will themselves to greatness through desire and muscle alone, of course. Someone had to drink what they sold, and their rapid advance was made possible by the thirsty drinking habits of their fellow European immigrants. In a sense, they packed their own consumers. Per capita consumption in Argentina rose from 23 liters a year in the late 1870s to 62 liters a year in 1914 (when 29 percent of the population was foreign born). By 1915, wine accounted for 8.7 percent of the average family's grocery bill, making it the third largest part, behind meat and bread. And, as Emilio Civit had predicted, those liters were increasingly of Argentine wine: in the early 1880s, two-thirds of the wine drunk in Argentina came from Spain, Italy, and France, but in 1915 less than 2 percent was imported. By that year, Argentina had become the world's fifth-largest producer of wine, behind France, Italy, Spain, and French Algeria.

The great fortunes to be won in Argentina's wine industry inspired an avaricious dark side in some aspiring moguls who, in typical boomtown fashion, took fraud's easy out. When immigrant *bodeguero* Domingo Tomba's brother and partner Antonio died from cancer in 1899, Domingo simply forged Antonio's signature on a fake will in order to gain control of the family *bodega*. After increasing the winery's production to 30 million liters a year, Domingo was sued by Antonio's suspicious son. Found guilty of forgery, Domingo returned to Italy broken and disgraced; he died as a municipal employee of the city of Rome.

More commonly, however, the *bodegueros* perpetrated the fraud on the very people who made their prosperity possible: Argentina's wine-drinking public. *Bodegueros*, distributors, and retailers began to habitually perform an oenological version of the miracle of the loaves and fishes, magically turning one liter into two without pressing another grape. By the time Argentina's inky reds got to their tables, consumers found that the once-dark wine had been watered down to pink. To add insult to oenological injury, wine counterfeiters who overdiluted their drink added ethyl alcohol and other products to bring back the kick. The obsession with selling as much as possible as cheaply as possible grew so feverish that people began adding honey, lime, and sulfuric acid to fix the product.

To try to save the industry from its own corruption and greed, government beverage inspectors dumped approximately ten million liters of tainted wine in 1902. The next year, Argentina formed a national commission to investigate the state of the wine industry. His tongue firmly in cheek, commission president Pedro Arata wrote of the dilution habit, "A white liquid is employed in these operations that some *bodegueros* refer to as 'correction' and others 'splitting.' There are some who, not being pretentious, call it 'water.'"

But Arata was not always able to summon his good humor. He spoke with eloquent sadness of the boom-time madness, evoking the lost opportunity of the United States' own New World Eden. "Many fortunes were made in the feverish activity of the first businesses. Mendoza and San Juan were synonymous with progress and wealth. The region of Cuyo was the new California, where the gold was hidden in the juice of the grape bunches gilded by the sun that blesses this Promised Land," he wrote. "Cuyo's wine industry is suffering a crisis that, having booby-trapped the foundation of the economic well-being that this region enjoyed, seriously threatens its future."

Petrified at losing the power and fortune they had so recently built, winemakers swung into action. In 1904, a self-appointed group of *bodegueros*—dominated by immigrant magnates like Giol, Gargantini, Arizu, and Tomba—formed the *Defensa Vitivinícola Nacional* ("National Wine Defense"), an industry group to lobby politicians on fighting wine fraud. Later that year, the national government came out with the *Ley Nacional de Vinos* ("National Wine Law"), meant to set rules and push the industry to make healthier stuff. Based in part on the advice of Pedro Arata, the law defined what could and could not be called "wine," which winemaking practices were legal, the fines and penalties for breaking the law (up to fifteen days in jail for each thousand liters of adulterated wine), and how foreign wines were to be sold to avoid counterfeiting.

It was a bold step for a country with a history of contraband trade. Perhaps the most telling sign of the depth to which fraud and bad winemaking had penetrated is the story of Elías Villanueva. As governor of Mendoza from 1901 to 1904, Villanueva had overseen the push for a law regulating the wine industry. He was, however, less eager to admit Pedro Arata's inspectors when they came to his own winery to check out his stock. The inspectors soon discovered why: he had on hand some hundred thousand rotten liters that would have been dangerous to their drinkers' health.

Of course, some Argentine *bodegas* aimed to produce high-quality wine. A few even won awards: wines from Tomba got top prizes in Paris, London, and Milan in 1905 and 1906, and Domingo Tomba himself was honored twice by the Italian king as a Knight of the Order of Work and a Knight of the Crown of Italy. Emboldened by such examples, Escuela

Nacional de Vitivinicultura de Mendoza oenology professors Enrique Simois and Gervasio Ortíz told the 1910 Congreso Científico Industrial Americano, "At the beginning, the only immediate necessity for *bodega* owners was to produce a lot of wine and sell it quickly, without worrying about the quality. They had an end: to make money, to make a fortune without worrying about the nobility of the means. But it must be understood that among them there were exceptions, exceptions that today are growing notably, and that augur a progressive mark toward the fineness and nobility of the product . . . As a result of tastings of wines of our region, it's been said that it was almost impossible to produce fine wines here. But the facts are starting to show the opposite."

After reaping a bonanza during the first quarter of the twentieth century—the nation grew to be one of the world's ten richest countries—Argentina saw its prosperity collapse with the global depression sparked by the Wall Street crash of 1929. The next year, a grossly corrupt military junta inaugurated the *Década Infame* ("Infamous Decade"). In its early years, the military government put into place a series of *juntas reguladoras nacionales* ("national regulatory boards") to support collapsing agricultural prices and prevent overproduction. In an example of how far the conservative government was willing to go to protect the business community from financial loss, the *juntas* paid to turn whole harvests of corn into train fuel, even though a significant number of Argentines were suffering hunger. Unemployment shot up, public employees went unpaid, and the country's agricultural economy collapsed, launching an almost biblical exodus to the cities and creating shantytowns on the outskirts of Buenos Aires.

The winemakers suffered alongside their countrymen as impoverished Argentines saved money by drinking less: annual per capita consumption fell from 62 liters to 33 liters between 1926 and 1932. With fewer buyers, overproduction and price collapses became the era's hopeless signature. The authoritarian government's *junta reguladora* responded with an extreme bleeding cure. To dissuade farmers from creating excess supply, new plantings would be charged a fine of up to 1,000 pesos per hectare (2.47 acres). And to cut back existing production, the *junta* bought farmers' wine before it could be sold, and they paid vineyard owners to yank vines producing some 200 million pounds of grapes. Again, confiscated wine ran like *bodeguero* blood in the west's irrigation canals.

Ironically, it was not massive deregulation or a new influx of immigrants that returned the wine industry to prosperity, but a politician whose interventionist ideology of prolabor laws and industrial regulation cut directly against the entrepreneurial grain of most *bodegueros*: an army colonel named Juan Domingo Perón. As part of a secret society of nationalist military officers, Perón helped overthrow the last *Década Infame* government in 1943. Working his way up the ranks of the new dictatorship, the pragmatic Perón built a constituency among the country's working class and the recently displaced rural workers who had moved to the cities to find jobs. Though he was far from a wide-eyed progressive, as secretary of labor Perón introduced social-welfare benefits for workers, raised wages, and took to organizing unions in industries that had traditionally not been unionized. After marrying a pretty but brittle radio actress named Eva Duarte, Perón was elected president in 1946 as an authoritarian champion of the common man, a kind of Mussolini Light.

Born out of wedlock and raised in poverty by the discarded mistress of a wealthy landowner, Perón's new wife Evita was a political blank slate when she met Juan. But she soon took to politicking with such vigor that she threatened to overshadow her husband. From her perch at the head of the Eva Perón Foundation, where she served as Perón's representative to Argentina's poor *descamisados* ("shirtless ones"), the couture-bedecked

Evita gave away everything she didn't have as a child. She distributed to Argentina's poor thousands of sewing machines, shoes, cooking kits, and wedding dresses. As vividly described in Argentine writer Tomás Eloy Martinez's *Santa Evita*, which mixes fiction and journalism in the telling of Evita's life, families made pilgrimages from the interior to Buenos Aires in order to take a number and wait in line at the foundation for hours, all on the off chance that they might have a moment to plead their case directly to the First Lady. "With Evita one never knows," one character says. "She's like God."

Indeed, shortly before her death of cervical cancer in 1952, at the age of thirty-three, she was officially dubbed the "Spiritual Leader of the Nation" by the Argentine Congress. Seen by the poor as an earthly saint during her lifetime, in death she came to represent something Christ-like (though not to all; when she was dying, the graffiti *"¡Viva el cáncer!"*— "Long live cancer!"—appeared in rich neighborhoods where resentment of the working-class uplift ran strong). So powerful was the cult that surrounded Evita and her corpse that when a group of conservative Catholic military officers overthrew Perón in 1955, they absconded with Evita's body, hid it in Italy for sixteen years, and decreed it illegal to mention the names of either Juan or Evita Perón.

Evita and her husband were largely unloved by Argentina's wealthy, conservative *bodeguero* class. But Perón's labor-friendly policies, which closed Argentina's income gap between rich and poor, were actually a great gift to the country's wine moguls. Under these new policies, huge masses of the new, urban working class found they had the money to buy a drink they quite liked: wine. And since they didn't have much experience in the finer versions of the stuff, they didn't seem to care what they drank as long as it got them tipsy.

To make sure there was abundant, cheap wine for these thirsty, undiscriminating followers, Perón's government pushed winemakers back to the process that locals cheekily referred to as "wine baptism." In the early fifties, wine inspectors began to demand that all wine shipped from the west have an alcohol level below 11.5 percent. Considering that the Andean zone's arid climate and intense sun inherently produced much boozier wines, there was only one way to comply: the *bodegueros* poured between 1.5 and 2 million liters of water a year into their wine before they shipped it east. Assuring that there was enough wine for the *descamisados* was truly urgent business; Evita herself personally exhorted winemakers to water down their product.

The diluted liquid probably qualified as some of the most expensive tap water ever sold. But to the newly solvent working class it did sell, and for decades. Annual per capita wine consumption in Argentina rose from 66 liters in 1950 to 80 liters in 1960 and 92 liters in 1970, when Buenos Aires was third only to Paris and Rome for per capita consumption in world cities. To keep up with the demand, vineyard land sprawled from 450,000 acres in 1950 to almost 900,000 in 1977, production exploded, and wineries that once had been artisanal shops became imagination-dwarfing fermentation factories. On urban construction sites, the indigenous descended laborers who had migrated from Argentina's impoverished north to the eastern cities—disparagingly known by the rich as *cabecitas negras* ("little black heads")—were said to typically consume a liter of wine along with a liter of seltzer water and a kilogram of meat each day. In the Palermo neighborhood of Buenos Aires, it became common to see a two-block line of wine tanker trucks pulled up to the curb, baking their product in the sun as they waited hours for their turn to unload at the clutch of bottling plants the industry kept there along a railroad spur. And as the maraschino cherry on Argentina's postwar wine boom, in 1972 the Peñaflor wine conglomerate inaugurated the world's largest wine tank, a 5.3-million-liter epoxy-lined cement behemoth with a diameter larger than the length of a football field.

As the 1970s rolled to a close, the offspring of the industry's immigrant founders could be excused for thinking that they had rejiggered the laws of physics and created a machine that would churn out easy profits in perpetuity.

# CHAPTER 3

# *LA CRISIS*

Héctor Greco (with sunglasses) in Mendoza, 1980. Courtesy of *Los Andes*.

IN THE LAST HOURS of April 24, 1980, the brothers Héctor and José Greco and their banker Jorge Bassil sat paging through the menu in the Pedemonte restaurant, a Buenos Aires landmark. Founded in 1890 by Italian immigrant José Pedemonte and famous for its artichoke tart, the restaurant was decorated with sumptuous stained-glass windows, beveled mirrors, art nouveau boiserie, an oak bar, and well-buffed bronze chandeliers. Just blocks from the Casa Rosada ("Pink House") presidential palace, it was the kind of place where political and cultural maestros went to do business and be seen.

The Grecos and Bassil had recently left a tense meeting at the Central Bank of their country, which was being run by yet another military dictatorship. At the meeting, Héctor had refused to sign a document demanded by the military junta's interior minister General Albano Harguindeguy and economy minister José Alfredo Martínez de Hoz, and a police Ford Falcon had been tailing them since. The Falcon had been the junta's model of choice for rounding up political enemies during the 1976–83 "Dirty War," in which up to thirty thousand leftist regime opponents were "disappeared." Its presence sent a clear message; the brothers were not surprised to be arrested at the Pedemonte.

Owners of Argentina's largest wine business, with almost half of the market, Héctor Greco and his associates were soon charged with monopolistic practices and the Orwellian crime of "economic subversion." The three businessmen were bundled off to prison, and their empire, with its twelve thousand employees spread across forty-seven businesses (including a newspaper, three banks, and three dozen *bodegas*), quickly ceased to exist.

Almost overnight, the Argentine wine boom ended.


The Grecos were the hood ornament on Argentina's postwar wine bonanza. The family started as *fraccionadores* in 1948, buying wine in bulk in Mendoza and distributing it in Buenos Aires. In the early sixties they got into making and selling their own wine by buying a winery on the eastern side of Mendoza, along with what would become the hugely successful wine brand Pángaro. When the oldest brother, Alberto, died in 1969, the next-oldest son, Héctor, assumed control, as was typical in traditional Italian families. A big man with a chin wattle and a pencil mustache above his fleshy lips, Héctor habitually wore dark sunglasses indoors and out in order to disguise a walleye. To those who didn't know him well, Héctor was mysterious, enigmatic, a bit Mafioso. It didn't lessen that impression that he traveled with an entourage of "advisers."

With his new winery in Mendoza, Héctor soon became a popular man among the region's wine and grape sellers: a man who respected the sacrifices of agriculture and, more important, paid well in good times and bad. "The grape growers are the goose that lays the golden eggs. We can't kill that goose," Greco said.

A crafty money manager, Greco grew progressively wealthier during a period of hyperinflation in the mid-1970s, when smart wine merchants stocked up on wine and then sold the product later for much higher prices. The real Greco windfall began in 1977, however, when the brothers bought a Mendoza bank, Banco de los Andes, from a group

of local notables. It was a great moment to be a banker in Argentina: that year the dictatorship had decided to liberalize the banking system by allowing banks to set their own interest rates and by expanding the amount of deposits the Central Bank would insure in the case of bank failures. Argentines began to deposit a flood of cash into new interest-bearing bank accounts. The result was a speculative boom as unknown banks tried to seduce this new mass of retail depositors with ever-higher interest rates.

The Grecos joined the party at Banco de los Andes. They offered interest rates 1 percent higher than those of their competitors and brought in a torrent of deposits. Believing that wine prices and consumption would continue to climb, they then lent themselves their depositors' money and went on a shopping spree. They bought wineries, vineyards, and large stocks of wine to corner the market, and a newspaper to defend themselves as they did so.

Greco chose a propitious time to wave around a full wallet: most of the country's family wine dynasties had reached the infamous third generation, in which an unwieldy passel of bickering grandchildren, many bereft of the hardworking immigrant ethic, were only too eager to cash out their share of the family business. Giants like the Arizus and Furlottis sold, as did many more. Only a few of the grand old names—ones like Bodegas López—remained.

Greco's Banco de los Andes quickly grew to be the largest private bank in Argentina, and Héctor and his brothers accumulated some 1.1 billion liters of wine—about 90 percent of Mendoza's annual production. At their height, they were selling some 50 million liters per month, or about 50 percent of the wine consumed in the country. But the wine didn't matter. The Grecos were just being capitalists, and their ploy was the natural end game of an industry that no longer cared about the product it sold. The drink they hawked was a basic manufactured good—almost a commodity—and their business plan was little more than a grand circus of financial engineering aimed at drowning the competing manufacturers in rising raw-material prices. Wine? Widgets? That wasn't the point.

As Héctor Greco grew increasingly powerful, salesmen began calling on his offices in the outpost of San Martín. An amply sized town on the east side of Mendoza, San Martín offers the weird mix of European class and provincial vulgarity that makes so many western Argentine towns feel like the set of a spaghetti western as imagined by a Frenchman. Hot, dusty, and generally charmless, San Martín's main drag is home to an anonymous run of retail stores and car mechanics but bears the cosmopolitan name of Boulogne Sur Mer, the fishing port in northern France where Argentine independence leader—and town namesake—José de San Martín died in 1850. It is not the kind of place one would expect to find the epicenter of Argentina's wine industry. Off the main artery, the town devolves into an almost interminable chain of square midcentury cement cube homes, interspersed with a few beautiful pre–World War II houses built in a French style, with elaborate iron gates and decorative stucco around the windows and doors.

The salesmen who tramped through Greco's headquarters offered him everything from a circus with which he could entertain his employees to a plane for vineyard fumigation, a Picasso (counterfeit) for general pleasure, and a Rolls Royce for transportation. In the end Greco did buy the Rolls, in which he was chauffeured everywhere. He also began to play the benefactor, using his money to start a foundation and fund charities. Usually out of deference, though sometimes also to disparage the Sicilian's sumptuous Rolls and mysterious shades, people began referring to Greco as *El Padrino*. The Godfather.

Those who dealt with Héctor Greco at the end of the seventies recall the era with unabashed nostalgia. As he poured money into the market, wholesale wine and grape prices spiraled upward. Greco offered such unbelievable prices that no one wanted to look under the hood. Héctor became a revered figure among winemakers and grape growers who had suffered a miserable three-year price trough from 1974 to 1977. Between 1978 and 1980 the portion of wine's retail price that went to Argentina's bulk winemakers almost doubled, from 45 percent to 85 percent. Arnaldo Carosio was working in Mendoza as a wine broker at the time, and he says he handled increasingly absurd sales as the industry lost touch with reality. "After Greco bought the bank, one day I sold the same wine five different times—and the wine never left the tank it was in. Juan would sell it to Pedro at 1 peso, Pedro to José at 1.30, José to someone else at 1.60, and then Greco would buy it at 1.80," Carosio says.

As Greco's price-raising ways endeared him to grape growers, it drove less well capitalized winemakers to ruin and forced many to sell their companies to him in desperation. "Winemakers had to pay Greco prices for grapes and wine. People were drowning," says Adriano Senetiner, the Italian-born cofounder of the Mendoza *bodega* Nieto Senetiner and, at the time of the Greco collapse, the president of a Mendozan trade group.

With this profligate and self-serving generosity, Héctor bought loyalty in addition to wine. One day when Carosio visited Greco to sign a contract for three million liters of wine, Greco asked him what he was doing driving a Ford Taurus. After the perplexed Carosio noted that it had only a thousand miles on the odometer, Héctor told Carosio to follow him to Mendoza. There they stopped at a Mercedes-Benz dealership. "I have to handle a few things," Greco told Carosio. "You choose a car." Unwilling to anger *El Padrino*—and unable to believe his luck—the baffled Carosio chose the cheapest Mercedes on the lot, a $46,000 red 280C Coupe, and left his Taurus as a down payment.

"I hid the coupe in the garage of our house because I didn't know what to tell my wife about how I'd gotten that car. She would have thought I was crazy,'" Carosio says. "Greco never charged me the rest of the price of the car. That's what he did to have you trapped. One day

I told Héctor that the difference never came out of my account. He said, 'Does that worry you?' Héctor Greco wanted all of his agents to have Mercedes-Benzes, to show his economic power. You have to remember at that time we commission agents had tons of money from selling the same wine five times; $100,000, $200,000 in our accounts. It was unreal."

In October 1979, Héctor Greco signed the deal that would crown him king of the industry: he would buy the table wine business of Argentina's largest *bodega*, Grupo Catena, which sold about 220 million liters a year. It was a kind of homecoming for the Grecos, since before they bought their own *bodega*, the Catena family had been their largest supplier of wine. The offer Greco made was so high—some $129 million, split into ten payments—that Catena could not refuse.

"I said to myself, 'For my *bodega*, this price will never be reached again,'" says the family firm's head, Nicolás Catena.

Catena was right. In March 1980, the bland-sounding "Regional Exchange Bank" (Banco de Intercambio Regional) went under, sparking fears of another Depression-like financial panic. Despite government deposit guarantees, worried account holders began a countrywide bank run, withdrawing their money before it disappeared. Within twenty-five days they had taken out more than half of Banco de los Andes's holdings, which exposed a glaring problem in Héctor Greco's business model: the Grecos had lent themselves a huge chunk of the deposits to buy wine, wineries, and vineyards—72 percent of the bank's loans had gone to them—and, though they had collateral in the form of property, they didn't have enough cash on hand to return their clients' deposits.

Eager to stave off a full-scale crisis, the military regime said it would lend money to Greco via the Central Bank. But after agreeing to what since-deceased Greco lawyer Salvador Sar Sar Chía characterized as reasonable terms, the junta changed its offer at the late-night Central Bank meeting and tried to strong-arm Greco into offering all his businesses as collateral. When the sunglass-wearing wine tycoon refused to sign away his empire and left the Central Bank to take refuge in the Pedemonte, the Ford Falcon on his tail showed that his fate had already been decided. The military put Greco behind bars, appropriated his empire and caused what he had built to vanish into the Mendozan sand.

The military-appointed managers who took over flooded the market with the wine Greco had stored in his *bodegas*; bulk wine prices fell off a cliff. Official statistics show them dropping some 82 percent between 1979 and 1982, while anecdotal evidence tells of an even steeper fall: Pedro Marchevsky, then Catena's vineyard manager, says the price of a liter of wine dropped from a dollar to two cents in 1981. "Imagine the industry then. It collapsed," he says. Thousands of vineyard and winery workers lost their jobs; the inexperienced and corrupt military-appointed overseers of Greco's businesses mismanaged the *bodegas* when they weren't stealing from them; and the *bodeguero* families who had sold to Greco but hadn't yet been paid watched their fortunes disappear.

Almost to a man, the industry was wiped out. Except, that is, for Nicolás Catena. Unlike the three dozen other *bodegueros* who had sold their businesses to Greco, Catena and his lawyers had negotiated a payment trigger under which the Catena family would not turn over majority ownership of their company until they received the final payment. If Greco defaulted on his payment schedule at any point, the Catenas would get to keep control of their company—and the cash Greco had already paid.

While negotiating his contract, Nicolás Catena says he noticed that although the Greco windfall was turbocharging the industry by transferring money from bank depositors to family *bodega* sellers, annual per capita wine consumption had actually been declining since it hit its peak of 92 liters in 1970. By 1975 it had slid to 84 liters, and in 1980 it fell to 76. Worse, the Argentine monetary system was a mess. Annual inflation was running at over 100 percent a year while the Argentine peso was getting stronger against the US dollar in real terms, which meant that Argentine wine was getting more expensive—and less attractive—to overseas importers every day. Argentine table wine exports fell from 67 million liters in 1978 to a mere 9 million in 1979 and 7 million in 1980. The Greco-fed boom was only papering over an industry in decline, one that had to sprint faster and faster just to stay in place.

"Prices went up and up, and Greco's businesses began to lose money," says Nicolás Catena. "I don't think they realized what they were doing. The crisis appeared when the bank went under, but I think it would have happened anyway, when they had to sell the wine they'd hoarded. I never understood the strategy of the Banco de los Andes. It wasn't thought out well."

According to one-time Greco partner Ángel Pedro Falanga, at the time of the Greco empire's implosion, the Catenas had received seven of the ten payments, or about $116 million of the $129 million total, which they got to keep along with a good chunk of the *bodegas* they had technically sold. "The contract worked out very well," admits Nicolás Catena. "Very well."

Clear-eyed insights like the one that led to his unique contract with Greco have made Nicolás Catena the most admired, innovative, and successful *bodeguero* in Argentina. They've also made him one of the most disliked. The recipient of grudging respect for this success and angry sniping about how it was attained, he is viewed a bit like the Goldman Sachs of Mendoza. That Catena was able to keep a large amount of money, as well as control of his *bodegas*, rankled many victims of the Greco collapse. Today he enjoys international acclaim as the father of Argentina's fine-wine industry, but in Mendoza, especially among those who lost money during the early 1980s, the name Catena can be a provocation.

"While most of the grape growers and wine producers lost their money, he ended up with double. That's how Dr. Catena is," says Gabriela Furlotti, the great granddaughter of immigrant winemaking giant Ángel Furlotti. "If you ask families from that era about Catena, they'll look at you like, 'No . . . Dr. Catena, the businessman of the year . . . the Mondavi of Mendoza? No.' They'd call him a criminal."

Some blamed Greco's fall on the astronomical price the Sicilians paid to Catena. Other darker theories swirled that after signing the deal with its unique payment trigger, Nicolás Catena asked friends in the dictatorship to shut Greco down so that he could keep both the cash and the *bodegas*. "Catena, who was very tricky, denounced Greco to the military as a monopolist, and Greco ended up in jail," says Adriano Senetiner, the *bodeguero* and ex-president of the Centro de Bodegueros de Mendoza trade group. "We [in the trade group] were always denouncing Greco in the paper for what he was doing, but nothing happened until *Catenita* armed the trap." According to a 2007 article by Gabriel Bustos Herrera in the Mendoza newspaper *Los Andes*, in a prison interview Héctor Greco himself said that, "Catena and [Interior Minister] Harguindeguy, who were associates, hatched traps to make us fail."

Adding fuel to those rumors, Catena, who has a doctorate in economics, had consulted for José Martínez de Hoz, the economy minister behind the dictatorship's liberalization of the financial system. But Catena calls these rumors absurd and denies that there was anything resembling a plot between him and the government. "I thought Greco was going to fail, but not for special information or because someone told me," he says.

Worse, Catena says, he lost money because the Grecos never finished paying him off, which stuck him with the plonk *bodegas* he'd been trying to unload—he later sold his remaining shares for cents on the dollar—just as the industry collapsed. "I didn't win anything, because they stopped paying me. It hurt me," he says. "I was left with shares in the businesses, but they weren't worth anything. No, I would have preferred that they'd continued to pay."

Even those who criticize Catena admit that there is no evidence of criminal deeds. "It was legal. Greco fell and the contract said if I don't make all the payments, you get to keep the *bodega*," Furlotti says. Similarly, Senetiner notes, "It was a scam, but from Greco, not from Catena. Catena took advantage of the stupidity of this guy who thought he was all-powerful."

There is a cultural reason for the mogul's awkward position in the wine community. Argentina offered prosperity for many hardworking settlers, but with the rise of invasive and corrupt governments after the Great Depression, achieving real wealth often required unfair backroom deals. In this context, a growing fortune is often not seen as something to be respected; rather, for many it *must* be a fruit of something unfairly attained. That Catena bested his colleagues didn't help, notes Miguel Brascó, the doyen of Argentine wine writing: *"Acá no lo quieren mucho. Hay . . ."* ("Here he is not well loved. There's . . ."), Brascó says—and then he rolls out a word in English for emphasis—"envy."


In person, Nicolás Catena is no colossus. Slight, soft-spoken, gentle, and a touch bowed, he explains himself slowly and precisely in the style of a professor. He uses logical signposts like "I came to the conclusion" with clockwork regularity. "He's very calm. He speaks to you very slowly. He listens more than he speaks. Then he comes out with a solution," says French winemaker Jacques Lurton. Almost preternaturally unimposing in a physical sense, Nicolás keeps his gray hair pulled back from his high forehead and, outside business meetings, sticks to an unremarkable uniform of white sneakers, khaki pants, and oxford-cloth shirts. Compared to the theatrical Greco, he is almost obsessive about not drawing attention to his wealth. Arnaldo Carosio, the wine broker for whom Greco bought a Mercedes-Benz, has regularly worked for

Catena; the two remain friends. One day when the pair walked out of Catena's Mendoza office, Catena noticed a high-end Chevrolet parked in the lot and asked Carosio who owned it. "I said, 'It's mine,' and he said, 'That's not a car, it's a slap to other people.' Because the concept for him was that there was no reason to show luxury," Carosio says. "I said, '*Gringo*, I do it for comfort, I drive five to six hundred miles a week to get your wine. If I had a Citroën like you do I'd never make it.'"

Most of Nicolás Catena's life after elementary school was spent in the classroom or office, not in the *bodega* or field, and the impression he gives is more that of an academic than a farmer or winery owner. Alejandro Vigil, the current chief winemaker at Bodega Catena Zapata, recalls that when he first interviewed at the winery, a small older man strolled in and out of the *bodega*'s administration offices. Assuming from the man's casual dress that he was an agricultural product supplier, Vigil asked his interviewer what company he was with. "Oh no," the interviewer replied, "that's Catena."

The story of this unassuming man's ascent to the summit of Argentina's wine industry starts like those of so many other Italian *campesinos* who became titans of Argentine wine. In 1898, an eighteen-year-old boy named Nicola Catena from the tiny town of Belforte del Chienti in Italy's Marche region—the same area, curiously, that produced the Mondavi and Gallo families—stepped off a steamer in the port of Buenos Aires. The youngest of six children of a family of vineyard workers, Nicola arrived with a small amount of money and the name of a family friend who had settled in the ranching province of Santa Fe, northwest of Buenos Aires. Living out of a borrowed room in the family friend's house, Nicola spent four years as an agricultural laborer—a *peón*—in area cornfields. In 1902, he moved west and set himself up as a homesteader in the only industry he'd ever known: wine.

With a tiny nest egg, poor Spanish, and an elementary-school education, Nicola purchased a 25-acre patch of land near the flyspeck town of La Libertad ("Liberty") in the flattening hills east of Mendoza. Five acres had already been planted with vines, but it was bad land—the only kind he was able to afford—hard up against the Tunuyán River. After building a small house and putting 5 more acres of vines into the ground, he was able to survive. While the Catenas do not figure in the books of top *bodegueros* prepared for the country's 1910 centennial, Nicola quickly progressed beyond subsistence, and by the time his son Domingo was born in 1910, he had joined what one might call the agricultural middle class. He brought his parents over from Italy, and by 1916 he had begun making his own wine, which Domingo started selling around the country in 150-liter barrels in 1928.

"What was interesting to me was that people always said that in that era there were only a few rich people and the workers were very badly off," says Nicolás Catena. "If they were so bad off, how did my grandfather do that? Without education or language, he did it."

Like many of the *campesinos* who had arrived with him, Nicola sported habits born from the poverty of his youth. Back in Italy, his parents had kept several cows to supply their large family with milk but, because the most expensive foodstuff at the time was beef, the Catenas led a cruel face-against-the-glass existence: when a cow's dairy-producing life was done, Nicola's family always sold the animal for needed income instead of enjoying the occasional steak from the small herd. But in sparsely populated Argentina, where the cattle that roamed the fertile pampas grasslands vastly outnumbered the human inhabitants, beef was a kind of protein birthright. Nicola celebrated his escape from Old World penury by taking up the rustic tradition of eating *bife con pan*—"beef with bread"—for breakfast, a daily ritual he continued until he died. "He became an addict of Argentine beef," says Nicolás, who was eighteen when his grandfather passed away.

Born on the La Libertad farm in 1939 as the second of four siblings, Nicolás recalls his primary-school years as an "exaggeration" of immigrant tough love. After morning classes in a country school alongside the children of those who worked in the Catena winery and vineyards, he would return to the small farm for afternoon chores. "The easiest job for a child was to feed and care for the animals. My grandparents had horses, goats, and cows, ducks, chickens. Later, when I turned seven or eight, I had to learn the work of the vineyard. And at ten I went to work at the *bodega*. I had to work a lot, too much for a child, I think," says Nicolás.

Nicolás's father, Domingo, was also born in La Libertad. A strong, balding man who grew corpulent in later years, Domingo played the executive role taken on by many children of *campesino* immigrants. Using the confidence afforded by the modern education his father Nicola never had, Domingo built his family's modest agricultural business into a regional empire. He designed a blended *vino tipificado* in which he combined wine fermented from his own vineyards with vintages from other *bodegas* to create generic blends for the urban markets; in his case, he sold barrels of "Buenos Aires A" and "Buenos Aires B," the first of which fetched several pesos more because Catena gave it a richer color and body by increasing by half the amount of ink-black Malbec he added to the cheap *criolla* grapes that made up the rest. In Argentina's major urban areas of Buenos Aires, Rosario, and Córdoba, *fracciona-dores* like the Greco family would then bottle the wine and sell it under their own brand. The invention of a consistent blend was an important step for the industry, and by the time Nicolás entered the business in the early 1960s, Domingo Catena was Mendoza's biggest wholesaler of blended table wine, with forty bottling clients. In 1965, he sold some 5.4 million liters of the stuff per month.

Although he labored in his wineries and held what would turn out to be prescient theories about viticulture—that Argentina's colder, higher-altitude locations would produce better wines, for example, and that Malbec could be great—Domingo Catena was foremost a business-man and a politician. He started his political activism young, serving as one of the signatories, at age eighteen, of the founding document of the conservative Partido Demócrata. "He didn't feel truly Argentine," Nicolás says about his father. "I think for children of immigrants, to enter into politics was to take part in the culture." Domingo also staked his claim to Argentina by marrying Angélica Zapata, a member of the Spanish-descended *criolla* aristocracy who worked as a headmistress at a local school.

For a second-generation immigrant like Domingo—the type of man who categorically did not believe in vacations—government intervention in business was an offense against his family's hard-won achievements. Like most winemakers and vineyard owners, he leaned right in his politics. Domingo Catena joined his fellow *bodegueros* in becoming an arch anti-Peronist after the election of 1946. Although Perón's wealth redistribution policies helped wine sales, Domingo would complain to Nicolás that under Perón any businessman who wanted to survive had to bribe government functionaries. When Perón was overthrown in 1955, Domingo celebrated. That year, the military government that displaced Perón appointed Domingo Catena mayor of the county seat of Rivadavia, a sleepy town of some twenty thousand people thirty-five miles east of Mendoza. (But Domingo was not strictly doctrinaire, according to his son; he used his position of power after the coup, Nicolás says, to keep a Peronist friend out of jail.)

When Guy Ruhland came to Mendoza in the early 1980s to consult at one of the Catena family's *bodegas*, he was given a bedroom just down the hall from Domingo. Living out of the Catena patriarch's house on the outskirts of Rivadavia, Ruhland discovered a close-knit society of grape growers, *bodegueros*, farmers, and laborers. They ran the gamut of social class, but they knew one another intimately from the earliest years of elementary school. Domingo's 1946 five-bedroom house, built in a "Californian" style, embodied the prosperity of this traditional small town in Argentina's west: a neat grid of low cement buildings—the finest ones tricked out with European cornices and pilasters—centered on a plaza circled by government and church buildings. Shaded by a neat grid of palms and London plane trees (a kind of sycamore), the plaza is the town jewel, a place to take pride in and to defend vigorously if an outsider suggests that a nearby town's plaza is more lovely.

The Domingo that Ruhland met was gnarled and stooped from age, but his sense of humor and reputation as a tough and demanding businessman remained intact. Carlos Vázquez, an agronomist who worked for the Catena family empire from 1980 to 2000, recalls one afternoon when he, Pedro Marchevsky, and a fellow vineyard worker led Domingo on a tour of the 750-acre La Vendimia vineyard, which they had recently worked into what they thought was agricultural perfection. After touring half the vineyard in silence—which Vázquez describes as a covert compliment—Domingo came across a stump where a vine should have been. When the vineyard workers couldn't explain why it hadn't been replaced, he barked at them, "Enough! Let's head back."

"But Don Domingo," his employees answered. "We're going to see the plantings."

"I've already seen too much," Domingo said. "Let's go!"

"He always found something wrong," says Vázquez, now the president of Mendoza's Altos Las Hormigas winery. "There was no way for everything to be okay."

Domingo's demanding nature was such that after a hip operation left him reliant on a cane, the sound of the cane hitting and scrapping along the floor would send his workers into absolute silence. When Domingo was not around, Vázquez says, employees would imitate the sound to frighten their colleagues.

Although he was tough at work, Domingo Catena was also a gregarious and popular man ("Domingo was wonderful," says Ralph Kunkee, an American oenology professor who visited Argentina in the late seventies. "All he wanted to do was make sure I got well fed."). He eschewed the apartment he kept in Mendoza city for business, preferring instead his private men's social club in Rivadavia. There, surrounded by a posse of old friends led by the town's undertaker Noé Ferreyra, he passed his evenings arguing politics while sipping *vino con soda* or shots of Fernet (a bitter, herb-based spirit) and playing *truco* ("trick"), a Spanish team card game based on bluffs, lies, secret facial signs between teammates, and irrelevant conversation meant to distract one's opponents. "The environment in his club was very, very competitive," says Ruhland, who now makes Korbel brandy and wines for other large California wineries. After losing a handful of games quite badly—Domingo and the other players diverted Ruhland's attention with a constant stream of anti-American political commentary—the innocent *yanqui* gave up. "They kicked my butt," he says. "I was too young and naïve to be any good at that game. You have to be a fairly good liar."

*Truco* was the perfect metaphor for business in Argentina, where an ability to game the system and get away with it—something called *viveza criolla*, or "Creole quick-wittedness"—is widely celebrated. While Ruhland found Domingo Catena to be an unfailingly charming gentleman, the kind of older man who jokingly gave the thirty-year-old Ruhland grief for supposedly botching things in the winery—"treating me like the kid I was," Ruhland says—he also knew that Domingo's skill at the *truco* table mirrored the acumen that had made the old man one of the most able strategists in the region. That reputation was driven home one night at a Mendoza nightclub, when Ruhland mentioned his employer to an acquaintance of his Argentine girlfriend. The man stepped close and began to rant at the stunned Ruhland, a big man who, at six foot two and two hundred pounds, was not accustomed to attempts at physical intimidation. Ruhland could recall only the constant repetition of the word *cobarde*. Later, his girlfriend—who knew the man's family—translated the word ("coward") and the explanation for the man's anger: his family had sold its business to Don Domingo during one of the industry's downturns, and they felt like Domingo had taken advantage of their weak position.

For his friends and family, however, Domingo's strategic skill manifested itself in a mischievous sense of humor. One day during Ruhland's visit, the American was driving Domingo to visit his vineyards during a broiling-hot siesta when his truck got stuck in the sandy wash at the bottom of a hill. Domingo had grudgingly accepted his daughter's prohibition on driving because of his advanced age, but the elderly Domingo couldn't help free the truck, so he got in the driver's seat and told Ruhland to push. Ruhland rocked the small Fiat truck through the sand bowl and Domingo pumped the gas. Eventually the wheels caught. Panting, the drenched Ruhland watched as his Fiat crested the next hilltop and disappeared. Ruhland climbed the hill under the midday Mendoza sun to find a laughing Domingo waiting for him halfway down the other side. Desert thirsty, Ruhland reached behind the seat and broke open one of the bottles of white wine that he had stashed there. If he was expecting an apology, he didn't get it.

"Domingo said, 'What the hell? You had that wine back there the whole time and you didn't tell me about it?'" Ruhland recounts, laughing. "So we sat there in the middle of nowhere, drinking white wine. He was truly an interesting guy."

Like many other third-generation immigrants in the wine industry, Nicolás Catena wanted to abandon the déclassé bulk-wine business. It was repetitive and uninspiring, the liquid version of a paper clip factory. After Nicolás finished elementary school at age twelve, Domingo and Angélica sent him to a military boarding school, the tough and very Germanic Liceo Militar General Espejo, from which he graduated at age fifteen. He loved the intellectual life and planned to follow it to its logical end. "My vocation was mathematics. I was good at it, and I liked it. I wanted to study theoretical physics. My mother was from a landowning culture, not one of work but one that valued intellectual attainments, and she believed that I should be an academic, an intellectual," says Nicolás. "But my father's influence was very strong, and he said that business used a lot of mathematics. He wanted me to one day be a businessman." In the end, Nicolás met his father halfway by enrolling in the economics department at the local Universidad de Cuyo, fully expecting to switch into physics after one year. But after falling in love with the mathematical side of economics, he stayed on to earn a doctorate.

During that era Arnaldo Carosio, the Mendoza wine broker, met Nicolás through Nicolás's younger brother Jorge. Carosio was impressed by Nicolás's unwavering studiousness. While Carosio and Jorge tried to grow crops on some of Domingo Catena's land to make a few extra pesos, Nicolás stayed home to read up on history. (Domingo would occasionally visit in his Chevy pickup to laugh at the novice farmers; "Domingo never said we were doing things wrong," Carosio says. "He said we needed the experience of failure to learn. And we failed.") As Carosio and his outgoing friends played at business schemes and dreamt of buying the coolest car, they also angled for the affections of Elena Maza, whom Carosio describes as by far the most attractive girl in the university. They were stunned when the lively Maza, an enthusiastic and skilled tango dancer, dated, and then married, the slight and shy Nicolás. It was classic Nicolás: while others were out glad-handing and chattering, Catena was at home reading up on the world's past mistakes, coming up with theories and testing them against reality. In the end it was the reserved economist who quietly claimed the prize.

In 1958, just as Nicolás was embarking on life in the academy, tragedy struck on one of the area's undivided two-lane speed alleys, where lumbering agriculture vehicles vie for space with whizzing subcompacts whose drivers show an Italian addiction to tailgating and speed. While driving to the city, his grandfather Nicola pulled into the path of a speeding agricultural truck and the car was crushed. Both Nicola and his daughter-in-law Angélica, Nicolás's mother, who was sitting in the front passenger seat, were killed. As Nicolás finished his economics PhD at the local university, the mourning Domingo lost his enthusiasm for business. The Catena *bodegas* began to suffer. Nicolás was faced with a choice between his dead mother's hopes and his live father's needs. After graduating, Nicolás decided to put his academic career on hold—he had been accepted into the PhD economics program at the University of Chicago—and, in 1962, took over management of the family business.

Although he'd been around winemaking all his life, Nicolás Catena was almost a stranger to the trade because he had never seriously considered it as part of his future. This lack of recent experience gave him an advantage over many of the third-generation *bodeguero* famiies; he could examine the business with an outsider's clear eyes, without the resentment of a child coerced into it from birth. Like the thwarted professor he was, Nicolás sublimated his academic ambitions into treating the industry as if it were a thesis project. "As I was used to acting like a student, I put my mind to studying everything about wine and vineyards," he says.

By bringing an economist's unsentimental logic to a business that was often run on intuition and tradition, Nicolás regularly clashed with the way things were done. During one of his first years at the company, the market price for grapes had been set at what he saw as an excessively high level, considering the large size of the harvest. He foresaw that a glut of wine would come to market and drive down prices, so Nicolás advised his father not to buy grapes from growers and to not even bother harvesting his own; it would be more profitable, he told Domingo, to wait for the market to crash and then buy and resell the resulting flood of cheap wine. "But he said he had committed to people. It cost him a fortune," Nicolás says of his more traditional father, who bought the grapes and lost money along with everyone else.

While he was foiled in that instance, Nicolás's economics-inspired ideas helped build the Catena business from a regional enterprise to Argentina's biggest wine power. At the time Nicolás entered the business, the local industry was divided between industrial wineries like

Domingo's, which made anonymous wine products like Buenos Aires A, and urban wholesalers who bought tanks of the stuff and bottled and sold the drink under their own brand, marking it up by astronomical percentages. Domingo's relationship with his forty *fraccionadores* caused him no end of angst, in part because of an industrial structure in which they received the lion's share of the profit for doing what to his eyes was so little of the work. "For my father," Nicolás says, "the enemy was the bottler who sold his wine, who never paid enough." From the outsider's perspective of the logical Nicolás, however, there was a simple solution to this struggle: change the game. "When I arrived, I had read and studied so much about economics and business, the first thing I said is that we have to bottle our own wine," he says. To this end, in the mid-1960s he convinced Domingo to buy Bodegas Esmeralda and Bodegas Crespi, two popular bottle brands in the Argentine market.

Fighting the bottlers on their own turf was a smart move, and the family empire's revenues blossomed. But while Nicolás's outsider ability to spot the unexploited angles was important, it was his intuitive marketing skill that set him apart. Most Argentine wines were essentially commodities at the time, and sold as such, but Nicolás saw that there was profit to be made in giving his wine an identity that differentiated it from the pack. The new Catena brand Crespi would be the guinea pig.

He began by selling science. After a history of dilution and several incidents in which people had died from consuming wine doctored with toxic *methyl* instead of potable *ethyl* alcohol, Argentines had reason to mistrust the wine industry. Catena's first commercial, in 1971, used the slogan "Crespi: Cared for by Experts." In the commercial, a parade of *bodega* technicians and agronomists explain the wine's chain of natural production, from the earth to the consumer's bottle. In that same year, Catena followed this up with what many call the most remembered commercial in Argentine history: In it, a young husband returning from work, played by rising Argentine actor Hugo Arana, is welcomed home by his wife. "We've been waiting for you," she says. Confused by the use of the plural, Arana asks "Who's the guest?" Arana's face quickly segues from incomprehension to wide-eyed joy when his wife points to a pair of tiny white baby booties on the kitchen table: *she is pregnant.* Arana holds the booties to his face and then embraces his wife—the dimpled Beatriz Galán in a conservative short shag hairdo—and the two celebrate with a glass of Crespi (a drink during pregnancy was not as *prohibido* then as it is now). "I associated wine with family life, to show that *bodegueros* were not suspicious people; they were good people," says Catena.

The black-and-white short is almost cliché in its naïve wholesomeness—a sensation not lessened by the jazzy show-tune twinkle of piano and harmonica in the background—but there was something so winningly honest about the couple that it struck a chord in an Argentina society. "That ad for Crespi was the most perfect TV commercial. People used to cry from emotion, and that generated a passion for the wine," says Pedro Marchevsky, Catena's viticulturist at the time. The Catholic Church was so pleased by the commercial that in 1972 it gave the Santa Clara de Asís prize to Catena for promoting the happiness of family life. "The church gave me a prize for selling alcohol!" laughs Catena.

The effect of the two commercials was nothing short of astounding. At the time, *bodegas* did not advertise on television, and Crespi's sales soared. Soon enough, competitors began to imitate Catena. "Everyone else starting doing similar ads," says Catena. So he doubled his efforts. "We did more publicity than Coke, than Sprite, than autos!" he says. By the end of the 1970s, Catena was Argentina's largest wine merchant, with 34 percent of the market, according to Nicolás.

The ninth-floor headquarters of the Catena business empire—which includes salt and bathroom fixture companies—looks down on Buenos Aires's Plaza de Mayo, where throngs of the working class famously gathered outside of the Casa Rosada to hear speeches by President Juan Domingo Perón and his wife Evita, and later where the mothers of those who were "disappeared" began a vigil of remembrance to the victims of the Dirty War of the late seventies and early eighties. Compared with the Italianate extravagance of the Casa Rosada, the Catena offices—like the man himself—are quietly low-key, with well-worn carpeting and boxy old furniture. The walls of the conference room are decorated with ends of the barrels Nicolás and his father used to ship bulk wines to their urban customers, painted with elaborately filigreed brand names.

His small frame nearly swallowed by a conference room couch, Nicolás Catena lays out his theories in a soft, slow voice with the logical clarity of a flowchart. Warm and gracious, with a retiring demeanor and a small, kind smile, Catena can give the impression that he is short on confidence or will. But Catena had the confidence and will to revolutionize an industry. Perhaps because he spent his youth outside the industry or because he was pushed harder by his father or because his family had fewer children than many, Catena is an anomaly in a business where generational leak is the norm. "First generation starts the business, second one builds it, and third one blows it. But Nicolás was the third generation—and he built it largely by blowing it up," says former Catena sales manager and education director Jeff Mausbach.

What makes Nicolás Catena a kind of photo negative of many Argentine businessmen is the way in which he shuns the spotlight—he works out at a decidedly middle-class sports club in Buenos Aires and would never drive a flashy car. Nevertheless, he makes moves that are inherently grand and attention worthy. This subtlety is most evident in his politics. Though less vocal than his father—a man with an oversize personality and girth to match—Nicolás inherited Domingo's dislike of Peronist populism. But instead of banging the drum for Mendoza's conservative Demócrata political party, as his father did, Nicolás cofounded in 1978 the Centro de Estudios Macroeconómicos de la Argentina

("Center for Macroeconomic Studies of Argentina"), or CEMA, a business school populated in part by "Chicago Boys," a group of University of Chicago–trained Latin American free-market economists who, among other things, developed the neoliberal economic plan employed by Chilean dictator Augusto Pinochet.

Quilting elaborate conspiracy theories is a national pastime in Argentina. In such an environment, Catena's mixture of introversion and backstage power has rendered him a blank canvas for people's worst anxieties. Employees at the Instituto Nacional de Tecnología Agropecuaria ("National Institute of Agricultural Technology"), or INTA, the government agrotech institute, used to refer to him as the *Monje Negro* ("Black Monk"); and one story traveling through local wine circles held that the rarely seen Nicolás Catena did not actually exist, says Catena head winemaker (and former INTA employee) Alejandro Vigil. His character had been invented by the Catena empire to scare others in the industry, the story ran, like an oenological Keyser Söze.

With their leader keeping to the shadows, Catena's employees have done much mythmaking on his behalf. "He liked to be referred to as *Dr. Catena*. He didn't make a big deal of it, but everybody else told me he liked that," says Steve Rasmussen, a California winemaker, now with Sierra Madre Vineyard, who consulted for Catena in 1995. Marina Gayan, who worked in marketing and exports at the Catena empire for seven years, was instrumental in creating Catena's public image. "Catena delegates things he would never do. He would never fire anyone. He would never stand and talk in front of people," says Gayan. "I used to speak for Catena a lot and put words in his mouth. We'd always tease him: 'If you only knew the things you said.'" The inherent clash between Catena's reticence and his employees' pride is reflected in the almost comical way his modesty is immodestly marketed on the Bodega Catena Zapata website: "Nicolás Catena would never use the word about himself—a less boastful spirit, it's hard to imagine—but he has been the quiet revolutionary in the Catena family history book."

...

Héctor Greco's arrest while checking out the menu at the Pedemonte was the end of the line for *El Padrino*. He spent four years in jail, first in Buenos Aires's Caseros prison, a hellish panopticon where he lost seventy-five pounds and had to wash his fruit in toilet water, and then in a Mendoza jail he described, comparatively, as a "club." Freed in 1984, the year after the dictatorship fell, he never rebuilt his empire, though loyal grape growers often would offer to help by giving him their products on credit. On a drizzly spring day in 1988, he died when his car slid on a wet Buenos Aires cobblestone street and crashed into another vehicle. His door popped open and he was thrown, headfirst, to the pavement.

For Catena, the industry's dark collapse presaged a new beginning. Bankrolled with the Greco sale and free from the management of his table-wine empire—and surrounded by a country mired in economic crisis and social conflict—Catena decided to take a sabbatical from the madness of Mendoza. "I didn't like doing things that weren't high quality," he says. "I didn't want to make something that wasn't pleasant to drink. And the wines we were making had very little aroma, very little flavor."

That's not to say he wanted to get out of wine. Catena had washed his hands of the family wine conglomerate with his sale to Greco, but he had retained one tiny part: the oldest vineyards, planted by his father and grandfather, and his one fine-wine *bodega*, Bodegas Esmeralda. If he was going to make wine, he reasoned, he would make a noble and fine one with those resources. It would be on a small scale, but it would be something worth doing.

How to get there was another question. While Catena traveled more than most Argentines, his country was still an island separated from the international community, a semi–pariah state isolated by a violent military dictatorship and a troubled economy. Inside the Argentine wine industry, isolation was exacerbated by complacency. Because the country had a government bureaucracy that regulated endlessly and a compliant and thirsty public that would quaff anything put in front of it, winemakers had little incentive to improve their product. "Until the 1990s, Argentina was a country where the influence of state regulation had an incredible weight," says Juan Viciana, a longtime Mendoza grape grower. "We had twenty or thirty years of a captive audience. We didn't have quality in mind; we had regulations in mind." For winery owners, the goal had long been to produce more for less, which instead of increasing quality contributed to its inexorable decline.

Although Catena harbored aspirations to quality, his company's wine was no better than the rest. Still, he had inklings of what he needed to do. While doing postgraduate work in economics at Columbia University at the end of the 1960s, Catena had begun to visit California, and in the mid-seventies he started taking his children to Berkeley from December to February each year so they could learn English. There, he learned of the University of California Davis's famous viticulture and oenology department; after Nicolás's brother Jorge went to UC Davis in 1976 to study winemaking for a year, Nicolás invited UC Davis professor Ralph Kunkee to visit Argentina.

Kunkee still speaks about the Argentina visit with the innocent wonder of a Hank Morgan, the nineteenth-century Connecticut Yankee who, after a blow to the head, awakens to find himself transported back to the court of King Arthur. In a Catena *bodega* that he visited in the province of San Juan, Kunkee was shocked to see continuous fermenters, an industrial system that, unlike current "batch" fermenters, which are cleaned and restarted after each tank of grapes, could stay in uninterrupted operation for months. Crushed grapes were pushed into the bottom of these huge tanks and worked their way to the top as they turned to wine. About halfway up, a platform and a press allowed winery laborers to extract the spent grape pulp and skins. For each liter of wine siphoned out, an equivalent amount of grapes was stuffed back in. For obvious reasons, this mass industrial process didn't allow one to develop the geographic and chemical personality—the *terroir*—of each lot of grapes. It was rather more like making Budweiser.

Argentina's use of continuous fermentation and other antiquated techniques led to sweet and murky "white" wines and bland or rustic reds with the thick feel of sherry, barely drinkable to all but those who didn't know better or care. To give them a touch of class, local reds were often sold under the false geographic appellation of "Borgoña"—Burgundy—and the whites as "Chablis." "They made lots and lots of wine," says Kunkee. "And the wines weren't very good."

Happily for Argentina's wine industry, Catena decided to spend his sabbatical from Mendoza at UC Berkeley, where his friend Carlos Benito, a fellow Argentine economist he'd known since college, was working on a research project in the university's department of agricultural and resource economics. Benito suggested that Catena come to pursue his economics studies. There, he would be just forty miles south of the Napa Valley, where another oenological revolution was just taking hold.

# CHAPTER 4

# BRINGING
# NAPA SOUTH

American winemaker Paul Hobbs, Argentine food and wine writer Fernando Vidal Buzzi, Nicolás Catena, and Argentine food and wine writer Miguel Brascó (left to right) tasting Catena's new Chardonnay in his Buenos Aires home around 1990. Courtesy of Paul Hobbs.

O N A S U N N Y P A R I S I A N afternoon, an expatriate English wine merchant named Steven Spurrier sat down in a room just off the patio bar at the swish InterContinental Hotel and prepared to watch nine Frenchmen sip, spit, and comment on wine. It was May 24, 1976.

Owner of the local Académie du Vin wine school and the Caves de la Madeleine, one of Paris's best wine shops, Spurrier had organized the tasting of recent French and Californian vintages as a celebration of the American bicentennial and the role France had played in America's independence. While he hadn't imagined the event as a Franco-American showdown per se—no one actually believed the American wines would win—Spurrier and his American assistant, Patricia Gallagher, had decided that the tasting would be blind. That is, the judges would not know the nationality and brand of each wine they tasted until the results were marked. Otherwise, Spurrier and Gallagher reasoned, it would be too easy for the French critics to find fault with the American wines. The French wines would still win, of course, but at least this way the judging would be fair.

For the tasting, the thirty-four-year-old Spurrier chose six California Chardonnays and six California Cabernet Sauvignons to compete with four white Burgundies and four Bordeaux reds. The French reds were a daunting group of top wines from the world's top wine region: two famous "first growths" and two "second growths" from the historic ranking done in 1855, when a Bordeaux trade group had classified the region's top wineries into five levels. The nine French judges were an oenophile who's who, including Pierre Tari, secretary-general of the Association des Grands Crus Classés, the trade organization of the French wineries classified in 1855; Christian Vannequé, the head sommelier of La Tour d'Argent, probably the most famous restaurant in Paris; and Odette Kahn, editor of *Revue du Vin de France* ("Review of French Wine"). Spurrier thanked the judges and told the assembled crowd that on recent trips to the United States he and Gallagher had discovered some unknown wineries that were producing wines the French judges might find interesting. With that, the tasting began.

As is memorably recounted by former *Time* correspondent George Taber in his book *Judgment of Paris*, the event quickly began to go sideways for the proud Gallic judges who thought they could discern high-quality French wines from the lesser American upstarts. "Ah, back to France!" one judge exclaimed after sipping a 1972 Chardonnay from the Napa Valley. "That is definitely California. It has no nose," another judge said after tasting a Bâtard-Montrachet '73, a white French Burgundy.

When the scores were collated and counted, the judges were stunned, some even angry. The top-scoring red was Stag's Leap Wine Cellars' '73 from the Napa Valley, and the leading white was Chateau Montelena '73, also from Napa. "French wines develop slower than California wines because of the climate, so the test was not completely correct," complained Tari. But when Taber's article on the tasting came out in *Time*, the balance of power began to shift. By noon the day after the article appeared, Manhattan's Acker Merrall & Condit, America's oldest wineshop, had sold the five cases of the two competing American wines it had in stock; another New York wineshop reported getting four hundred calls about the winning wines the same day; and *New York Times* wine writer Frank Prial devoted two columns in a row to the tasting. By debunking the assumed preeminence of French wine, the United States had drawn first blood in a war that would force France to rethink how it made a beverage fundamental to its national identity and, more important for Argentina, would offer New World wines a fair shake in the international marketplace.

When Nicolás Catena moved his family to Berkeley for the spring semester of 1982, he had not yet read about the 1976 tasting and America's shocking wine victory over France. And he might not have cared. For a *bodeguero* from Argentina—the most European country in the New World—it would be insane, even offensive, to suggest that one would go to the whiskey- and beer-drinking United States to learn how to make fine wine. In the late 1960s, while Catena was a postdoctoral economics student at Columbia University in New York, the Argentine prejudice against American wine was such that when the Argentine consul invited him for a series of lunch meetings to discuss exporting Argentine wine, Catena and the consul drank wines exclusively from Bordeaux—Lafite, Latour, and Margaux. Tasting top French vintages he had only heard about from his father was an eye-opening experience for the economist, but since the oenological tour didn't extend to domestic American bottles, it did little to expand his appreciation for New World wines. Even when Catena and his student friends were footing the bill and looking for lower-end tipple, they religiously steered clear of the US national swill. While the wealthy Catena could have afforded expensive French wines, it would have been tacky to spend so much in front of his poorer academic colleagues, so instead they stuck to inexpensive vintages he knew from his country's Andean neighbor, Chile; Undurraga was a favorite. California was not even an afterthought.

"It was a coincidence that I went to Napa then. I didn't go to California to investigate wine," Catena says. "I didn't know or respect American wines. All the people I knew in the wine world—Argentines, Italians, Spaniards, and Frenchmen—all had the theory that French wine was the best. After that, it was like there was nothing. Far below was the Italian wine, and then wine from the rest of the world. Everyone agreed that no one could make a wine as good as a French wine. It was like saying you could make a Boeing airplane in Africa."

That's not to say that Catena did not want to make *better* wine than he had up to that point. Before his trip to California, Catena had already spent several years dabbling in ways to improve the quality of his own products. But the local market wouldn't pay for quality, his winery equipment was dilapidated and out-of-date, and his winemakers weren't trained in contemporary techniques. Not only had Argentina's economic and cultural isolation limited his resources; it had capped his aspirations as well. Argentina was so cut off from the rest of the world that its consumers, winemakers, and *bodegueros* had grown accustomed to their vulgar gaucho wine. In such a limiting environment, even a man like Catena, who had traveled and tasted a good deal, could only imagine making his wine incrementally better in the Argentine/Italian style he was familiar with. French quality, as everyone knew, was outside the realm of possibility.

"When I arrived in Napa, I thought I was making a great wine in Argentina. The most prestigious wine in Argentina, my Saint Felicien brand, I thought was a great wine," he says. "I had already started remodeling Bodegas Esmeralda to make premium wines, but in the old form, the old 'premium.' It was a kind of wine that had its attraction. The concept was more or less the idea of sherry or port, a strong, accelerated oxidation that produced a certain flavor that was attractive, that wasn't ugly, but that had nothing to do with the flavor of fruit. I was going to make wine in that style, but better and better."

The 1976 tasting in Paris heralded the triumph of a revolution nearly a hundred years in the making. The California legislature had established a Department of Viticulture & Enology at UC Berkeley in 1880. It closed during Prohibition, only to reopen at UC Davis in 1935, two years after the Twenty-First Amendment ended America's thirteen-year experiment with forced sobriety.

The program was conceived as a departure from the Old World winemaking schools in France and Italy. Because they couldn't assume top quality of their grapes as a Bordeaux winemaker might, the department founders discarded the centuries of tradition that had separated the study of viticulture from that of oenology. The unified viticulture and oenology program was a pioneer, and it is now the oldest in the United States. California did not have centuries of empirical *terroir* knowledge to fall back on, so early UC Davis professors like Dr. Albert Winkler and Dr. Maynard Amerine—widely considered the fathers of American viticulture—began experimenting to discover which grape varietals were best suited to various areas in California's wide range of climates. Unburdened by the rigid appellation rules that regulate grape growing, wine blending, and alcohol levels in the Old World, the school also experimented with winemaking and viticulture in ways that were not possible—or even legal—in France. That the state's best vineyards were just an hour's drive away in the Napa Valley made it all the better. The department quickly earned a reputation as the go-to place for creative winemaking, an intellectual hothouse ideally suited to New World winemakers who needed to invent their own industry.

It was for this reason that on a visit he made to California a year before moving there in 1982, Catena turned to his old acquaintance Ralph Kunkee and asked him to suggest a UC Davis graduate who might be willing to spend some time in Argentina. Not long after, Guy Ruhland found himself being interviewed by the reserved economist in Berkeley. Barely thirty years old, cocky and immature, Ruhland had spent time in high school in Spain and worked in Mexican wineries. He was well educated and single, spoke some Spanish, and had just enough self-confidence to consult in a wine hinterland ruled by a military junta. When Catena asked if he would come, Ruhland said yes.

When Ruhland flew to Mendoza a few months later, in the harvest season of 1981, one of the first things he noticed was the high frequency of reckless and drunk driving on the region's notoriously dangerous two-lane roads ("I didn't think the police existed," he says). A fellow winemaker told him that the pulverized car crash debris he saw littering the roadway shoulders was, like so many things in Argentina, an economizing jury-rigging—a way of reminding drivers to ease off the gas without spending too much money on police surveillance. It is a mentality that has not changed much in the intervening years: "It was almost like the Wild West," says Greg Adams, a viticulturist who worked in Mendoza from 1992 to 1998. "In the US, I had trained myself on keeping my eyes pegged in the rearview for police, but in Argentina you have to have your eyes looking forward to avoid cars and people and animals. As long as you can manage your vehicle, you can go as fast as you want."

The laissez-faire highway protection was a good introduction to Argentina for Ruhland. The same anarchy ruled inside the region's *bodegas*. There, the goal was to manufacture a beverage no worse than the competition with the least possible outlay on manpower, machinery, or upkeep. For a foreign winemaker like Ruhland, accustomed to the competitive craftsmanship of the American industry, there was something inexplicable about the Argentine mentality. But it made sense in context: in an isolated and underfunded country gripped by a tangle of regulation, one got by with what was at hand. Argentina didn't have the privilege of worrying too much about achieving greatness. Looking at the Argentine industry at the end of the 1970s, Ruhland saw the ravages that several decades of this mentality had wrought: although the technicians were intelligent and well trained, their winemaking procedures suffered from a chain of shortcuts that started in the vineyard and extended all the way to the bottles in the store. Argentine *bodegas* not only suffered from technological backwardness but were often unhygienic and ill-maintained. Indeed, it would have been hard to find much that was done *correctly*. It was as if the system were designed to make the wine bad.

Still, while the problems Ruhland saw were complicated and far-reaching, they at least could largely be traced back to one basic cause: oxygen. In a simplified sense, grapes can be broken into two parts: pulp, which stores the sugar that, through fermentation, defines a wine's alcohol level; and skins, which contain phenolic compounds, the chemical building blocks that define color, taste, and mouthfeel and are said to improve the health of those who drink a daily glass. (The pulp contains some phenols as well.) One of the basic precepts of modern winemaking is that, except for during fermentation, phenolic compounds should not come into contact with oxygen until the drinker pours his wine into a glass. The reason is simple: when oxygen is present, an enzyme called polyphenol oxidase causes phenolic compounds to oxidize—that is, to turn brown and lose their flavor. It's exactly the same process that causes a cut apple to go brown and bland if it's left on a counter.

To combat this problem, modern winemaking protocol calls for picking and gently pressing grapes at a cool temperature and then quickly combining the resulting juice and solids (the "must") with yeast in a cool tank. Handled this way, the phenolic compounds suffer minimal oxidization. The chemical reason is that cool temperatures slow oxidation and the fermentation of sugar to ethyl alcohol is an anaerobic (oxygen-free) process that releases carbon dioxide, driving out the oxygen. Without excess oxygen around, the phenolic compounds can be safely transferred from the skins into the juice without fear of turning the wine brown and bland. After fermentation finishes, oxygen again presents a danger, but a fermented wine that is aged, bottled, and stored in a cool, oxygen-free environment is safe. It even has the chance to rise to sublimity . . . if it's made from great grapes.

But what happened during Argentina's *vendimia* grape-picking season looked more like a massacre than a harvest, as if the *bodegas* needed to extract revenge on their fruit for prior sins. Instead of picking in the cool early-morning hours and quickly transporting grapes to the *bodega* in stackable plastic boxes designed to protect them, field hands harvested slowly in the heat of the day and tossed the pounds and pounds of grapes into large open-topped dump trucks whose bays had been lined with plastic tent tarps. Left to molder in the summer sun until the trucks were full, these massive fruit mountains crushed themselves: as the pickers piled on fruit, the resulting tonnage would squash the hot bottom grapes. Once the full trailers were finally driven to the winery (often after the drivers let the grapes marinate a bit longer while they took their lunch and siesta on the sweltering roadside), they would wait their turn in a long line of trucks until the laborers could jump atop the listing mountain of fruit—the bed had been tilted to enlist gravity's help in moving the grapes—and begin shifting the fruit from the truck bed to the destemmers and pressers, stomping the bunches with their feet and hacking them with shovels.

The image of laborers standing atop precarious hills of grapes, one slip from tumbling into a running screw conveyor and becoming part of the product, still remains a shock to Ruhland thirty years on. "Isn't that the scariest thing in the world?" he asks.

Under these conditions, problems were almost unavoidable. Oxidation started early, when the accidental grape crushing in the truck beds exposed the phenolic compounds to oxygen. This original sin was exacerbated by temperature. Grapes in Argentina were picked in the heat, left to sit in the heat, and then hours later crushed in hot presses at the winery. High temperatures extract phenolic compounds from skins faster than low temperatures do—just as hot water leaches color from a tea bag faster than does chilled tap water—so when the must is hot, there are more phenolic compounds available to oxidize. Compounding these problems, the equipment inside Argentine *bodegas* was uniformly dilapidated—the result of four decades of government policies that had almost closed the borders to imports. Many of the presses, pumps, and destemmers were poor domestic copies of European machinery that had been imported in the 1920s. By coarsely pounding and grinding the skins to a mash, these harsh antiques extracted phenolic compounds faster than gentle modern presses do. To get a sense of the violence done to the flavor of the grape, imagine the bitter taste of tea when the bag is squeezed harshly.

The damaged juice, heavy with oxidized phenolic compounds, then went to the fermentation tank. Connected as they were with obsolete pumps and aged tubing, the trip to the tanks in Argentine *bodegas* probably qualified as one of the least hygienic voyages on earth. Bacteria hid in the cracks of unwashed tubes, in the seals of old bronze pumps, and in the crevices of the tanks. One strain in particular turns alcohol to vinegar in a process called acetic acid fermentation. In an effort to kill these bacterial colonies and slow oxidation, Ruhland says that Catena's winemakers were adding two to three hundred parts per million of sulfur dioxide—an all-purpose disinfectant and antioxidant—well above the industry norm. Looking around the antiquated *bodega*, Ruhland understood why they would want to add so much. But the problem with this fix was that excess sulfur dioxide gives white wine a pungency that seems to physically burn a drinker's sinuses; at extreme levels, it feels as if it's going to blow your head off.

The more Ruhland looked, the worse it got. The wines were fermented in epoxy-lined concrete pools as large as bank vaults, whose size and construction made the temperature of the wine inside almost impossible to regulate. Temperature in the pools was especially important to Ruhland because as yeast turns sugar into ethyl alcohol and carbon dioxide, it raises the temperature of the fermenting liquid. Temperatures nearing a hundred degrees kill the yeast before it has converted all of the sugar to alcohol, leaving a wine that's susceptible to invasions of bacteria

or unwanted wild yeast. Keeping temperature down is especially important when making white wine. Oenologists generally prefer to ferment
white-wine grapes below sixty-five degrees Fahrenheit in order to get a
clean, fresh flavor and avoid heat-browning. In earlier times, Bordeaux
winemakers cooled their fermentation vats with blocks of ice. Today,
winemakers lower the temperature inside stainless steel fermentation
tanks by cooling their insulating jackets. With huge concrete pools, however, the most common way to take the fermentation heat out of the juice
is to pump it out of the pool and through what's called a heat exchanger,
a tube of wine that is surrounded by an outer tube filled with a refrigerat-
ing agent such as ammonia, Freon, or ice water.

There was no inherent problem in this mode of operation—the technique is common in wineries around the world—but in an antiquated
*bodega* like the one Ruhland was using, all this moving the wine from
one place to another meant the liquid would have to spin through antique
pumps, tubes, and gaskets that were leaky, moldy, and dirty. "Our equipment was very precarious," says the Catena ex-winemaker José "Pepe"
Galante.

After fermentation, premium reds like Catena's Saint Felicien were
insulted again by being aged for several years in *toneles*, huge oak
casks that had been bought in the early 1900s from men like Adolfo
Fruhinsholz, a merchant based in the northeastern French region of
Nancy. Every seven years or so, each *tonel* would be drained and given a
good scraping to remove a layer of wood so that the next round of wine
would have more flavor-inducing contact with fresh oak. Not only was
this the traditional Italian way of making wine, it was economical. As
opposed to the 225-liter French oak barrels one sees in modern wineries, which are used four or five times at most before being discarded or
turned into end tables, a typical 10,000- or 20,000-liter *tonel*, with regular care, can last a century.

One does not need graduate-level oenology training to realize that
making wine in huge oak Methuselahs doesn't lend the product the

freshest taste. Temperature was again a problem. In Mendoza's arid, hot environment, the huge *toneles* were stored in uninsulated and un-air-conditioned warehouses. All woods are membranes that allow oxygen to pass through. Even dead wood breathes, and the combination of high temperatures and low humidity cooked the wine and sucked the evaporated moisture through the wood into the outside dry air. This lost liquid is replaced with oxygen from the outside. Again, like fruit that browns when left out of the refrigerator, this oxidative "rusting" ironed over wine's naturally bright fruit flavors and colors and replaced them with the heavy smoothness of port or sherry, a mouthfeel winningly described as *terciopelado* ("velvety"). Of course, small oak barrels are also porous and go through a similar process, but in most other parts of the world winemakers age their product in wood for a far shorter time and keep their barrels in cooler, more humid environments.

The sheer age of the *toneles* also meant that their insides were like high school science projects. No matter how much the winemakers might clean them, the casks had decades of microorganisms hidden in their wooden pores. *Acetobacter* transforms wine into vinegar, for example, while the grungy *Brettanomyces* can give it the unpleasant flavor of horse sweat. Each microorganism had its own deleterious effect on the wine; the combination could be disgusting.

The wine was subjected to two final insults before the consumer could "enjoy" his bedraggled beverage. When Ruhland traveled to Buenos Aires to inspect the Catena company's bottling line, he discovered that they were "hot-bottling" their wine—a process in which the liquid is heated before bottling to kill yeast and to guarantee that there's no refermentation of the remaining sugar. This process destroys flavor and furthers browning, making the wine even uglier in the glass. "If it wasn't brown before they did that to it, once they bottled it at 130 degrees and let it cool it sure was. Yeah, it killed every bit of yeast and bacteria, but it sure did a hellacious job on the color," says Ruhland.

Finally, when the bottles of wine at last arrived at Buenos Aires *par-*

*rilla* steak houses, they were often stored in the crammed kitchens' last available spot: next to the grill. There they cooked until a customer asked for a bottle of his country's finest to go with his steak.

Notes of horse sweat notwithstanding, for many Argentines there was really nothing wrong with the much-battered Argentine wine. Argentina's population had learned to accept its harsh tannins and even to prize the velvety, oxidized feel it gained with aging. Because Argentines generally consumed their wine with meals—not as a cocktail—the harshness of the wine's tannins was muted by the flavor of the food. In addition, Argentine wine's voluptuous oxidation fulfilled an image of bygone luxury that Italian Argentines had brought from their native land. "The wines had a brick-red color, and more brick color made it seem older to consumers," says Pedro Marchevsky, then Catena's viticulturist. It reminded many of a homeland they had never seen.

Catena's desire to make wine in the traditional style but better was like aspiring to be the world's tallest midget. Of that he got his first inkling a few weeks after moving his family to a house near Berkeley's Tilden Regional Park. Elena and Nicolás saw the birth of their daughter Adrianna there in February 1982—fourteen years after the birth of their second child, Laura. They soon began to suffer the reverse hostage crisis that is being the parents of a newborn. Eager to find a weekend outing for the entire family, Catena drove to Napa, where some of the wineries were engaging in the new practice of opening their doors to tourists. Heading north past the Bay Area suburbs, Nicolás and Elena soon found themselves in a familiar landscape. California's wine country had not yet become today's *Sideways* pilgrimage, a viticultural theme park where amateur Robert Parkers and twentysomethings cruising for free booze clog the St. Helena Highway and fill tasting rooms. In the early 1980s, the towns of Napa and Sonoma still anchored sleepy agricultural communities where the vineyards were owned by dirt-nailed farmers, not gourmet celebrities, and the tourists were mostly San Franciscans looking to escape their city's cold fog and enjoy the touted health benefits of Napa's hot springs.

A friend of Catena's had suggested that he stop at an especially ambitious winery that by happenstance was run by Robert Mondavi, a man whose family had also emigrated from the Marche region of Italy that had produced the Catenas. While Mondavi's wine hadn't been chosen for the 1976 Paris tasting that launched Napa into the world's league of premier wine appellations, the winemakers behind the two winning wines—Mike Grgich and Warren Winiarski—were both Mondavi alumni. By the time of Catena's 1982 visit, the energetic Mondavi was already a legend in California for his evangelical passion for New World wine. He also had attained the rare combination of critical acclaim and commercial success. After being painfully ousted from his family's Charles Krug winery in 1965, Mondavi had—at the entrepreneurially geriatric age of fifty-two—launched his winery inside a California mission-style structure with an iconic bell tower he commissioned from the architectural father of the California ranch house, Cliff May. At the time there were only several dozen wineries in Napa, and most churned out unexceptional plonk palatable only to the few Americans who drank wine. Mondavi aimed higher. His 1967 launch of oak-aged Fumé Blanc—a dry, crisp take on Sauvignon Blanc, which until then had been considered a poor-quality sweet wine—was a marketing coup and financial success that proved the viability of his premium-wine dream. His winery's sales exploded, from some 2,600 cases in 1967 to nearly 100,000 in 1973. Mondavi's 1980 announcement of the Opus One joint venture with Baron Philippe de Rothschild (head of Château Mouton Rothschild in Bordeaux's Médoc region) established him not only as a winemaker who could sell Americans plenty of moderately priced wines, but also as a man to be taken seriously on the international stage as a maker of quality vintages.

In other words, he was just the man that Catena wanted to be.

...

On their way up to the Mondavi winery in Oakville, Nicolás, Elena, and their infant daughter passed through the county seat of Napa and then, about fifteen minutes later, pulled off Route 29 into the tiny town of Yountville. There, Nicolás recounts, they sat down to eat at a seven-table bistro in an oblong two-story brick-and-stone building that had at various times been home to a saloon, a brothel, and a laundry—Yountville's famous French Laundry restaurant. At the time it was owned by Don and Sally Schmitt, the town's onetime mayor and his wife—it would be more than a decade before Thomas Keller turned it into the destination for culinary pilgrims it is today—and Catena was happy to learn that it sold Grand Cru ("great growth") French wines almost at cost. After making this happy discovery and finishing their repast, the Catenas drove the final four miles north to Mondavi's signature winery.

While the Napa Valley that Catena found was much like the rustic western wilderness he knew from his birthplace of Mendoza, Argentina —agricultural and quiet—the wine he discovered at Mondavi was from another universe. Instead of an America subservient to French greatness, he found a New World in full rebellion against Old World elites. "We tasted Cabernet in barrels and Sauvignon Blanc in bottles. And to me, the fruit of those wines, the touch of wood, impressed me. I had never tasted that flavor in my life. It was a shock: at that moment they tasted to me better than the best French wine I'd ever had," Catena says.

In keeping with his modest style, Catena had not announced himself as a winery owner. But in the excitement of oenological epiphany, he blew his cover. Soon he was taken behind the tourist curtain into the barrel room, where a candy store variety of wines made his mind explode with possibilities. "In the conversation with the guide it came out that I was a *bodeguero*. And he said to me, 'If you know wine you have to check *this* out,' and he made me taste a lot of wines. I said to myself, this is something we've never done," Catena says. "For the first time I heard a challenge to this French hegemony."

After this epiphany, Catena began visiting Napa obsessively. Every few weeks, he, Elena, and Adrianna dropped by the *bodegas* that opened their doors to tourists; Nicolás learned about the 1976 tasting and met American wine revolutionaries like Caymus's Charlie Wagner and Stags Leap's Warren Winiarski (whose '73 Cabernet Sauvignon had won the 1976 "Judgment of Paris"). And, through a mutual banker friend at Wells Fargo, he finally met Robert Mondavi and his sons.

"I knew from the first meeting that Nicolás had that same very curious mind and wanting to excel. Just making good wine was not good enough for him," says Mondavi's son Michael, ex-CEO of the Robert Mondavi Winery and now founder and head of Folio Fine Wine Partners. "It was almost embarrassing, he was so complimentary of what we were doing."

In California, Catena not only found wines that thrilled his palate. He also found an open professional culture that allowed him so much access that he felt like an industrial spy. "Immediately I put myself to studying how these people did this, how they challenged the French," he says. "I began to study everything from the vines, the plants, the soil, the climate, the *bodegas*, asking everyone. It was a rigorous study."

Every time he visited a winery, he asked the winemaker for his secrets, from planting techniques to winery design. And they would tell him. In a kind of New World pact against French domination, Napa's winery owners even allowed him to take photographs of their systems so that he could re-create them in Argentina. "I remember asking where they bought oak, and they brought out a pamphlet and told me everything," Catena says. "It was information you couldn't buy. Because very few years before, at the end of the sixties, Napa was like we were in the eighties."

Napa was indeed the polar opposite of the French wine culture. The

French rarely shared their expertise, in part because of French secrecy, but also because some French winemakers no longer knew the whys of their tradition. Unlike Californians, they hadn't had to personally create their industry from the dirt up. Michael Mondavi describes it thus:

> In the late sixties and seventies, when I started to go to France, the first three or four visits with an individual they'd ask questions and want answers; and when you asked questions, they'd tell you well this is just the way we do it. "Why?" you'd say. "Because my father did it this way." "Why did he do it?" "Because my grandfather did it." Either they wouldn't share with you, or they didn't know the technical reasons. Our attitude was that we had no secrets. The wine industry here is quite unique in that. We're quite competitive from a sales and marketing perspective, but qualitatively we're synergistic. Even though making wine is the second oldest profession, we're always learning. And Mother Nature's in charge; we're not. So if we can learn how they do things, whether it's in the Rhine or Bordeaux or Mendoza, we will say, "Well, *that's* interesting. Maybe we should try that here."

After each of Nicolás's investigative expeditions through California wine country, the Catenas ate at the French Laundry. At each lunch, his mind in analytical fervor, Catena says he bought two bottles of wine—one from Napa and the other a French Grand Cru—in order to compare them. He fell in love with American Cabernet Sauvignon.

"My period as a professor was supposed to be a kind of vacation," he says. "And my vacation lasted three weeks. Because that's when I visited the Napa Valley. After I went to Napa I realized there was another world I didn't know. I saw this all close-up, and I realized that our style of winemaking was from the past. It wasn't going to continue. And that's when I began to put together the new project."

After his Napa epiphany, Catena realized that to escape his industry's downward pull, he needed to change his tack. No longer would the *bodeguero* put his energy into improving on something that was uniquely Argentine, to "make wine in the old style, but better and better." There was no point: That wine had no clients outside the shrinking market that was Argentina.

"Catena came back from California and told us, 'These wines would be impossible to sell in the international market.' The difference between what we were producing then and what was in the international market was huge," says José "Pepe" Galante, Catena's winemaker at the time. "Catena brought us some bottles from the US, and you tried a Chardonnay or Cabernet with the varietal flavors, the color, the freshness. How those wines made you feel! We couldn't do anything like them."

Catena saw that competing on the world stage would require a complete gut remodeling of his company. Everything from the raw materials to the culture, techniques, and marketing would have to be replaced. But how? There was one place in the New World that had turned its oceans of plonk into fine wine. And as the academically inclined Catena knew, the good thing about a successful model is that it can be re-created. So Catena put himself to copying California. "I wanted to do something equal to Napa," Catena says. "I didn't want to invent anything."

Though he knew people would say he was insane to try—"like saying you could make a Boeing airplane in Africa"—Catena was not dissuaded. From tasting California wines he had learned a powerful lesson: competing with the French was possible. "I saw that the Americans had done in 10 years," Catena told the *New York Times* in 2001, "what the Europeans took over 300 years to do."

"The fact that my father received critical success early on inspired Nicolás," says Robert Mondavi's son Tim, former head winemaker at the family firm and now the winegrower at Continuum Estate. "He said, 'If he can do it there, I can do it here.' And he set about doing that."

...

"Doing that" would require a lot more than desire, however, especially in 1980s Argentina. Argentina's wine industry was suffering a perfect storm of isolation and poverty. High import barriers meant that most winemakers had no idea what was going on in the rest of the world, and the violent military dictatorship had divided the country. Worse, the Greco empire's 1980 collapse had sucked some $500 million out of the western economy, and wine drinking was in free fall. After annual wine consumption peaked at 92 liters per Argentine in 1970, it fell some 35 percent over the next fifteen years. "In Argentina, we were penned in," says Ricardo Santos, whose family owned Mendoza's Bodega Norton from 1956 until 1989.

Farmers were desperate. Rather than care for vineyards whose fruit was worth less than it would cost to pick, landowners frantically pulled vines that had survived for decades in the Mendozan heat, shrinking vineyard acreage from its 1977 peak of 875,000 acres to a bottom of 525,000 in 1990. With cruel irony, grape growers reserved special violence for the kind of plants that are most prized today: gnarled old Malbec vines. Tending to seventy-five-year-old vines that produced sparse quantities of highly concentrated, flavorful grapes was a luxury almost no one could afford.

Malbec, which had covered 120,000 acres in Argentina at its 1960s peak, only covered 25,000 in the 1990s. "There was little differentiation between low and high quality, and when I came to the country the highest-quality vineyards were being taken out of production because they weren't economically feasible," says Greg Adams, the American viticulturist who worked in Argentina from 1992 to 1998.

After clearing their land of these treasured old Malbecs, the vineyard owners who wanted to stay in the game planted high-producing bulk-wine vines like *cereza*, *criolla*, and *Pedro Giménez*, while the rest gave the land over to vegetable production or, if they were close enough to Mendoza, took advantage of the city's expansion by penciling lines across their property plan and selling off the partitions as suburban lots.

Argentina's wine industry had to find new markets if it was going to survive. "The need to export is suddenly urgent," Eduardo Pulenta, part of the family that owned industry giant Peñaflor, told the *New York Times* in 1984. But exporting meant producing what Argentines self-deprecatingly refer to as "export-quality" wine—that is, better than the low-quality plonk they would accept at home.

Catena began his export-quality revolution with the raw materials at the bottom of the production chain, planting fine-wine varietals just as the rest of the country was ripping them out.

Concentrating on the vines played to Catena's strengths. Like many Argentine *bodegueros*, his grandfather had come from a family of vineyard workers. Although Argentine wineries were often backward and unhygienic, they nevertheless had generations of hands-on experience with the land. And though the plantings may not have been trellised in the most modern style and the vines may have often been the mediocre *criolla* variety that evolved from the vines brought by the conquistadores and abandoned to nature, one thing was undeniable: Argentine vineyard care was first-rate.

"What was interesting to me was not a reputation like Bordeaux or Burgundy or Tuscany, but the quality and health of the way the vineyards looked. I looked for uniform vines, proper cleanliness, weed control, things like that," says Michael Mondavi, who made his first visit to Argentina in the mid-eighties. "And their vineyards were *beautiful*."

Electing what to plant was straightforward enough for Catena. He chose Napa's best weapons in its war with France: Chardonnay and Cabernet Sauvignon. Starting in 1983, he planted some 20 acres of Chardonnay and Cabernet each year, mostly at what is now known as his *La*

*Pirámide* ("The Pyramid") Vineyard in Agrelo, an area that was considered Mendoza's top vineyard zone. The plantings were done on guesstimate, as no one really knew where these French varietals—especially Chardonnay—would grow well in the high desert. Catena planted, and waited. It would take two years before the first small harvest could be gathered, and several more before he could determine if it made successful wine.

"The most important variety that we had in Argentina was Malbec. All of our important vineyards were Malbec. The first ones my grandfather planted were Malbec. We had some beautiful vineyards. But I said no. I put myself to planting Cabernet and Chardonnay," says Catena. "I planted them in the areas that supposedly were the best for wine. But you have to wait five or six years to see how they turn out. We had no information."

What made this retiring academic take such a leap of faith was the realization that to fight French wine hegemony, he would have to do so on France's terms. The king and queen of the grape world would always be the white Chardonnay of Burgundy and the Cabernet Sauvignon that dominated red Bordeaux blends. Revered for their complex flavors and aromas, these varietals loomed high above bit players like Malbec. When Napa went up against France in 1976, it did so with Chardonnay and Cabernet. And when great Tuscan winemaking families wanted to prove they could compete internationally, they went against regional regulations and made "Super Tuscans" by blending their traditional Sangiovese with French stalwarts Cabernet Sauvignon, Merlot, and Cabernet Franc. In Argentina's case, selling the world on its iconic Malbec grape would have to wait until it had proven that it could make wine in the first place.

"Nicolás focused on Chardonnay and Cabernet because he, like my father, saw that they were the most highly esteemed wines in the world," says Robert Mondavi's son Michael. "And if you want to get into the company of those top wines, you need to play in that arena. Nicolás and my father came to the same conclusion very early: if you want to compete with the best, you can't make a motorcycle when everyone else is comparing Ferraris."

By the mid-eighties, Catena's efforts began to bear fruit, both literally and figuratively. *Vendimia*, the picking season, brought in the first sparse grapes of the newly planted vineyards. While the first harvests rarely produce great wine, their arrival created a palpable sense of progress. In fits and spurts, Catena's wines improved as his viticulturist Pedro Marchevsky and winemaker José Galante avoided some of the most obvious problems—the use of *toneles*, for example—in order to introduce Argentina to the previously unknown wonders of fruitiness and freshness.

"The first new fine wine we commercialized was a 1986 Saint Felicien Cabernet," says Galante. "The only thing we did was bottle it young and fresh without oxidation, and it was a commercial success. In the moment, it was revolutionary. But all we did was protect it from oxidation and bottle it with a brilliant red color, with all the fruit, with smooth round tannins. There was no comparison here in Argentina."

Marchevsky recalls the wine as a similarly clear break from the past: "It was very rounded from being bottle-aged for two years; it went straight to the bottle from the cement pool, without going into a *tonel*," he says. "The wine was a shock. It had color, fruit. Something completely new."

Getting from vine to bottle with consistent quality proved to be a fraught process, however. Despite rare successes like the 1986 Saint Felicien, high-quality Argentine wine continued to be the exception, not the rule. The limiting factor was that few *bodegueros* were eager to join Catena's foolhardy crusade. While per capita annual wine consumption had fallen precipitously, the diminished amount was still about six times what the average American consumes today. Insulated from the world by Argentina's trade walls and thirsty local market, the majority of the *bodegueros* who had survived the Greco putsch were still more than happy to collect their ample, albeit diminishing, slice of the domestic plonk market. As they cashed their checks, they had little motivation to change.

"Many people thought we were crazy because we were the only ones preoccupied with the potential of Argentine wines," says winemaker Galante. "Everyone calmly sold their wine on the local market, and we were trying to do something different."

Without a doubt, Catena was the most committed revolutionary in Argentine wine, the only one with the right mixture of money, desire, and foresight to make big moves. But it bears noting that he wasn't alone in his quest to do something different. A small group of other *bodegueros*, viticulturists, and oenologists had also been trying, in fits and starts, to make Argentine wine internationally viable. Though their means had been too limited and their numbers too few to make an important splash, these early trailblazers had marked the path that Catena widened into a highway.

Named the Best Twentieth Century Winemaker in Argentina by the Bordeaux-based World Association of Wine & Spirits Writers and Journalists, the demanding and feisty Raúl de la Mota—a karate blackbelt—first traveled to France in 1965, and in Bordeaux he became friends with Jean Ribéreau-Gayon and Émile Peynaud, the French fathers of modern oenology. Through them, he learned a radically new type of winemaking based on hard science and exactitude. "I never knew that winemaking required so much investigation," he said years later. "I realized that we were in diapers." Implementing their new techniques—importing high technology, cutting back grape yields, and making wines purely from recognized French varietals—was difficult in an economically depressed Argentina. "It was a big struggle with the accountants of the *bodegas*, who wanted low cost wine made from bulk *criolla* grapes," De la Mota said in a 2007 interview with the Argentine newspaper *La Nación*.

De la Mota worked with several big *bodegas* to improve their wines within these economic and technological limitations. But his greatest fame came from his work at Bodega y Cavas de Weinert. When Brazilian transportation executive Bernardo Weinert made the quixotic decision to open a Mendoza fine-wine *bodega* in 1975, De la Mota jumped at the chance to oversee the operation. "He asked me what I wanted to do, and I said I wanted to make the best wines of Argentina. He laughed because Brazilians always wanted to be the biggest," Weinert says of De la Mota, who died in 2009 at age ninety. "He was able to live his dream, of making the best wines, which he couldn't do before because the other *bodegueros* didn't give him the chance."

De la Mota made the best of his boss's Brazilian ego. He had Weinert buy high-end equipment such as French Gasquet-brand presses. He then braved the threat of late-summer hail in order to pick at the last possible moment, pruned back vineyards to create high-intensity grapes, and went through the time-consuming process of using small boxes for gentle harvesting at a time when, in the words of his son Roberto, "it seemed madness to do so." Bodega y Cavas de Weinert began exporting in 1978, first to Brazil and then to the United States and the United Kingdom. Though the wine still hewed to Italian tradition—it was aged in *toneles*, for example—De la Mota's passion achieved full-throated recognition. "This wine competes with the finest red wines made anywhere in the world . . . I unequivocally believe that this estate from Argentina is making the most profound red wine in South America," critic Robert Parker Jr. wrote of Weinert's 1977 Malbec. A decade later Parker went even further: "I have made no secret of my belief that Bodega Weinert is indisputably South America's finest wine producer."

For Bodega Norton owner Ricardo Santos and winemaker Francisco "Pancho" Giménez, the inspiration wasn't France or Napa, but a desire to sell Argentina's identity. A goateed 1961 University of Virginia graduate who still evinces the overgrown kid's mischievousness that defines many in Argentina's aristocracy, Santos worked in architecture in Los Angeles before returning to his family's Mendoza *bodega*. Back in Mendoza, Santos and Giménez, a friend and former colleague of De la Mota, read the works of American wine importer Frank Schoonmaker. Convinced that New World wineries would never be respected until they abandoned the provincial practice of borrowing European names like Burgundy or Chablis, Schoonmaker pushed the use of single-varietal wines (for example, Merlot) in the New World. Following Schoonmaker's advice, Santos and Giménez experimented with a varietal for export, one whose fruity freshness had not been dulled with a *tonel*. They did so with a grape that screamed Argentine pride long before that became fashionable. According to Santos, this wine, the 1971 Norton Mendoza Malbec, was the first Argentine varietal exported to the United States.

And at table-wine giant Peñaflor, the owning Pulenta family intuited that the Argentine industry would have to export long before anyone else. In 1970, the Pulentas put together Vinos Argentinos, an uneasy conglomerate of five competing *bodegas*—including Greco—to export to the United States. From a Manhattan office on Fifty-Fourth Street between Park and Madison Avenues, their US representative Byron Tosi attempted to sell Americans on Argentine wine. It wasn't a success. The oxidized style of Argentina's wines and the country's constant battles with inflation and devaluation crippled the venture; family member Carlos Pulenta, now the owner of Mendoza's Bodega Vistalba, refers to it as an exporting "apprenticeship." Peñaflor's four partners all dropped out by 1981, having either gone under or been sold. But the Pulentas continued to work toward international-quality vintages—with wines like Trapiche Medalla, created in 1983—and to export the brand that the conglomerate had invented, Andean Vineyards, giving Argentina its first toehold in America; in the 1980s, Andean was the Argentine wine most widely sold in the United States.

By the late 1980s, Catena and this small cadre of fellow progressives had established themselves as a budding revolutionary corps. But the great leap forward would require another decade of work and an influx of techniques and technology from the outside world. It would also require assistance from foreign wine artists who could change the ingrown habits of Argentina winemaking culture and provide inspiration that would turn the industry on its head.

# CHAPTER 5

# THE NEW
# CONQUISTADORES

Winery worker Fernando Oltra, winemaker José Galante, winemaking consultant Paul Hobbs,
agronomist Pedro Marchevsky, and Hobbs's translator, Mariel Romagnoli (left to right), in
Bodegas Esmeralda, filling new French oak barrels with Chardonnay juice for
barrel fermentation in 1990. Courtesy of Paul Hobbs.

ONE JANUARY DAY DURING France's freezing winter of 1988, the phone rang in Bordeaux's Château Fontenil and Dany Rolland picked up the line. The speaker, a hotel operator from Madrid, announced a call for her husband, Michel. A call from an Argentine hotel guest.

"It's for you Michel, from a South American in Spain. Do you want to take it?" Dany said, holding out the phone to Michel. Michel shrugged and took the receiver. "*Soy Arnaldo Etchart. Soy de Salta, Argentina,*" a voice said. Rolland recognized the words as Spanish, a language he did not speak. The only word he understood was the country name, but geography eluded him. He continued to listen. "*Es en el Sur, donde hacemos vino* [It's in South America, where we make wine]," Etchart said. "*Y necesitamos un consultor* [And we need a consultant]."

The Frenchman and the Argentine talked past each in their respective languages. Occasionally the operator tried to clarify the conversation. By the time he hung up, Rolland was pretty sure he had agreed to visit Etchart's *bodega* in several months' time. It seemed that he would soon be receiving a plane ticket—two actually, as he had asked for one for his wife, also a winemaker. He would be paid. It was all rather vague.

Every morning, Arnaldo Etchart takes his breakfast alone—save for a flock of birds awaiting the crumbs he tosses them—at an outdoor café on the main square in the Argentine mountain wine village of Cafayate. Each day after coffee he returns to his hillside *bodega* home, which, at 6,700 feet, offers a heart-stopping view of his 50 acres of Malbec and Cabernet vines, many of which are more than sixty years old. There, off a dining room that sports a huge diorama of stuffed wildlife, he reads poetry from the likes of French Renaissance humanist François Rabelais and eleventh-century Persian Omar Khayyam, and pens the occasional political essay. (A quotable man himself, Etchart's classically piquant phrases include, "If you don't read poetry, your wines will taste like crap.") Rotund, with long gray hair, cowboy boots, tinted glasses, and a cravat held in place by a brass grape-bunch clip, he resembles Ben Franklin with a scowl. Born at the *bodega* founded by his French Basque ancestors in 1850, Etchart has been an oenologist himself for fifty years. When he speaks about wine, he expects others to listen.

Etchart was not happy when he called Rolland. In fact, his unhappiness had been simmering for a while. Several years before, on the advice of his American importer, Bernhard Horstmann, he had embarked on several wine-tasting trips to France's Bordeaux and Burgundy regions, and the more he tasted the worse he felt. "I spent a *lot* of money buying and tasting wines in top French restaurants. And when I realized what the best French wines were like, I realized that I could not be satisfied with the wines I was making," Etchart says.

When a container of wine his 140-year-old *bodega* had shipped to a northern European customer was returned because the color had faded from red to rosé—the fault of winery technicians who didn't know how to use a unique rotating fermenter they had had specially designed—he lost patience. "I'm going to find someone who knows what he's doing," he barked at his winery staff.

In December 1987 he explained to Horstmann that he needed a French winemaker to instruct his winemakers—a Frenchman from Bordeaux, not Burgundy. When Horstmann asked why, Etchart explained that Burgundy wines were Pinot Noir based, and Cafayate Pinot Noir was terrible. "Maybe we can't achieve a Bordeaux here, but at least Bordeaux wines have some similarities to ours," Etchart said. A short time later, after consulting with friends in France, Horstmann called Etchart back with the name of an up-and-coming winemaker: forty-year-old Michel Rolland.

A handsome, stocky man with a sweep of dark hair who smokes *cigarillos* and has a touch of rosé on his nose and cheeks—the kind of gourmand the poetic Etchart describes in a crescendo as "an enthusiast of wine, an enjoyer of wine, *a celebrator of wine!*"—Michel Rolland comes from a small-time Bordeaux wine family. After attending the University of Bordeaux's oenology school—where he met Dany—Michel bought a small Bordeaux oenological laboratory with Dany and the two became consultants. Winemakers brought samples to Rolland's lab to verify that their wine's alcohol and acidity levels complied with the convoluted French rules of appellation. Not exciting work, but profitable.

As recounted by William Echikson in his book *Noble Rot*, the sociable Michel soon realized that he hated the confinement of the lab and took to picking up the samples from their winery customers. He quickly saw how unhygienic the wineries' cellars were and coaxed the owners to invest in stainless steel tanks with temperature controls. The charming lab owner would get himself invited to dinner, and soon he was working as a full-blown cellar consultant. But even after he fixed the wineries' dirty cellars, the wines remained inconsistent. Some years they were thin and watery, reminiscent of the pale Claret for which Bordeaux was known until the eighteenth century, while other vintages were rich and flavorful.

This began to change in 1981, after the critic Robert Parker Jr. made a chance visit to the lab in the hope that Michel and Dany could help him plan some wine tastings for the *Wine Advocate*, his new consumer's guide to fine wine.

On the surface, the awkward American reviewer and the dapper French consultant made an odd couple. A middle-class kid from rural Maryland, Parker attended a small-town public school named Hereford, hung out with kids who belonged to the Future Farmers of America, and didn't taste wine until age eighteen, when he tried a fortified sweet bubbly called Cold Duck and promptly threw up. After graduating from the University of Maryland School of Law in 1973, Parker spent a decade working as a lawyer for the Farm Credit Banks of Baltimore. He was heavy, naïve, and American. And he went by the most prosaic of monikers: "Bob."

Parker's was far from the typical backstory of a wine aficionado. But along the way—in December 1967 to be exact, on a visit to his high school sweetheart and future wife, Pat Etzel, during her junior year abroad in France—the Maryland son of a dairy farmer discovered that he had a freakishly perceptive nose.

Admittedly, it was an inherited gift. His father could detect someone's garlicky breath from the other side of a room. For Parker, the family skill had always been little more than a parlor trick. But then, during the France trip, he visited Strasbourg, where Pat was studying. There, as the genesis story goes, Bob and Pat ate several haute cuisine meals with a doctor who had befriended Pat. They drank fine wines. And Bob began to pick apart the flavors.

"Oh, that's good!" Bob said. "There's a little taste of grapefruit there, and a little taste of lemon, and a little taste of . . ." The doctor evidently eyed Parker and then, after taking a moment to calm his surprise, asked, "Do you know that you have just defined the main components of a Riesling?" At that very moment, Bob Parker supposedly had an epiphany: he was blessed with the palate of a tasting savant.

In William Langewiesche's excellent December 2000 profile of Parker in the *Atlantic Monthly*, which recounts the pivotal trip, Parker explained how wine affected him. A classic supertaster—people whose taste bud density is up to a hundred times that of normal folks—Parker does not fumble around with vague words to describe what he puts in his mouth. Nor does he have to guess whether a wine's flavors include a touch of grapefruit or orange. Flavors present themselves to him in hallucinogenic Technicolor. He has to name them by their proper titles. They simply will not be ignored.

"A wine goes in my mouth, and I just see it. I see it in three dimensions," Parker told Langewiesche. "The textures. The flavors. The smells. They just jump out at me. I can taste with a hundred screaming kids in a room. When I put my nose in a glass, it's like tunnel vision. I move into another world, where everything around me is just gone, and every bit of mental energy is focused on that wine."

Parker can, he told Langewiesche, remember every wine he has ever tasted.

The trip to France opened Parker's eyes to his savantlike palate. It also knocked the scales from his eyes. As the capstone of the visit, Bob and Pat treated themselves to dinner at Maxim's, the Parisian temple to fine dining. They were shuttled off to a back dining room reserved for unimportant foreigners. The staff was condescending. The food was attractive, but it was mediocre. The wine was mediocre too. And everything was overpriced. Parker was offended by the service, of course, but more so by the deference paid to overrated and ordinary comestibles. With his freakish powers, then, Parker vowed he would do more than just describe wines. He would *democratize* them by cutting through the fatuous reverence for nobility that passed for the era's criticism. If a wine was ordinary and overpriced, he would say so, even if it came from a pedigreed château with a top spot in the official 1855 classification of

French *crus*, or "growths." He simply didn't "give a shit," he said, about a château's history. When he launched his *Wine Advocate* journal in 1978, he kept true to his word.

In an industry as rigidly stratified as French wine, ranking a wine on its current quality was a belligerent act. Since Bordeaux wine brokers had ranked the region's top Bordeaux wineries into five *crus* in 1855, the classification had taken on the power of scripture. But it was no longer accurate. The classification had been based on the prices of the wines in 1855. This was not an entirely arbitrary way to rank the wines, as the prices reflected their quality and the wine hierarchy had stayed fairly constant over the previous century. But in the century following the classification, the wineries had evolved. Some had improved while others had slipped, and still others not listed at all had risen to greatness. And yet, a winery's reputation and the price it could charge were still largely defined by its *cru*. For obvious reasons, the Bordeaux *crus* that had made it into the classification, especially those in the upper classes, were loath to submit themselves to anything as base and mutable as an honest reviewer's opinion.

Parker's decision not to bow before the 1855 rankings made him a natural ally of Rolland. As William Echikson explains in *Noble Rot*, advances in pesticides in the sixties had enabled Bordeaux winemakers to vastly increase their grape yields, and therefore their wine production. The increased grape yield seemed to make for thin, weak wine, but the Bordeaux old guard didn't care. The prices they charged were defined by their place in the 1855 hierarchy, so every extra bottle they could produce was like printing money. Rolland wanted to show this lazy aristocracy that the ever-increasing amount of thin wine they were pumping out wasn't "noble" or "austere," as sycophantic critics claimed; it was just bad. In a globalizing world where customers could demand real quality and not just a name, château owners would need to modernize just like any other business. Conversely, while Rolland wanted to save the château owners from their own greed, Parker aimed to save the global consumer from overpraised crap. Parker would tell them what to buy and what to avoid. He saw himself as a consumer advocate, the Ralph Nader of wine.

Like garrulous lost brothers, the two stocky oenophiles immediately clicked. They were impatient with the wine world's deference to aristocracy, and they both wanted to bring science and merit to the hierarchy of wine. Parker and Rolland were hardworking heathens, drinkers on a mission who could spend twelve hours a day tasting upwards of two hundred wines while somehow staying reasonably sober. It didn't hurt their budding friendship that they had the same image of high-quality wine: fruity, rich, and concentrated as blood. They were believers with the same god.

The timing of their meeting was propitious. One year later, Rolland predicted that the 1982 vintage was going to be exceptionally fruity, full, and dense, just as he and Parker liked. The 1982 harvest had come after a dry year with an unusual amount of sun, which had led to smaller crops of more mature grapes that were especially high in sugar and complex tannins. Tipped off by Rolland, Parker said the 1982 vintage would be one of the best vintages he had ever tasted. Other critics, especially Brits, heartily disagreed. They found that the previews of the 1982 wines were too dark, strong, and heavy (one American called it "oafish"). But when the vintage was released for consumption in 1984, Parker and Rolland were proven right by almost unanimous opinion.

Parker's clear-eyed style of criticism was a revelation for consumers. Before his arrival, wine criticism and marketing had been chummy sports rife with backroom corruption, and the buyers had been the marks. The layman fine-wine buyer bought as high up the 1855 classification as he could afford, and he paid accordingly. If he wasn't entirely enamored with the wine he got, he figured maybe his palate wasn't sufficiently fine. When it came to determining the quality of the vintages he was buying, he had little on which to base his decision besides historical reputation. The English critics who traditionally interpreted

French wine for him were almost no help, as Echikson notes in *Noble Rot*. "In traditional English wine criticism, bad wines didn't exist," he writes. "There were just varying degrees of wonderful and more wonderful." Worse, many of the same critics who praised the wines were in the industry's pocket. "There was one grower in Burgundy who used to have cases of Grands Crus prepared for me every year," says Pierre-Antoine Rovani, a wine critic who worked for Parker for a decade. "And every year I would say, 'I can't take those,' and he'd say, 'Everyone else takes them, why not you?'"

Many of the 1982-vintage Bordeaux wines sold out; prices doubled on the auction market. By the time other critics began to change their tune, Parker's reputation had already been made. Those who had listened to him and purchased the 1982 vintage got a good deal on very nice wine, and wine speculators who had followed his recommendation made a nice profit by buying undervalued wine and selling it in the ensuing boom. Oenophilia is about taste, of course, but it is also very much about money. Wine, unlike other beverages, is treated as an art form—it's sold in auction, for example—and top wineries often hold back part of a vintage in the hope that rising prices on the auction market will increase its value. For speculators, straightforward advance information like Parker's offered a competitive advantage. While Parker has said that "speculation" is a "dirty word" in the world of wine, and that wine is meant to be drunk and enjoyed, market players saw his prescient ratings as a stock-picking tool.

After seeing the 1982 vintage's greatness, Rolland realized that the trick was getting similar grapes every harvest. He figured out that Bordeaux vineyards produced too many grapes and harvested them too young, and he soon shifted his consulting eye from cellar sanitation to vineyard yield. Rolland began preaching a gospel of deep pruning in winter, "green-harvesting" to reduce the quantity of grapes, leaf trimming to keep the grapes exposed to sun and air, and very late harvesting. The mere suggestion that grapes could be improved by man was radical in a region of aristocratic families that worshiped at the altar of their *terroir*, the belief that a mythic mix of soil, weather, and history made one château's wine intrinsically better than that of its neighbor.

As time went on, the two stocky wine rebels saw their fame and power grow concurrently. Although Rolland's new theories on the improvability of winemaking did not make him many friends among the old guard, it helped industry pioneers and up-and-coming *garagistes* (low-production winemakers whose tiny wineries resembled garages) produce riper grapes, sometimes nearly shriveled to raisins because of late harvesting. The Rolland-inspired fruit had high sugar and tannin levels, and it produced dark, fruity, concentrated wine. And following Rolland's advice often meant kind words from Parker, who was proving that he could make a winery's market with one positive review.

Not everyone thought this new style was an improvement. Some complained that these "hedonistic fruit bombs"—a term Parker approvingly used—were just candy for the Coke-drinking American masses, and that Rolland, via Parker, was creating a globalized wine recipe of big, anonymous wines. They even had a word for this army of alcoholic, jammy creations: "Parkerization." In a sentiment often heard among those who resist the form, former Bodega Norton owner Ricardo Santos says, "Michel Rolland makes very good wines, but he makes his Merlot in a hundred different countries. He makes *his* wine in many parts of the world. You can't blame him for it. But it's not a wine with a regional personality."

Still, Parker's reputation as an honest broker grew. He did away with the opaque prose that defined wine writing of the era. In its place, he spoke to his readers as one plain-spoken if slightly overwrought American to another, describing wine flavors with easily understood adjectives ("opaque purple," "jammy," "full-bodied"). And he traded English critics' old 20-point scale for a 100-point version that appealed to Americans weaned on high school number grades.

Such change didn't always endear Parker to Bordeaux traditionalists. While the writer William Langewiesche was in Bordeaux researching his *Atlantic Monthly* article, people talked to him openly about setting Parker up for a drunk-driving arrest. And some in Bordeaux went beyond talk. The angry manager of a famous château named Cheval Blanc allowed his schnauzer to attack and draw blood from Parker's leg after Parker had given Cheval Blanc's wine a poor review. With so much faith being put in his endangered tasting skills, Parker took out $1 million in insurance on his olfactory abilities—his nose.

He couldn't have known it, but by launching his new style journal just as Americans were beginning to drink wine, Parker set off a wine publishing frenzy. Other magazines copied his 100-point scoring system and plain-speaking style. Today, a cacophony of voices has diluted the value of those reviews, however. Aided by the ease of web publishing, a growing number of self-appointed experts have entered the fray. With the realization that high point ratings are those most widely disseminated by stores that want to sell more wine—meaning free publicity for the reviewer who gives them—a kind of grade inflation has crept in. And often buyers don't know which experts to trust.

"I think we're suffering from point fatigue," says Tyler Colman, an economist and author who runs the popular industry website DrVino.com. "People are starting to realize that wines are sold on points, and they're often not as good as they might appear to be. Points just tell you about one person's opinion. It's a very limiting perspective."

With so many voices demanding attention, the competition for reviews by the most trusted writers has grown fierce. This is understandable: a 2003 UC Davis study found that every extra ratings point a wine got from the *Wine Spectator* added eighty-three cents to its price. So worried are wine buyers that this fierce competition between wineries will lead to tainted reviews that oenological website chat rooms practically glow with indignation when a reviewer is caught in a perceived conflict of interest. A typical blow-up is the one that erupted onto the pages of the

*Wall Street Journal* in 2009 when it came out that Parker's *Wine Advocate* reviewer for South America, Jay Miller, had accepted trips to Argentina, Chile, and Australia paid for by local trade groups; Parker defended Miller but posted online that he would no longer allow such junkets to Argentina. Beyond the verifiable stories, the outlandish nature of some of the industry's whispered tales shows how much is at stake in positive wine reviews: one especially salacious rumor holds that a top wine writer asked that the number of women be doubled when an Argentine *bodega* offered to hire him a prostitute.

Those issues were still in the future when Rolland's techniques and Parker's words changed the industry in the 1980s and '90s. Desperate for high scores from the increasingly powerful *Wine Advocate*, a growing number of wineries hired Rolland. By 2001, Rolland was making $2 million a year. Though he still works as hard as ever, Rolland's ample girth and dandyish affection for fat gold cufflinks attest to his love of the good life.

When Michel and Dany Rolland arrived in Buenos Aires in the last days of February 1988, Arnaldo Etchart took them to the Jockey Club, one of the British-style dining and sports clubs that testify to the influence of the English and Scottish immigrants who arrived to build railways and run *estancias* in the late nineteenth century. Founded in 1882 by Carlos Pellegrini—who became Argentina's president eight years later—the club has been housed since 1966 in two adjoining turn-of-the-century French/Italian-style mansions on the city's toniest street, Avenida Alvear. There, Etchart introduced Michel and Dany to a group of Argentine food and wine journalists.

Argentina's thirty most prestigious wines sat atop a long table, lined in a queue of increasing fame. For the French couple's benefit, each was accompanied with an index card that noted its popularity, annual sales, and other trivia. Dany begged off the tasting, too tired to go through thirty bottles after the fifteen-hour flight from Paris. She asked her husband if he would mind winnowing them down to five.

Michel and the local scribblers began to sip. Aware of being a guest in a proud country whose language he did not speak, the amiable Michel tried to remain upbeat and friendly. But the wines kept pulling his smile into a frown. Most of them suffered from technical defects. It wasn't that he disagreed with the taste they were aiming for, but that he tasted unsanitary conditions, incorrect storage temperatures, and underripe fruit. They tasted as if the Argentines who made and served wine had lost the touch for it—an impression that was deepened when, several days later, Michel went to a traditional *parrilla* steak house and was served a bottle of wine that had been stored next to the grill and arrived at his table downright warm.

Once Michel and the journalists had thinned the herd to five, Dany began her abbreviated tasting. After she sipped and spat from the final wine—supposedly Argentina's most prestigious one—she turned and spoke to Michel in French. "Did you really *like* this wine?" she asked. "Because it's very bad." Michel shrugged. "Honestly, it's frightening," he said. "But it's the most famous in the country. It's their best."

Such was the state of Argentine wine in 1988. "The majority of the wines were of middling quality, or just bad. There were only a few bottles that allowed one to think of interesting possibilities," Rolland says today. "And there wasn't even one good enough for the export market."

At eight o'clock the morning after arriving in Cafayate, Michel Rolland emerged from the guest bedroom at Arnaldo Etchart's winery home and presented himself for work.

"Are you doing the harvest now?" he asked Etchart.

"Yes."

"Fine, I'll taste the grapes you're harvesting. Can you give me a little truck and an employee to take me around to the fields?"

"But what about the laboratory and the *bodega*?" Etchart asked, thinking, as any winemaker would, that his wines' faults lay in their elaboration.

"Later," came Rolland's reply.

"All the oenologists and technicians were waiting for him in the laboratory, and this guy says, 'Let's go out to the vineyards.' So they *all* went out to the vineyard. And he starts to eat grapes," says Arnaldo's son Marcos, a facsimile of his father in earlier years, replete with saggy corduroys, expensive new cowboy boots, and glasses that go dark in the sun. Today Marcos runs the San Pedro de Yacochuya winery, a partnership between the Etchart family and Rolland. "It's funny, in those days the winemaker never went into the field and the agronomist never went into the *bodega*. And now they walk around inseparable," Marcos says.

Trailed by a procession of confused agronomists, technicians, winemaker Jorge Riccitelli, and a translator, Rolland absently nibbled on grapes as he strolled alongside Arnaldo Etchart through the vintner's high-altitude mountain vineyard in Cafayate, the breathtaking mountain desert seven hundred miles north of Mendoza that's best known for the citric white wine Torrontés. The vineyard was planted in a fashion that most contemporary winemakers knew largely as an example of what was no longer done. The plants were trellised in a "pergola" style: rows of vines trained to guideposts about seven feet high and woven across an overhead grid so that the grapes could be picked quickly by workers walking underneath the canopy. The grid sagged, pregnant with thick bunches of fruit. "They preferred high production above all else," says Rolland. "No one talked about quality."

Rolland waved away the folders that had been prepared for him on the region's soil, grape varieties, and unique climate. At the vineyard's highest point he paused and stared at the mosaic of vineyards sprawling across the desert below him. Turning to Etchart, he spoke a sentence in French. "He doesn't want to read anything," the translator said. "If the landscape is this beautiful, the wine will be wonderful."

...

After their vineyard stroll, Rolland and Etchart sat down to a country lunch. While the cuisine in immigrant cities like Buenos Aires and Mendoza tends toward European staples such as pasta and steak, food in Salta and the rest of Argentina's northwest sticks close to its indigenous roots. Etchart served Rolland a pair of Salteña classics: *humitas*, fresh cornmeal cooked with spices, lard, and a touch of sugar and then steamed to delicious consistency inside corn husks; and *empanadas*, meat pies. Usually baked in an *horno de barro*—an igloo-shaped clay oven whose interior can stay hot for a day after being heated with a small inferno of wood—a Salteña *empanada* is a spicy, handheld feast hearty enough to see a vineyard worker through a day of picking: hand-cut steak, cubes of potato, green onion, hardboiled egg, and hot pepper flakes, folded into a small pastry shell the shape of a half-moon, all cooked with beef tallow.

"Your property is very beautiful," Rolland said as they worked through their lunch.

"Yes, yes, of course it is," said the impatient Etchart.

"But there's a problem."

"Oh? And what is that?" Etchart said.

"You are harvesting grapes that aren't sufficiently mature."

"How are they not *mature*?"

"They're not sufficiently mature," the Frenchman said. "The tannins are not ready. You're fifteen days short. *At least.* If I were you, I'd suspend the harvest."

Several hours later, Rolland stood in the winery lab facing the restless crowd of agronomists, lab techs, and winemakers. Many of them had been flown up from an Etchart property in Mendoza, Argentina's main wine region, for an audience with Rolland. They already had their doubts after his snacking vineyard walkabout. Who did this arrogant European think he was, lecturing them on how to make wine in their own country?

"When do you harvest grapes?" asked Rolland.

One of the junior winemakers from Mendoza shrugged. "When the grapes are mature," he said.

"Correct," Rolland answered. "And when is it mature? In what moment is it mature?"

"Right now," the winemaker said. "That's why we're harvesting."

"How do you *know* it's mature?"

"Well, that's what the lab measurements say."

In the silence that followed, Etchart winemaker Jorge Riccitelli—who has since gone on to become the head winemaker at the mega-*bodega* Norton—noticed that Arnaldo Etchart was grinning like a Cheshire cat. "Look, *jefe*, don't smile so much," he said to Etchart. "You're a winemaker and you don't know either. Or maybe you *do* know. So why don't you answer?" Etchart laughed. "I'm not going to answer. Rolland has to," he said. "I brought all of you up here so that you can discuss this with him. I'm just going to listen. If he says it's not mature, it's not mature in my opinion."

Rolland had chewed Etchart's grapes to see if the seeds were toasted and crunchy, not green, and if the tannins had begun to grow concentrated and complex, which improves the taste, color, mouthfeel, and ageability of the finished wine. He had, of course, not found any of those things. At the time in Argentina, Etchart and many other winegrowers simply ran lab tests on sugar and acidity levels in the grapes and harvested when they reached a certain level. Because grape sugar levels rise quickly in hot environments and Argentine wine country is generally very hot, the sugars can reach high levels early in the long harvest season. But because the vineyard managers rarely pruned the grapes and usually irrigated as much as they could—both methods to maximize volume—the fruit tended to be immature in every way except for their sugar. That is, it tended to be watery and bloated from overirrigation, and the phenolic compounds that give wine its color and taste tended to be underdeveloped and raw. The end result was watery wine with a weak but rough flavor—just the problem that Etchart wanted to correct.

"To make a good wine, well concentrated, one has to wait, and wait, and wait," Rolland told the assembled Etchart employees. "And when you've finished waiting, wait some more." As simple as that sounded, what Rolland was suggesting was a radical move into the unknown. At the time, Argentina had a shrinking economy and inflation of over 300 percent. While Etchart eagerly wanted to improve his wines, his huge winery's ubiquitous brands had legions of dedicated local drinkers. To abruptly change his recipe at such a precarious moment meant taking a huge risk. After a pause, Etchart spoke. "Tomorrow we're going to stop the harvest."

"All the technicians were opposed to the Frenchman," says Marcos Etchart. "In the beginning they said, 'It's unheard of for him to come here and charge money to eat grapes. If we did lab analyses of maturity, why are you going out to eat grapes?' And now? Every one of the same technicians and winemakers checks maturity by going out there and eating grapes."

Rolland had planned only to observe local winegrowing techniques during his first Argentine visit, but after two or three days he had seen so many practices that directly contradicted his convictions that he felt compelled to push for changes. As he and Dany wrapped up their stay in Cafayate, Michel Rolland gave winemaker Jorge Riccitelli a blueprint to start the evolution of Etchart wines: twenty steps toward cutting-edge Bordeaux. Rolland's most radical suggestion was that Riccitelli prune the vines, even though it was later than one would normally "green-harvest" or "drop fruit." Lowering production even for a short period would allow the remaining clusters to develop better. The amount of water used in irrigation—which was done by a traditional "flood" method, a process by which an irrigation canal is diverted into a vineyard for several hours—was also to be severely cut. Finally, the vinery's huge vineyard—over 700 acres of grapes, says Marcos Etchart—was to be split into zones, and each was to be fermented separately.

"We used to mix everything together, and Rolland said we'll do the vineyards from above in this tank, the ones from below in that tank, and so on," says Etchart's son Arnaldo Jr., who runs the *bodega*'s sales and marketing. "The idea was to see where the best wine was in the *finca* [farm]."

Upon reading his instructions, Riccitelli eyed the Frenchman skeptically. "I'll do this," he said. "But if this doesn't work and I get fired, you better find me a new job."

Most important, Rolland said that the best grapes, which came from the high-altitude Yacochuya vineyard, should be separated, subjected to extended maceration (a process in which the grape skins are left in contact with the juice for several weeks after fermentation in order to leach more tannins, colors, and flavor compounds from them), and aged in small oak barrels to create a premium brand. It sounded simple enough, but caused great consternation. One basic problem: there were no new French oak barrels in the country, sending the winery's oenologists to scrounge used ones at other *bodegas*.

But it was the request for extended maceration that was too much for Riccitelli, a proud man who, at thirty-eight, had already spent nine years as the head winemaker at Etchart. He called Arnaldo Etchart. "Boss, the crazy Frenchman wants us to end up with vinegar," said the flustered winemaker. "Why do you say that?" Etchart asked. "Because he wants us to macerate for *three weeks*," Riccitelli replied.

At the time, Argentine wines were rarely macerated after fermentation because, unless vigorously controlled, the long process risked spoiling the wine.

"Okay," Etchart said. "Is it a lot of wine?"

"No."

"Then do what he says."

...

"The neighbors thought it was idiocy that my father was paying a fortune to this Frenchman," says Marcos Etchart. "People were saying, 'Look at this *pelotudo*—this jackass—and the money he pays to watch that other *pelotudo* eat grapes and toss fruit on the ground.'"

In the end, though, it paid off. "Of course, we got a wine with a lot more body and color," Marcos says of the first vintage of the premium wine, which was named after his father: Arnaldo B. Etchart. The next years were even better. When the 1990 Arnaldo B. Etchart premium red hit the market, Parker's newsletter, the *Wine Advocate*, called it "a beautifully made wine with considerable complexity and richness." The praise continued in a near parody of purple wine prose. "It displays a dense, saturated plum color, and a nearly outstanding set of aromatics consisting of cedar, licorice, smoke, jammy cassis, berry fruit, and a notion of prunes," the review gushed. "This medium to full-bodied wine exhibits admirable concentration, low acidity, a fleshy, nicely-textured and layered mouthfeel and a plump, opulent finish."

In Jonathan Nossiter's controversial 2004 wine globalization documentary *Mondovino*, Arnaldo Etchart gives Michel Rolland credit for the oenological revolution.

"He changed the face of Argentine wine," Etchart says.

"Michel himself?" asks an incredulous Nossiter.

"Yes."

"One man?"

"Well, Michel *and* I," says the proud Etchart. "Because I brought him."

In March 1988, just as Rolland was threatening Riccitelli's job with his viticultural prescriptions, thirty-four-year-old American winemaker Paul Hobbs was saying his prayers in a car piloted by Jorge Catena, Nicolás Catena's younger brother. Jorge had spent a year at UC Davis taking courses in the mid-seventies, while Hobbs was getting his degree in the winemaking program there. It wasn't a bad time for Jorge to be outside of Argentina, where left-wing rebel groups had been raising money by kidnapping rich business people like Carlos Pulenta, a member of the family that then owned the huge *bodega* Peñaflor. Slight and quiet, Jorge bears a passing physical resemblance to the 1950s cartoon character Mr. Magoo, and his voice, which sounds almost as if he were talking through a trumpet mute, gives him an air of shyness.

As they descended the steep cross-Andes route from Santiago, Chile, to Mendoza, Argentina, Jorge stomped the brake at each switchback's 180-degree turn, bringing the car to a grinding standstill, and then jammed the accelerator into the straightaway. The wheels of his tiny Fiat slipped over the puckers of the packed-dirt road and the loose-shake shoulders. Pebbles shot from beneath his spinning tires and launched over the edge of the switch, skittering and bouncing before settling to rest hundreds of feet below. "A lot of the time we were off the road as much as we were on it," Hobbs says. "Jorge's vision was not very good."

"I had driven that road a lot, so I was accustomed to the switchbacks," says Jorge Catena, laughing. "But Paul wasn't. There's a lot more security on the roads in the US."

Hobbs hadn't planned to visit Argentina, much less die there. But then again, much of his South American adventure hadn't worked out as planned.

Handsome in a Greg Kinnear way—like a Hollywood cowboy, with a cleft chin, roughhewn features, a mop of dirty-blond curls, and eyes so blue they are almost fluorescent—Hobbs is the perfect winemaker mix of farmer and fop: a bit too pretty to be a roughneck but at the same time too rugged to be fey. He speaks with enunciated care: he clicks on every "t" in words like "little" and "literally." Hobbs talks with his head pulled back and slightly cocked, and he wears a constant smile.

The second oldest of eleven children, Hobbs grew up near Lake Ontario, in western New York, on farmland heavy with apple, peach, and cherry orchards. It was a tough, though not impossible, existence: when money was tight after a bad 1959 harvest, the family rented out the farmhouse and lived in the barn. In 1969, when Hobbs was fifteen, his father—a wine enthusiast—brought home a bottle of 1962 Château d'Yquem, a famous French Sauterne, and poured it into little Dixie paper cups that he shared around the family dinner table. While the rest of his siblings gave the wine a perfunctory sip, it was a pivotal moment for Paul. The bouquet and flavor fused onto the sensory receptors that one finds asymmetrically hyperdeveloped in winemakers and perfume designers, and Paul, like the apostle on the road to Damascus, was converted to wine. Driving through the family orchards next to his father on the front seat of their station wagon, Hobbs had learned that fruit tastes like the specific patch of land that grew it. And after tasting the Château d'Yquem, he needed to apply that knowledge to grapes. He soon convinced his father to uproot a section of their apple orchard and replant it with wine grapes, and to put him in charge of the project.

Later, while a pre-med student at the University of Notre Dame, Paul's passion for wine blossomed, fertilized by tastings hosted by his botany professor, a former winemaker at the Christian Brothers Winery in California. After graduating in 1975, he traded medicine for the graduate winemaking program at UC Davis. There, his innovative thesis—a study of how phenolic compounds are extracted from oak into wine and of the chemical differences between French and American oak barrels—led to a job as a research technician at Napa Valley's Opus One, the Robert Mondavi and Baron Philippe de Rothschild venture that produced America's first ultrapremium wine. Rothschild's involvement in the joint venture, which was launched in 1980, gave an air of respectability and European dash to the burgeoning Napa wine region.

After the 1984 vintage, Hobbs left Mondavi and started working as an assistant winemaker at the Simi Winery, a Sonoma County winery in the town of Healdsburg, about seventy miles north of San Francisco's Golden Gate Bridge. Located in what was then a California hinterland, Simi was small enough that Hobbs could aspire to be its head winemaker someday—an opportunity he would never have at the Mondavi juggernaut, where Robert Mondavi's son Tim controlled winemaking.

Hobbs's use of extended macerations and gentle fruit handling soon helped bring the winery critical attention: Simi's 1985, 1986, and 1987 Cabernet Sauvignon Reserves all got "Outstanding" ratings of at least 90 points from Robert Parker Jr. Hobbs moved up quickly and would be appointed vice president and winemaker in 1989.


In March 1988, Hobbs was supposed to be in Chile, studying Chilean wineries. Instead, he was hurtling down the side of the Andes cordillera in Jorge Catena's Fiat. For years, both Jorge Catena and Marcelo Kogan Alterman, a professor of botany at Chile's Catholic University and an old friend of Hobbs from Davis, had been selling the rising Californian star on a visit to South America. Like the *bodegueros* of Argentina, Chile's winemakers were hoping to catch some of California's lightning in their own bottles.

From what Hobbs had heard from his former UC Davis professor Ralph Kunkee—who had visited Argentina at Nicolás Catena's invitation —Argentina's future wasn't terribly bright. Argentina, Kunkee had told Hobbs, was like California's Central Valley: a great place for making cheap, high-volume wines. It was just too hot in Argentina to make good wine. "It's a wine wasteland," Kunkee told Hobbs. "They only make plonk."

But by the mid-eighties, Hobbs had begun hearing good things about Chile. Wedged between two geographic extremes—the Atacama Desert to the north and the Patagonian ice field to the south—Chile's central valleys had a Mediterranean climate that was attracting the attention of winegrowers. They were starting to say that it might have the world's best winemaking climate and could be the next great viticultural region. Like Argentina, though, it wasn't yet known for the quality of its products. But it was courting investment and had begun to export solid table wine at an ever-increasing clip.

Before Chile's early-1988 harvest season, Hobbs called his old friend Kogan and asked him to set up several winery visits. The timing could not have been better: March was the slow season in California's wine valleys. Because of the flipped seasons of the Southern Hemisphere, Chile was enjoying the last days of summer. Beautiful, sunny, and warm.

At the time of Hobbs's 1988 visit, Chile sat at an inflection point between its past as a tin-pot dictatorship and its future as a poster child of emerging free-market democracy. A 2,700-mile-long ribbon of land wedged between the Pacific Ocean and the Andes mountain range—averaging barely 110 miles in width—Chile was about to emerge from General Augusto Pinochet Ugarte's fifteen-year dictatorship. Pinochet had taken over the country in a bloody 1973 coup that culminated in Socialist President Salvador Allende's death. After the murder or "disappearance" of some three thousand political opponents, Pinochet's regime had frayed by the late eighties; Chileans had tired of life under a pariah regime. For several years his government had been launching market-oriented reforms and allowing more trade union and political freedoms in a bid to remake its image. But in October 1988, Pinochet's attempt to win a new eight-year term by relatively democratic referendum ended in a loss of 56 percent to 44 percent.

When Hobbs arrived, the military presence was still palpable. Driving down Ruta 5 near Santiago, he saw turrets perched over the road—like prison watchtowers—bristling with rifle-holding soldiers.

"It reminded me a bit of Eastern Europe," says Hobbs. "I remember not feeling very comfortable. Military trucks would stop, and guys would jump out and swarm the street with machine guns. You never saw what happened afterward."

The 1970s under Allende and Pinochet had been terrible for Chilean wine sellers. Battered first by socialist land redistribution, high taxes, and social policies meant to combat alcohol consumption, and then by the foreign disapprobation of Pinochet, wine exports stood at only 93,600 cases in 1980, representing barely 0.3 percent of the US imported table-wine market. Some countries where wine purchases were controlled by the state (especially in Scandinavia) decided to boycott Chilean wine entirely.

But unlike Argentina, where leaders like Catena and Etchart were just beginning to create "export-quality" wines for sale overseas, Chileans had already reversed their fortunes. By the time of Hobbs's visit in 1988, the Chilean wine industry had invested in high technology, and by the end of the Pinochet dictatorship, exports had begun to take off. They more than doubled, from $17.5 million in 1987 to $35.4 million in 1989, and within a decade Chile would account for 13 percent of the 38 million cases of table wine imported by the United States—more than Germany, Spain, Argentina, Portugal, and a half dozen other countries combined.

Instead of being impressed by the industriousness of the Chilean vintners, however, Hobbs felt oversold. Many of the vines in Chile were planted ten to twelve feet apart, as in the cheap grape zone of California's Central Valley, so that industrial tractors could drive down the rows. And the winemakers seemed beholden to money in an unhealthy way. At the first winery he visited, Hobbs says, the owners were trying to up their profits by labeling a wine as Pinot Noir even though it contained no Pinot Noir grapes. The winemakers he met with even committed the abomination of drinking Coca-Cola—not wine—with lunch. "Nobody seemed to be anything more than commercial," he says today. "I didn't see any passion."

Unlike the products of most other industries, good wine is meant to express the culture in which it was created. Wine buyers do not want an anonymous product, no matter how perfect it is. They want wine to express a lifestyle in which an obsessive peasant grower pours his soul into grapes that an aristocratic winemaker lovingly transforms into the blood of his homeland. They want a wine from France to distill centuries of history of its Bordeaux château. Whether it is possible to put lifestyle in a bottle is questionable, but it is how wine marketers justify the prices they demand. And in that amorphous desire for "passion," Chile had failed.

"The countries that export are ones that drink a lot and export their tastes. France exports the French lifestyle, the Italians export the Tuscan style," says François Lurton, the fifth generation of a prominent Bordeaux wine family. "Chile is the only country that makes copies of [the] rest of [the] world. Chileans say, 'You don't like it? I'll make what you want.' They don't care about their own tastes."

At a prosaic level, Hobbs had discovered that Chile lacked a basic wine-drinking culture. With less than half the population of Argentina, and an immigrant constituency that skewed more toward Germany and eastern Europe than Italy, Chileans drank much less wine per capita. Chilean wine held no romance for winemakers weaned on France, Italy, and California. It was a rich man's game, composed of huge *bodegas* often founded by oligarchs who had originally made their money in Chile's mining industry.

"There were big wineries and big vineyards, and a big gap between the wealthy people who owned the wineries and the poor people who made the wine. The feeling was more like business," says Alberto Antonini, the former head winemaker at Italy's legendary Marchesi Antinori wine company who visited Chile in the same era.

Without a captive audience like Argentina's, Chile's industrial winemakers depended on the export market. And so they did what any intelligent industrialist would do: they quizzed potential customers on their tastes and made a product to suit. That meant producing tankers of agreeable, low-cost wines for bargain-hunting Americans, not risking the farm on high-priced, low-production standouts that would thrill connoisseurs and sell oenophiles on the romance of Chilean culture.

Soon after his arrival in Chile, Hobbs had called his old acquaintance Jorge Catena. Hobbs didn't expect to see Jorge; he wasn't an expert in geography, but traveling to another country for a dinner seemed excessive. But Jorge had driven across the Andes and rented a room in a Santiago hotel.

Saddened by what he had found in Chilean wineries, Hobbs's thoughts turned to his friend. Hobbs had so far been unable to get together with Jorge because of his winery tours. Jorge had suggested that he could go along on the visits, but Hobbs would answer no, on orders from his host, Marcelo Kogan, an imposing man with wild Einstein-like hair who Hobbs says had explicitly told him not to bring Argentines in the wine business into Chilean *bodegas*.

Chile and Argentina had been at loggerheads for much of their existence, with Chileans mocking their Italianate neighbors for their European pretentions and their corruption, and Argentina looking down at Chileans as vulgar, mercantilist hicks. Chile was Germany, Argentina was France, and the wine industry was their disputed Alsace-Lorraine. That Pinochet had aided Britain during Argentina's 1982 attempt to wrest the Falkland Islands from the United Kingdom was only the most recent insult between the neighbors.

Tired of dull wineries and annoyed about having to deny his friend because of a cultural spat he didn't understand, Hobbs invited Jorge along on his visit to the Viña Canepa winery. Word quickly got back to Kogan. Later that night, after, Hobbs says, his host lit into him for breaking their agreement, Hobbs decided to add a country to his trip.

"Fine," Hobbs said to Jorge. "Let's go to Argentina."

...

As the Fiat crested the Andes from Chile and shuddered down the Argentine side, Hobbs immediately saw the great challenge of the country's Andean west. Looking at an aerial photograph of Argentine wine country is like seeing a moonscape. The great storms that boil in from the Pacific Ocean just a few hundred miles to the west empty themselves before they reach Mendoza, dropping their rain and snow on the Chilean side of the Andes. By the time the few clouds that survive reach the Argentine side, they are dry puffs of cotton. Here, the vaulted firmament is a cowboy's dream, a cloudless and celestial blue expanse, empty as a fall Wyoming sky.

From the windows of the Fiat, Jorge and Hobbs could see the road easing onto flat desert pan. But they were not greeted by the Saharan glitter of silica quartz. Instead, spread in front of the car's dashboard was a wash of green, all made possible by the irrigation system designed by the Huarpe Indians five centuries before. It looked like a sea of vineyards.

Jorge pulled over and led Hobbs into one of his family's new vineyards, a spread of five-year-old Chardonnay and Cabernet Sauvignon vines, the international varietals Catena had instructed Marchevsky to plant in what's now known as the *La Pirámide* Vineyard in Agrelo.

Hobbs shook his head: even from the road he could see that the vines were outmoded in terms of modern technique. Though not planted in the overhead "pergola" style Rolland had found in Salta, these vines were planted in an equally antiquated style that Mendoza's Italian immigrants had brought at the end of the nineteenth century. The vines were trellised just above the ground with out-of-control foliage burying the fruit in moist, mouthlike cocoons. It was a way of protecting the grapes from the harsh sun and even harsher hailstorms, but in these fields Hobbs saw a breeding ground for mold and underripe fruit.

And yet, his heart leapt with excitement; the sight of the vines made his trip worthwhile. Though stylistically outdated, the vines were closely spaced, one meter apart, with just less than two meters between rows, as in Europe and Napa. More important, despite some grape rot, the vines themselves were beautiful and healthy. And the soil was amazing. It was poor in the way winemakers love: sandy, dry, and full of rocks, just the type to challenge a grapevine to transcendence. "I fell in love with the land," Hobbs says. "From the moment I drove over the mountains and went into the first vineyard with their scraggly vines, I just loved it."

"Jorge," Hobbs said. "I am blown away."

The fields may have been romantic, but Argentina's urban areas were a different beast. On the way to the top Catena winery, Bodegas Esmeralda, Jorge drove Hobbs through the city of Mendoza. As they entered the sprawling metro area of about seven hundred thousand people, Hobbs could not have been farther from the quaint wine capitals in Tuscany, Bordeaux, and Napa. "Mendoza was butt ugly as far as visitors were concerned," says Norm Roby, a wine journalist at *Decanter* who visited the city in its first boom years.

Inside the government-owned Plaza Hotel—now a Park Hyatt—the decorations were drab leftovers from the 1930s, like some two-star Moscow hotel of the Khrushchev era, and the rickety pipes shuddered within the walls when you turned on the bathroom tap. The waiters in the hotel's café were dressed like all Argentine waiters, as if by law, in white shirts and black bow ties. If correctly inspired, they could be counted upon to bring an order of coffee within thirty minutes. To make the Soviet reference more pronounced, the streets were plied by trolley buses that Mendoza had received from the USSR in exchange for tankers of wine.

Leaving behind the layers of urban sprawl built atop Pedro Ruiz del Castillo's sixteenth-century settlement, Jorge Catena and Hobbs drove east.

Until the early nineties, most Argentine wine was shipped by rail or truck to Buenos Aires for bottling. At the time of Hobbs's visit, when one visited a winery one usually visited Buenos Aires, where the *bodegas* had offices, tasting rooms, and bottling plants. The winery itself was almost never seen; it was a place for country people. In Bodegas Esmeralda's case, the winery sat in a rural zone called Junín on the southern outskirts of San Martín, a county seat twenty-five miles east of Mendoza. There, Jorge led Hobbs through the winery, which his family had bought in 1965. Founded by Don Juan Fernández and named for his daughter, the winery was built in the style of a Spanish hacienda and painted Pepto-Bismol pink, a traditional Argentine color historically achieved by mixing whitewash and cow's blood for protection from humidity.

Despite Nicolás Catena's multiyear modernization project, little had changed since Ruhland's 1981 visit. It was harvest season, and Hobbs spied containers of just-picked grapes, many of them weakly red or an unripe green, covered with bugs and leaves. There was an old wooden incline drainer and a continuous screw press, juicing tools that would qualify as artifacts in many other parts of the world. The pumps and hoses were cracked and speckled with black mold, the few steel tanks he saw were epoxy-lined behemoths, and nothing was automated. In the lab, it looked as if something had exploded on the walls. The *bodega's* medieval equipment and disregard for hygiene almost ensured the brown stain of oxidation. "It was like going into the dungeon at Edinburgh Castle," Hobbs says.

Jorge led Hobbs through the offices and past a huge table where *bodega* workers ate a communal lunch of homemade pasta or *asado* (traditional Argentine BBQ) and wine. In the cellar, Jorge began passing glasses to Hobbs, who sipped, swished, and spat. Despite the advances made after Catena's Napa moment, the wines were still high in sulfur, oxidized, and astringent.

"These are some of the most god-awful wines," Hobbs says he exclaimed. "What do you people *do* to such beautiful grapes to make wine like this?" That was the problem, Jorge told him: they didn't know. Looking around, Hobbs saw what Jorge meant. "They had nothing. *Nothing*," Hobbs says. "I had never seen anything so antiquated and dilapidated that you could still consider commercially viable."

Jorge cut to the chase. He offered to change Hobbs's flights to add a detour through Buenos Aires, where the family business headquarters was located. "My brother Nicolás wants to meet you," he said.

At the appointed hour, Hobbs sat down to lunch with Nicolás Catena at his apartment in the upscale Buenos Aires neighborhood of Palermo Chico. Where Jorge was awkward in his shyness, Nicolás's habit of quiet, smiling observation was charming and solicitous. He let conversational partners reveal themselves until he was ready to speak, a friendly aspect in his gaze.

As they sat down at a casually elegant table on the apartment's terrace, which overlooked a small pool and yard, Nicolás, dressed in a relaxed blue shirt, settled into his role as listener and asked Hobbs to tell his story. As Hobbs and Catena worked their way through the pasta course, Nicolás finally began to explain his problems. For ten years he'd been trying to make his wines good enough for export. And he was still not happy with his wines, even his top one, Saint Felicien, a Cabernet Sauvignon he had launched in the sixties. It was his best wine. It was a high-priced wine. And it had improved a bit with some of the lessons Catena had brought from California. But it wasn't selling well enough. And it was still somehow being oxidized. *All* the wines were. A frustrated Catena explained that not only was he eager to develop wines good enough for export, but he also wanted to start a new brand good enough to call "Catena"—a name as yet unknown to those outside the industry. He wanted to make his name known.

"With the climate and soil you have, I'm sure you could make some wonderful reds here," Hobbs said. Nicolás shook his head. "No, Paul, I want you to focus on Chardonnay production. We'll make a Chardonnay," he said.

Hobbs looked at Nicolás with curiosity. He didn't think the Argentine was joking—not exactly—but he did think Nicolás naïve to believe it was possible to make a high-quality Chardonnay in Argentina. Hobbs also seemed like a strange target for the request. He was best known for the Cabernet Sauvignon work he had done at Opus One and Simi Winery, and from everything he knew about Argentina, it was simply too hot to turn out a top white. But Nicolás had his reasons. A good Chardonnay requires high technology; it would prove that Argentina was a member of the First World of winemaking. Nicolás would not be swayed.

"And if we can show the world that Argentina can make a high-quality white wine," said Nicolás, "they will automatically accept that Argentina can produce high-quality reds." As an added advantage, a Chardonnay would remind the world of Napa, the New World wine hotspot that had first inspired Catena's modernizing project for Argentine wine.

The Argentine paused. "Why don't you come back next year and show us what to do?" Nicolás said. It sounded like a crazy challenge; Hobbs agreed.

# CHAPTER 6

## TURNING THE SHIP

Robert Mondavi and Carlos Tizio Mayer (left to right) at the 1991 lunch at
the Robert Mondavi Winery. Courtesy of Carlos Tizio.

IN 1991, AS SUMMER drew to a close, a group of some thirty Argentine winemakers and viticulturists arrived at Robert Mondavi's iconic winery. They had been invited for lunch with the master of New World wines, and they were humbled by the honor of the opportunity. Pedro Marchevsky was there, as was Jorge Catena's son Marcelo, along with representatives from Bodega Luigi Bosca, Peñaflor's fine-wine brand Trapiche, and other prominent Argentina wineries. Their leader was Carlos Tizio Mayer, an English-speaking Argentine UC Davis graduate who worked as a viticulture investigator for the National Agricultural Technology Institute, or INTA, in Mendoza, where he had run Argentina's first vineyard varietal census in 1990.

The lunch was the grand finale to a two-week California wine tour organized by INTA and the Asociación Argentina de Consorcios Regionales de Experimentación Agrícola ("Argentine Association of Regional Consortiums for Agricultural Experimentation"), or CREA. For many of the Argentines on the tour, the visit represented an inflection point: it was their first time behind the curtains of cutting-edge winemaking. The tour took the group to some of California's legendary sites: Tally Vineyards, Inglenook Vineyards, Clos du Bois, Beringer Vineyards, Clos du

Val, Sterling Vineyards (reached by an aerial tram), Simi Winery, and a host of other wineries and grape producers. They visited UC Davis and its Oakville Experimental Vineyard, and participated in master classes with top viticulture professors Nick Dokoozlian and Mark Kliewer. They marveled at the informality of American professors, who wore sneakers and Bermuda shorts. Most important, the Americans revealed the secrets of their sudden success.

"To me, the Americans were crazy because they opened up *every-thing* they had discovered and learned," says Marchevsky. "I could pass a few hours with a technician and ask whatever question I could think of, and he would answer every one without restrictions. A girl doing open-tank fermentation of Pinot Noir showed me everything. We went to Opus One, participated in the tastings, and they asked my opinion. They showed us *everything.*"

Grouped for their lunch on an outdoor patio at a cluster of tables decorated with sunflower centerpieces and shaded by broad white umbrellas, the Argentines soaked up the possibilities personified by Mondavi. "He was a visionary with a very clear idea of where consumer tastes were going, and his winery was the best developed and most competitive business we'd visited," says Juan Viciana, a Mendoza grape grower on the trip. The visitors tasted Mondavi's wines, as well as ones they had brought to demonstrate their own skills. When a group of Japanese visitors eating inside the nearby winery learned that Mondavi's guests were Argentine, one sat at the piano and played a tango. "The conversation was like a spa treatment. The ideas of quality, of the long term . . . ," rhapsodizes Viciana. It was idyllic.

Not long before, Robert Mondavi had visited Argentina, and he and his wife Margrit had toured Mendoza's wineries. They had gorged themselves at *asado* barbecues and learned to drink Argentina's bitter *mate* herb drink. The trip had made an impression. As the lunch in Napa came to a close, Mondavi stood. He had taken off his soft brown leather jacket, showing off his red striped oxford shirt, with shirtsleeves casually rolled and several buttons open at the neck. As he began to speak, it became clear that he was not there to give his visitors a congratulatory pat on the back. Instead, the master of American wine launched a challenge. "Gentlemen, if you want to have a significant wine industry," he told them, "you must make products of quality."

Argentina and its wines had the potential for greatness, he said, but Argentine winemakers had had it easy for so long that they'd gotten lazy. Three decades of selling to a captive audience had made them soft. A lot of wines were being damaged in the wineries from a lack of effort and care, and that inconsistency was killing them in the international market. They had to improve the quality, he told them; they had to pick up their game. "It was a cordial lunch, but he was very severe," says Viciana.

"In 1991, the *bodegueros* needed a kick in the ass," says Steve Rasmussen. "Mondavi cut right through the bullshit. He understood them as only a fellow Italian could." Rasmussen is a former Mondavi employee who had been consulting at Argentine wineries since 1989 and attended the lunch. "It was a really inspirational talk. He cut right to the chase. That was a turning point, like Steve Spurrier's 'Judgment of Paris' tasting."

The speech was classic Mondavi, down to his famously quotable enthusiasm: at the end of his talk, he told the assembled Argentines that he wanted to make wines with "the smoothness of a baby's bottom and the power of Pavarotti."

"My father would always challenge people, whether it was my brother or myself or other winemakers, encouraging them to try to improve," says Michael Mondavi. "I think the only people he didn't encourage to improve were Domaine de la Romanée-Conti and Château Lafite Rothschild, who were doing pretty well on their own."

As the lunch came to a close, Mondavi remade his challenge into an expression of New World solidarity: if anyone wanted to come by his winery the next day, they were more than welcome to visit and learn. "And if you're going to come, don't dress up," he said. "Remember to wear comfortable old clothes so you can work."

...

Mondavi's exhortation was still two years in the future when Paul Hobbs arrived for his first two-week consulting visit to Catena's Bodegas Esmeralda in 1989.

Whereas Rolland was known mostly as a kind of "grape whisperer" and magic blender, Hobbs's fame leaned more to that of an alchemist who could do amazing things inside a winery (though both, of course, did plenty of everything). Catena specifically wanted Hobbs to turn the 1989 harvest into a modern Chardonnay, and Hobbs arrived with a Dr. Feelgood laboratory inside his suitcase to make that happen. Among other things, there was a spectrophotometer, meant for measuring the chemical composition of wine as it went through the fermentation process, and there was something called MCW bacteria, which converted tart malic acid to smooth lactic acid in a process called malolactic fermentation, a secondary fermentation, often used in California Chardonnays, that gives wine a round, creamy mouthfeel. Luckily for the future of Argentine winemaking, the customs agents at Buenos Aires's airport didn't choose Hobbs's bag for a thorough search. "That was all illegal as hell," says Hobbs.

Hobbs quickly learned that his job would be tougher than showing off shiny gadgets. There were good reasons why people in the industry were loath to change. The Argentines were proud of who they were and of the success they'd had. They came from winemaking cultures in Italy and Spain—they had vines and wines in their blood—and for centuries they'd been making wine in the New World. For decades they'd been making good money off it too, so while consumption might have been a little off, they certainly didn't need a foreigner—a *yanqui* who couldn't speak Spanish, no less—to teach them how to ferment.

Luckily for Nicolás Catena, Paul Hobbs would prove the perfect drill sergeant to upend the status quo, the right man to inculcate Catena's technicians with a fear of oxygen and a hatred for sloppiness as he brought them up to speed on the latest international technology, techniques, and styles. Hobbs can be disparaging to those who leave a hose dirty or otherwise do not follow his instructions to the letter—a management style that can sit poorly with the sometimes tender Argentine pride—and he has a penchant for educating his fellow technicians in ways they do not forget.

"Paul micromanages dramatically. How they clean the floor, everything," says Marina Gayan, who worked in marketing and exports at the Catena empire from 1993 to 2000.

In short, like many top winemakers, Hobbs is hands-on, demanding, and detail oriented. His perfectionism stems from a simple philosophy: the smallest moves are what make, or break, a wine. "I recall clearly what Paul said: 'The success of this kind of wine is a series of small details,'" says former Catena winemaker José Galante.

Hobbs was right to worry. The first Chardonnay he fermented in oak barrels, the 1990 vintage, entered the bottling process bright and fruity and came out brown, flat, and oxidized. The American hit the roof. "Imagine all the work we went through, and then to destroy it in the filtration was a tremendous blow," says Galante. The problem was partly technical—the staff had old bottling equipment—but the larger problem was that Catena's technicians had not been educated in the most contemporary industry procedures because there had been no need. When Hobbs asked viticulturist Pedro Marchevsky for the oxygen measurements so that he could analyze what had gone wrong, Marchevsky had no reply. "We didn't know what he was talking about," Marchevsky told the *Los Angeles Times* in a 2006 story. Perhaps worse, "He didn't know what we didn't know."

To show Catena's winemakers how old pumps and pipes, bad hygiene, and inattention were destroying their wines, Hobbs brought an oxygen meter and started measuring the levels in the wine before and after it was moved through the winery's antiquated centrifugal pumps. "When we began to measure oxygen, we saw the tremendous errors we'd been making," says Galante. "The oxygen meters drove us nuts because they made you see how much oxygen the old filters, bronze accessories, bad seals, and centrifugal pumps were putting in. No one had been paying attention." To make that lesson stick, Hobbs had golf shirts embroidered with the logo "Anti-Oxidation Team" for Galante and other members of the winery crew. Mariano Di Paola, the recipient of one of those shirts and now the head winemaker at Mendoza's Bodega La Rural, says he learned his lesson quickly: oxygen was the enemy.

"Paul had this philosophy of 'No Mistakes Allowed.' That was kind of foreign to the Argentine way of thinking. There's no siesta going on with Paul Hobbs," says Nicolás Catena's daughter Laura, a San Francisco–based doctor who now is the president of the family's Bodega Catena Zapata.

With his bizarre-seeming obsessions and hands-on philosophy, it was inevitable that Hobbs would run into conflict with Argentina's traditional winery hierarchy. His success would depend on how well he overcame that conflict, specifically on how well he seduced and co-opted Catena's leaders: Galante and Marchevsky. The two proud professionals were a study in contrasts. The neat, round-faced Galante wore a cryptic half smile, was unfailingly polite, rarely told jokes, and stuck to rigid routine (he always lunched at one thirty in the afternoon on the dot, Hobbs recalls). Galante's foil was the impulsive, opinionated, and well-read Marchevsky, the type of man people describe as being unafraid to speak his mind.

In an era when winemakers were the aristocrats of the winery, Galante was a very skilled and traditional one. He had been with Catena for thirteen years and was understandably proud to be the author of some of the best wines in Argentina's fine-wine market. The Saint Felicien he turned out for Catena at Bodegas Esmeralda was the company's most expensive wine, and it commanded about a 20 percent market share of the country's admittedly small fine-wine shelf (only about 5 percent of the market).

The grandson of a viticulturist who had emigrated from Venice, Galante was keenly aware of the winery's well-drawn territorial boundaries: he did not venture far from the winemaker's office and lab area, and he expected others to steer clear of his domain. In that, he was typical for his era. "We didn't have tasting rooms, and oenologists didn't taste much," says Pedro Marchevsky. "They knew what alcohol, color, acidity they needed. They dressed in lab coats and managed the levels. And that was wine." Such an arrangement served corporate flowcharts more than wine quality because it gave the winemaker and agronomist contradictory goals. "There was a divorce between the vineyard and the winery," says Daniel Pi, chief winemaker at Trapiche, part of the giant Peñaflor conglomerate. "The general manager would ask the agronomist for quantity, and the winemaker for quality."

For foreigners accustomed to winemakers and agronomists who regularly stepped on each other in the quest to produce the best wine, this was a bizarre arrangement whose elimination would be one of Argentina's greatest steps toward success. Jacques Lurton, a mischievous fifth-generation Bordeaux winemaker who worked in the Catena *bodegas* in the early 1990s, nicknamed Galante "White Shoes" for his apparent phobia of leaving his lab area and dirtying his blindingly white tennis sneakers. "Galante never moved from his office," laughs Lurton. "He'd write a little note and give it to the cellar hand and tell the cellar hand to take a sample from this tank. The cellar hand would bring the sample to the laboratory, and White Shoes would go to the laboratory to taste the sample. Then he would write a decision and give the cellar hand a note, and the cellar hand would go do what it said."

For Galante, growing fruit was Marchevsky's domain. A descendant of Ukrainian Jews who had arrived in Argentina in 1902, Marchevsky had started his career teaching soil and irrigation studies before coming to Bodegas Esmeralda in 1972 to oversee the planting of high-yield bulk-wine vineyards. Marchevsky's relationship with plants bordered on preternatural. "Marchevsky has a green thumb. I've seen rare things with his relationship with the vines," says Argentine wine journalist Miguel Brascó. "Whenever he goes to the vineyard, the vines stand at attention, like what happens with old English women and rosebushes. You have to see it to believe it."

Where Galante was a distant manager who respected the wine business's boundaries, the outspoken Marchevsky divided his colleagues into those who revered him and those who avoided him. "He was a very secure man," says Greg Adams, the American viticulturist. Marchevsky loved to argue and to step into other people's bailiwicks in order to expand his craft, and this mix of intellect and pride made him a perfect officer in Catena's campaign to upend tradition and create a great Argentine wine. "He loved to bust people's balls. He ranted and raved. He was the *commandant*," says Hobbs.

A rigorous investigator with an omnivorous intellect, Marchevsky has little time for accepted wisdom. When he and I first met in March 2010, Marchevsky immediately unclicked the magnet that connected the nosepiece of his mod reading glasses and launched into a diatribe against catchall winemaking rules like "later harvests are better" (easily swallowed bullshit created for journalists) and the reverence paid to *terroir* (human intervention being such a big part of winemaking).

After Marchevsky left Catena's winery and, with his then wife, Susana Balbo, founded the Dominio del Plata Winery, the viticulturist continued with the obsessive investigations that spoke volumes about his distrust of conventional wisdom. "On vacations they would go to wine regions and visit other wineries, which for most winemakers is the last thing you'd want to do," says Scott Peterson, a winemaker who consulted for Catena for several years. At the time, many vineyard owners protected their vines from Mendoza's regular hailstorms with antihail netting, and they always used one color of netting—black—because it

172

was readily available. But simple availability wasn't enough to convince Marchevsky. He dug up a government investigative grant and had vineyard workers install antihail netting in four colors over various vineyard parcels in order to test whether color made a difference. It turned out that black netting cut light intensity by 15 percent, while white cut the intensity by only 5 percent, which meant that grapes under different colors had to spend different amounts of extra time on the vine to mature. (Green acted like black, and red like white, though the red netting tended to disintegrate in the sun, Marchevsky says.)

This new knowledge enabled vineyard managers to use the right color, depending on how much longer they wanted to keep grapes on the vine in hail-prone areas. Admittedly, almost everyone stuck with black. But at least they *knew*. Marchevsky also noticed that the usual way of installing antihail netting—wrapped like a girdle around a row of vines—made it hard to get at the grapes, so he adapted the tentlike antihail canopy system used on fruit trees into what is still known by many in the region as "Marchevsky netting."

Beyond his agronomy skills, Marchevsky was famous for lunchtime *bodega* lectures in which he explained the problems of the Soviet Union. "He would be talking to a crowd of people, cellar hands, secretaries, accountants, lab girls, and the winemaker Pepe. We could only listen to him. And he would talk about Karl Marx. He was very fond of Marx. He was permanently telling us that the USSR was a mistake because Karl Marx would have never wanted it. It was just a misinterpretation of Marx's ideas," says the aristocratic Frenchman Jacques Lurton. "I called him Marxchevsky."

A reputable producer of Napa Chardonnay would pick grapes in small bins and harvest at dawn before the day's heat entered the fruit. But Hobbs could not make that happen—his powers as a consultant did not extend to remaking Argentina's workweek—so he pressed Catena to buy a modern (and more gentle) French pneumatic press and a tube-in-tube must chiller (must is freshly pressed grape juice that contains skins and seeds) to lower the temperature of the grapes. The chiller was especially important to Hobbs because temperatures during the blistering-hot March residence harvest varied between eighty-five and a hundred degrees Fahrenheit. If the field heat is not removed from the grapes before fermentation begins, the white grape juice becomes irrevocably brown, and its flavor burns off. "The picking was only by hand, so it could only be done during the day," says Jacques Lurton. "So on hot days of ninety-five or a hundred degrees, the grapes would arrive in the winery at eighty-five degrees. If you press a white grape that hot, the juice gets oxidized in one minute and loses all of the flavor components."

Necessary or not, however, the chiller and the press would only arrive the next year. Importing technology to Argentina took time. In a country that suffered lacerating economic volatility and operated almost entirely without a credit system, the ability to improvise with what was at hand—something known as *atalo con alambre*, or "tie it with wire"—was the Argentine's most prized business skill. And so in 1989, the perfectionist Hobbs did his best *atalo con alambre* with Catena's grapes. To get the best juice for his Chardonnay, Hobbs asked Galante and his technicians to siphon off just the first few minutes of delicately squeezed natural runoff (known as the "free-run" juice) from the winery's screw press before they torqued the bull-like press tight and hammered the grapes into a cake. To get the coldest fruit possible, Hobbs begged the vineyard managers to pick his Chardonnay grapes first in the morning and deliver them when they had loaded the tarp-lined dump trucks only a quarter full. And to protect the fresh juice from heat-inspired oxidation, he quickly pumped it from the winery's cement pools into the handful of epoxy-lined steel tanks that sat in the *bodega*'s so-called cold room.

"Making the first wine was very tough," says Hobbs. "Nicolás boasted about having the most modern cold fermentation in Argentina, which consisted of a room full of epoxy-lined steel tanks and a thermostat. He was proud of that room: 'We have temperature control.' Which for there at the time was modern. But the fact is, we had very antiquated equipment."

Inside the medieval lab, Hobbs instructed Galante in contemporary techniques that were popular in California and France—like how to manage malolactic fermentation, the secondary fermentation used to give wines a rounder, creamier mouthfeel; and wild yeast fermentation, the hazardous practice of allowing yeast naturally present on the fruit or cellar equipment to start fermentation instead of adding commercial yeast. "We did things that would be considered risky even in California," says Hobbs.

At the end of his visit, Hobbs packed up several bottles of the developing wine and flew back to California. Soon after, Hobbs entered the Chardonnay in one of the blind taste tests organized by his boss at Simi Winery, Zelma Long. Against barrel-fermented whites from California and from France's Burgundy region, Catena's Chardonnay claimed second place. It was a shock, in no small part because it hadn't had the advantage of any aging time in oak, as the other wines had. "It was like, 'This wine's from Argentina?!'" Hobbs says of the reaction.

On the heels of this unexpected success, Catena acceded to Hobbs's request to buy a shipping container of about 150 new 225-liter François Frères French oak barrels so that the next year they could start barrel-fermenting Chardonnay. White wines fermented in barrels are thought to have better-harmonized flavors, with hints of cinnamon, vanilla, or cloves. But barrels were expensive, some $430 each in the United States at the time, and more in Argentina, and the idea of spending such cash on Argentine wine had until that moment existed only in the realm of the absurd. The silliness of the idea was compounded when the shipment of barrels was delayed for months by Argentina's customs authorities. Galante spent hours on the phone with the government explaining exactly what the barrels were for. The customs officials had no idea what tax to charge because Argentina had not imported oak wine containers—either 225-liter barrels or 10,000-liter *toneles*—for more than half a century. On the customs form there was no box to check.

After his first visit, Hobbs began to travel regularly to Argentina, teaching contemporary techniques and international styles to Catena employees for several weeks at a time. Hobbs ate with the employees and slept at the Catenas' residence. For entertainment in the evenings, the crew would break out their guitars and Hobbs would show off his dancing skills. As he spent more time with Nicolás Catena and his family, the relationship between the young man and the elder businessman grew into something paternal. Hobbs regularly stayed at Nicolás's house, and he accompanied Nicolás's wife Elena to Mendoza's *vendimia*, the annual harvest festival where the Queen of the Harvest is crowned. "It reminded me of that scene in *Pulp Fiction*," Hobbs jokes. "Where John Travolta had to entertain the boss's wife, [played by] Uma Thurman."

Many nights, Hobbs and Catena would dine alone at the rural Mendoza house where Nicolás had been born. At these dinners, Nicolás waxed nostalgic about the history of Argentina and his family, while Hobbs regaled the older man with stories of his experiences working with Robert Mondavi and insights on how Mondavi marketed and sold wine. It was a kind of perfect symbiosis: Nicolás offered Hobbs a unique chance to make his name, while Hobbs tantalized the Argentine with the possibility that he could be the next Mondavi.

"Nicolás was a very reclusive man. I remember taking Nicolás to the airport to fly back from Mendoza to Buenos Aires once. He waited for everyone to board the airplane. And then he walked to the back stairway and waved goodbye, like a lone soldier," says Hobbs. "He never liked mingling with Argentines. It's like he didn't feel comfortable in his own country. He many times said to me, 'They won't understand what we're doing.'"

Choosing the stardom offered by being the man who helped "make" Argentina, Hobbs decided to leave Simi in 1990. But not without a backup plan: with Nicolás Catena as an investor—the *bodeguero* put in $200,000 for a 40 percent stake—he opened Paul Hobbs Winery in California's Sonoma County in 1991. As part of their agreement, Hobbs would spend several months a year in Argentina. Bound together by ambition, wine, and money, the two men—Argentine and American, *bodeguero* and winemaker, father figure and de facto adopted son—would be together for quite some time.

Hobbs's relationships with Catena's managers were sometimes tumultuous, but as the demanding American and the proud Argentines came to understand the benefits of listening to one another, their teamwork started to bear fruit.

Hobbs soon learned that José "Pepe" Galante was a talented winemaker and an open-minded student. After seeing the possibilities offered by Hobbs's method, the quiet and meticulous Galante broke with the cliché territoriality of Argentine winemakers and embraced the inevitability of the future. "Pepe was great," says Marina Gayan, the Catena marketing and export manager. "Imagine you're a chief of a winery and a guy from outside comes in, which was not a practice in Argentina. Any other winemaker would have thrown a fit."

Relations between the self-assured Hobbs and the opinionated Pedro Marchevsky—who spoke English fairly well and often acted as Hobbs's translator—were also fruitful, though not as smooth. To ensure that the winery got better grapes with more sugar and mature tannins, Hobbs tromped into Marchevsky's vineyards with a list of changes. "Pedro was not used to that," Gayan says.

Hobbs's basic demand, like Rolland's in Salta, was that Marchevsky deep-prune early to harvest fewer, more concentrated grapes. This mandate led to personality clashes between the men. Winemakers like Hobbs advocate the practice of "dropping fruit" because experience has shown that when vines have fewer grapes on which to concentrate, they act like protective parents of only children and endow the remaining grapes with more of the chemical building blocks of flavor, color, aroma, and mouthfeel.

The problem was that, while such low-production grapes were wonderful for perfectionist artisanal winemakers and oenophiles, for Argentine grape growers who had historically sold their grapes by weight, tossing out half one's fruit in the unguaranteed hope of higher quality and prices at harvest looked a whole lot like burning money. For a corporate head agronomist as proud and talented as Marchevksy, dropping fruit he had worked so hard to grow felt like cutting out a chunk of his heart. "Imagine when Paul said, 'Pedro, we're going to prune grapes and throw to the ground.' Pedro went crazy. After all he had done to grow the grapes, Paul was going to throw them out," says Galante.

Marchevksy was not alone in this sentiment. During his first years in Argentina, Paul Hobbs was also hired by Tincho Bianchi to consult at Bodegas Valentín Bianchi. There, when Tincho's oenologist father Enzo discovered that his workers had been tossing grapes on Hobbs's orders, he was so angry that he refused to speak to his son for ten days. Enzo's relationship with Hobbs did not improve when the American impregnated and then married his secretary. "For my father, throwing out a kilo of grapes was a sacrilege. And his secretary was like his daughter. 'The gringo's throwing out my grapes *and* he's taking away my secretary!'" says current CEO Raúl Bianchi, roaring in imitation of his father. "My old man saw him as the enemy."

Controversial as it might have been, cutting back grape production was one of the key steps to creating wine that Argentina could sell on the world market. During the bulk wine boom of the 1960s and '70s, Argentine growers had superirrigated their vines and produced north of 35,000 pounds per acre (in the 1960s, there was a competition to see who could produce 45,000 pounds, says Nicolás Catena). But once you go above 10,500 pounds per acre, the aroma fades, and then the flavor, says Carlos Gei Berra, a Mendozan grape grower who harvests about 250 acres. "The color and the alcohol stays, but it's not the same wine," says Gei Berra, a descendant of Spanish Basque and French emigrants.

At the time of Hobbs's arrival, the quantity-first mentality was so ingrained that even employees at wineries aiming for quality would over-water from habit. A day after Paul Hobbs asked Nicolás Catena to tell one of the field hands that a certain vineyard should go a week without water, the two drove by the vineyard to witness the same worker water-ing the vines. The mild-mannered Catena pulled the car to the shoulder, ambled over to the fence, and waved the field hand over to him. "If you don't stop irrigating," he said quietly, "I'm going to fire you."

Smart *bodegueros* learned they had to work within the culture to fix this problem, and they did so by tweaking the economic incentives of grape growing: they began to contract with owners of the best old-vine vineyards in deals in which the growers were paid by the acre, not by the kilo. Freed of motivation to inflate the grapes with water, growers started to follow the winemakers' instructions. For some independent growers, the competition today has even become who can be contracted to produce the *least* amount of fruit per acre, low yields being a sign that the grapes will go into top wines. That shift in thinking came into high relief at a lunch conversation Laura Catena describes having several years ago with two growers contracted by Catena. "The one who had a much younger vineyard said to me, 'Why do you let me have much higher yields than him?'" she says. "He was so upset. We couldn't tell him the other guy had a better old vineyard and that reducing his yields wouldn't get me to a $100 wine. Thinking 15 years ago that that would ever happen . . ."

Today Gei Berra's vineyard production is down to an average of about 8,000 pounds per acre. He grows premium grapes for Trapi-che, Catena, and a host of small *bodegas*. His grapes became Trapiche's superpremium 2004 Malbec Single Vineyard Viña Carlos Gei Berra (in giving it 93 points, *Wine Advocate* reviewer Jay Miller wrote, "If I were a young collector, I'd be stashing these away in my cellar"). Some purists prune even further than Gei Berra did: in a bid to achieve small, concentrated grapes from vines where the leaves and bunches are in perfect low-production equilibrium, Carlos Tizio—now general manager at Mendoza's Clos de los Siete, a sprawling multi-*bodega* project overseen by deep-pruning advocate Michel Rolland—aims for vineyards that produce as little as 4,000 pounds per acre.

Mondavi's 1991 exhortation of his Argentine visitors to make products of quality—to improve or perish—marked an immediate turning point in the urgency Argentina's *bodegueros* felt in their quest for "export-quality" wine. Catena agronomist Carlos Vázquez says that upon returning, he and Marchevsky immediately removed the second story of grapes that Argentines habitually grew on their vines. Mondavi's speech also came just as the arrival of foreign advisers was turning from a trickle to a flood. Early consultant Steve Rasmussen first visited Argentina in 1989, when Boston-area importer Dick Tosi hired him to bring wine from Bodega Norton and his other Argentine clients in line with international expectations. Viticulturist Greg Adams met the Argentine tour in California in 1991 and was invited down because of his mix of UC Davis education and Spanish language skills. And European winemakers Jacques Lurton and Attilio Pagli were professional friends of Hobbs who, intrigued by his talk of Argentina's possibilities, came soon after. Their effects were profound and immediate.

"The consultants had a lot of effect in the sense of training people fast," says Nicolás Catena's daughter Laura. "If you have to learn by doing in winemaking, that's ten years of making mistakes. And we didn't have ten years to make mistakes. The great thing of the consultants was adopting the knowledge sooner."

Even after Argentina's great leap, the foreign consultants continued to serve as a necessary destabilizing influence, albeit not as intensely as in the beginning. "Working with outside consultants is a way to keep ourselves up-to-date, and it gives us another view on what we do," says Trapiche chief winemaker Daniel Pi, who worked with Michel Rolland between 1996 and 2004 and now consults with Alberto Antonini. "The person who spends the entire day looking in the mirror ends up thinking he's pretty."

The first meetings between the foreign consultants and the local winemakers were often not easy, however. A cultural gulf divided the Argentines and their visitors. Mendoza vineyards witnessed a showdown between Anglo-Saxon obsession with control and a Latin recognition that some things—too many things, to the American consultants' eyes—were out of man's dominion. Ángel Mendoza, a leading Argentine oenologist who headed winemaking at industry giant Peñaflor's top Trapiche brand, describes the lessons taught by this clash as simple but necessary.

"The consultants would say, 'We need a sample. We're going to walk the *entire* vineyard and get two hundred grapes.' An Argentine would get all the grapes from the edge of the vineyard. They would say, 'We need ten leaf buds per plant,' and then they would prune back to ten. The Argentine would say, 'We'll leave twenty because the frost will come and kill ten.' But if the frost didn't come, he'd never prune," says Mendoza, a short, big-bellied man with a Hells Angels handlebar mustache who today runs his own Domaine St. Diego winery. "They brought a bit of Anglo-Saxon philosophy to the Latin world, more rigor and discipline."

Almost to a man, the consultants ran into the same problems that Paul Hobbs had experienced at Esmeralda. After graduating from UC Davis in fermentation science in 1981, Steve Rasmussen had worked with Hobbs at Mondavi for several years. Today the winemaker at the Sierra Madre Vineyard in California's Central Coast region, Rasmussen, like Hobbs, has a detail-oriented mind-set that ran into conflict with the Argentine *no pasa nada* ("nothing's going to happen") mentality.

At the time of Rasmussen's arrival, winemaking programs like the one at Davis taught their students that one of the most fundamental steps in wine creation was analyzing and correcting pH, a measure of acidity that runs from 0 (pure acid) to 14 (pure alkaline). Adequate acidity makes it hard for spoilage bacteria to survive through fermentation, acts as a preservative afterward, and provides the tartness that makes a wine's flavor bright in the mouth. Conversely, a wine without enough acid—one with a pH above 3.6 or so—will often spoil, age badly, turn an ugly brown, and have flat, flabby flavors. Amazingly, considering the availability of pH meters and the usefulness of this simple test, Bodega Norton owner Ricardo Santos says (perhaps slightly hyperbolically) that Rasmussen was the first person to do pH analysis of wine in Argentina. And it wasn't from a lack of technology. "All the wineries had pH meters that sat in the corner collecting dust—a lot of dust. And when I asked to use them, they didn't work. They were just there for show," says the tall and lanky Rasmussen, whose graying blond hair gives him the aspect of a Californian Ichabod Crane.

Similarly, while inspecting a crop of nearly ripe Cabernet Sauvignon grapes that Santos was thinking of buying for a top export wine, Rasmussen found that the vineyard owner had flooded his fields several days before harvest. Grape growers loved to do this because it artificially fattened the grapes and thereby increased their profits, but it is a winemaking no-no because the excess water dilutes the ensuing wine's flavors, sugar, and intensity. Argentine growers and winemakers learned this the hard way: Rasmussen had the grape buy canceled, to the farmer's considerable dismay.

Considering how much foreign wine consultants did to remake the Argentine wine industry's culture and technique, it's tempting to attribute the country's wine boom exclusively to them. Indeed, within ten years of their arrival, the country was producing scads of internationally acclaimed wines. But while the consultants certainly accelerated the process, the Argentine wine revolution was very much a local thing. Argentina's oenological backwardness had been caused by the country's multidecade shell of political and economic catastrophe, not by a failure of intelligence or skill. In reality, Argentina has a longer and more ingrained wine culture than the United States could possibly imagine. As far back as the beginning of the twentieth century, its *bodegas* sported well-educated local winemakers, often graduates of the French academy at Montpellier or one of Italy's royal schools of viticulture and oenology in Conegliano and Alba. In that era, foreign visitors were consistently impressed by the skill of the country's grape farmers and by the quantity and quality of the fruit they were able to produce in a desert.

"The agronomists and winemakers were super-well-educated. It was not about teaching the fundamentals of winemaking. It was all cultural," says Jeffrey Stambor, winemaker at Napa Valley's Beaulieu Vineyard, who worked at Mendoza's Bodega Navarro Correas for several years beginning in 1999.

And to be fair, the culture was far from all bad. While Argentines' casual relationship with schedules and procedures drove many foreigners to distraction, the looseness lent the locals a freedom and creativity that more rigid cultures did not always have. "Argentina has negative things like the lack of organization, but the upside is that people keep an open mind. With the loose organization and schedule, you can stop to talk to someone who interests you," says José Alberto Zuccardi, the head of the giant Familia Zuccardi winery. "Of course, 15 percent Japanese blood wouldn't hurt us. We have excess Italian blood."

Empowered to revamp the industry in an environment they did not know, the foreign consultants inevitably made mistakes that locals would have avoided. Through a mixture of hubris and ignorance, the consultants would assume that their Napa or Bordeaux techniques would also work in Mendoza, often to be proven decisively wrong.

The peculiarities of the soil, climate, and people of Argentina's desert west made the place hard to understand for someone used to California or France. One of the greatest differences between Argentina's traditional vineyard zone east of Mendoza and Bordeaux or Napa is that the hot climate tends to ripen grapes rapidly. Hot-temperature ripening burns off a great deal of malic acid, one of the two main acids inherent in grapes. Complicating matters, the soil's high potassium content can cause a good portion of the other acid—tartaric acid—to precipitate out of the juice during fermentation. Argentine winemakers learned early that one had to add shocking amounts of acid to make the wines drinkable, but for the foreign consultants, adding gobs of acid seemed like a lazy fallback. This became a point of contention between Hobbs and Marchevsky in the early years, as the American consultant told the headstrong Argentine not to add too much acid to the recently arrived harvest.

"Paul told me we didn't need extra acid, because the grapes entered with 7.5 grams per liter of tartaric acid. Then after the fermentation he tasted it. 'It's flat,' he said. 'Let's add some acid, but just a little.' Fifteen days later he tasted it. Still flat. We had to do that five times," says Marchevsky. "Then one day, we went to harvest a premium vineyard. It was a Friday. We sent the grapes to Pepe Galante to fill the tank. They filled it halfway, and he added enough acid to correct the whole tank's acidity because on Saturday we were going to send him the other half of the grapes. But it rained, so we couldn't harvest. Monday, the tank's fermenting, we've put in double the acid Paul wanted. Paul tasted it. 'Blech, what's this?' 'We put in double acid,' we said. 'How crazy! What a thing!' Paul said. Three months later, we tasted it again. And we liked it. So we said, 'Time for a blind tasting, Paul.' He went through the samples and said, 'Flat, flat, flat,' and then, 'This one! Which one was it?' It was from the mistake." Marchevsky shrugs. "One learns." Indeed, all the consultants did.

"I was with a bunch of consultants at Catena," says Marchevsky's ex-wife Susana Balbo, who worked in exports for Nicolás Catena before launching the Dominio del Plata Winery with Marchevsky. "Correcting acidity was a point of conflict with all of them. But in the end, they chose the wine we'd corrected."

Similarly, French winemaker Jacques Lurton ran into problems with his lack of local knowledge when the UK supermarket chain Tesco commissioned him to create the "International Winemaker" series, a line of wines from various countries around the globe, including Argentina. A friend of Paul Hobbs, Lurton chose to make his Tesco wine at Catena's winery in 1992 because, through Hobbs's involvement, it was the only one equipped with a "tube-in-tube" chiller and other gear that Lurton needed.

Over some of what he describes as the famously bad coffee brewed in Bodegas Esmeralda's lab, Lurton explained his Tesco project to Catena. The pioneering *bodeguero* quickly offered to charge him for only the wine he made—and not for use of the winery—if he decided to use Bodegas Esmeralda. "I said, 'That's fantastic,'" Lurton recalls. "He had the chiller, which I needed, and an unbeatable economic offer."

As the 1992 vintage began, Lurton began to see that nothing came for free. At Esmeralda, he often worked with an Australian winemaking assistant who stayed in Argentina while Lurton saw to his other wines around the world. The two handled the entire winemaking process themselves, from adding yeast to siphoning wine between tanks. While this didn't require a lot of effort on the part of the Esmeralda employees, they seemed unhappy with the arrangement. Part of the problem was that Lurton was crossing boundaries; in Argentina, the aristocrats of the winey—winemakers like Lurton—did not get their hands dirty in the cellar. But it also occurred to Lurton that he had been given a good deal on winery usage because he was expected to act as a kind of unpaid professor: Catena had offered Lurton use of his facilities in part so that his winery workers could look over his shoulder and pick up the well-traveled Frenchman's techniques without paying a cent. And Jacques was thwarting that strategy. "They didn't like it very much, because they couldn't see what we were doing," says Lurton.

Of course, there are two sides to every story, and the Argentine side to this one shows the cultural gulf that separated the foreigner from the locals. While Pedro Marchevsky agrees that he found the French-man's aversion to gratis instruction annoying, he says his real anger was caused by Jacques's dangerous lack of understanding of Argentina's *atalo con alambre* style. The light sockets near Bodegas Esmeralda's roof, for example, were dodgy and often spit off sparks—they didn't have a neutral ground wire, for one thing—so while all the locals knew not to plug in pumps there, foreigners like Lurton didn't. "Our equipment was fairly precarious and primitive," Marchevsky says. "I didn't want him to get involved, because he was used to working in the First World and this wasn't the First World."

One day, Marchevsky watched as Lurton plugged in one of the *bodega*'s old pumps and then ran around to open the valve on the tank himself instead of having a *bodega* hand help him. "As a good Frenchman, Jacques didn't want to teach anything. He didn't want to tell us what to do because he didn't want to pass on information," says Marchevsky. The pump immediately began pressurizing the tube between the pump and the tank as Lurton sprinted toward it, and before the Frenchman could reach the tank valve, the tube exploded. "Jacques, now this is finished," Marchevsky yelled at Lurton. "You don't touch a single thing anymore in the winery. You tell us what you want us to do and we'll do it for you."

"Pedro and I had an incredible fight," admits Lurton.

In another cultural contretemps, the viticulturist Marchevsky arrived at the *bodega* to find Lurton spraying nitrogen into a *pie de cuba*, a chunk of fermenting must and yeast that's borrowed from one tank of fermenting juice to start fermentation in another. Curious about Lurton's technique, Marchevsky asked the Frenchman why he was adding nitrogen instead of oxygen, as one usually does to kick-start the yeast. Lurton answered that Marchevsky was mistaken: he was spraying oxygen, as per normal procedure. "But the tubes were switched, and only we knew that. He didn't understand the Argentine mentality," says Marchevksy. "The tubes were all painted the same color but *we* knew which side was oxygen and which was nitrogen. He was putting in nitrogen because he didn't want to teach us."

In the end, the relationship between Lurton and Catena proved mutually beneficial. From their time in Argentina, Jacques and his brother François fell in love with the country's potential and bought 455 acres to found Bodega J&F Lurton. And from watching Lurton, Catena's winemakers learned how to cold-ferment white wine to create tropical fruit flavors, and how to economically create an oaky flavor in table wines by using wood chips instead of oak barrels. "He made his wine," Marchevksy says, "and we learned without paying him."

From the late eighties through the mid-nineties, Nicolás Catena's Bodegas Esmeralda continued to be the locus for the most progressive work going on in Argentina. Not only did Catena have a forward-thinking mind-set, but he also had plenty of cash from the well-timed sale of his bulk-wine business to Greco. Catena was financially secure enough to ride out the inflation that was impoverishing the rest of the industry, and thus he had enough money to invest in new technology and foreign consultants. His Bodegas Esmeralda was the first Mendoza winery to install individually temperature-controlled stainless steel tanks, for example, and to buy small French oak barrels in bulk. Catena could also afford to build an overseas distribution network while exporting at a loss. Most of the other wineries were merely trying to survive.

"We started with the idea of doing great wine in 1989, but hyperinflation meant we couldn't buy stainless steel tanks for the *bodega*. So we had to use cement pools," says Alberto Arizu Sr., head of the family-owned Bodega Luigi Bosca. "The economy stabilized in 1991, but banks still lent at 25 percent interest. So the local manufacturers took loans abroad for 6 percent, and we took loans from them and paid their interest. Then we grew *rapidísimo*."

Others were not so lucky. "With inflation like it was by the time our distributor paid us four months after the sale, it wasn't worth it to take a streetcar to pick up the check. You couldn't even think of making investments. Later, when the changeover began, a lot of the traditional *bodegas* were sold because the original owners didn't have the money to invest in stainless steel, in barrels," recalls former Norton owner Ricardo Santos, who says inflating costs forced him to stop exporting his varietals and eventually sell his winery in 1989.

Just a few years after Santos was forced to sell, the Argentine wine revolution began to spread. What allowed the nascent fine-wine revolution to expand so quickly was not merely increased knowledge brought from overseas, though that certainly helped. It had more to do with a man from western Argentina blessed with mutton chops large enough to make the entire decade of the 1970s turn green with envy.

In May 1989, Argentines elected Carlos Saúl Menem as their president. A member of the political party founded by Juan Domingo Perón, Menem was the son of immigrants from what is now Syria; he had been constitutionally required to convert from Islam to Catholicism to become president. Faced with absurdly high inflation (some 5,000 percent in 1989), Menem trotted out several failed economic stabilization schemes before he and his economics minister, Domingo Cavallo, pegged the peso to the dollar in a system called *convertibilidad* ("convertibility"), lowered trade barriers, and launched a wholesale privatization binge, selling off the state oil company, post office, and the telephone, gas, electricity, and water utilities. As a result of these plans, inflation fell to the single digits by 1993, and foreign investment flooded into Argentina. "Until convertibility, Argentina was like Albania, a totally closed country," viticulturist Carlos Tizio told *Newsweek* in the mid-nineties.

While all parts of the Argentine economy felt the effects of this sudden rush of oxygen, the western wine regions especially benefited. Low inflation and a stable currency pegged to the dollar meant that many more winemakers could afford to travel to learn the recent advances in their fields. The flood of foreign funding gave the surviving *bodegueros* the money they needed to invest. Less regulation freed winemakers to try something new. And lower import taxes and the dollar peg made the stainless steel tanks, oak barrels, and modern pumps much more accessible.

Hervé Birnie-Scott, the French director of Mendoza's Bodegas Chandon, arrived in Argentina in 1991 to work as a winery assistant. At the time, Birnie-Scott would get together with oenologists from other *bodegas* to compare the success of their requests for new equipment. "There were no new oak barrels here," he says. "When we would get together we'd say, 'I got to buy sixty,' 'I got thirty,' 'None yet for me.' Five years later it was, 'Container,' 'Container,' 'Six hundred.' In the beginning it seemed crazy to the owners to buy barrels for $500 each instead of using big *toneles* that you shaved every once in a while to get 'national-quality' wine."

During the decade beginning in 1991, some $1.5 billion would be invested in the Argentine wine industry. Showing a realization of the importance of exports for the survival and growth of Argentine *bodegas*, 70 percent of that money went to funding production for the international market. Argentina's *bodegueros* imported top-quality vine clones, small oak barrels, stainless steel tanks, bladder presses, modern cooling systems, destemmers, and bottling lines.

Today Menem is scorned for the inept handling of the privatization of Argentina's "patrimony," his administration's glib corruption, and the deep recession that began at the end of his second term. But his sudden deregulation of Argentina's economy arrived at just the right time in the

Andean west, where rich pioneers like Catena had laid the groundwork for an entirely new industry. "The father of the change in Argentine winemaking is named Carlos Menem," says Ángel Mendoza, "because he brought stability."

A few short years after Paul Hobbs's arrival in Argentina, the first reviews rolled in. And, at least in Catena's case, they were great. The *Wine Spectator* called his 1990 Cabernet Sauvignon "an exotic and arresting Argentine wine." It went on, "Beautifully concentrated fruit flavors of currant and black cherry are accented by mint and anise in this very dry and tannic, full-bodied red wine." Catena's 1991 Chardonnay—the first barrel-fermented Hobbs project to make it to the export market after the disastrous destruction of the 1990 vintage—won even more unequivocal praise. "This may be the beginning of some more upscale wines from Argentina . . . I was immediately impressed by the chardonnay for its full bodied, fruity style with nice hints of oak," wrote Tom Stockley of the *Seattle Times*, the *Wines & Vines* 1990 Wine Writer of the Year. The *Wine Spectator* was even kinder. "The best Argentine wine we've tasted," it said of the Chardonnay. "Ripe, spicy and smoothly balanced, with a solid core of pear flavor shaded by vanilla, nutmeg and toast notes. A seamless, harmonious wine." Money would soon follow. Argentine fine-wine exports, a mere $7.7 million in 1990, almost doubled to $13.7 million in 1993 before exploding to $35.4 million in 1996 and $72.1 million in 1997.

Sadly, the Catena family experienced grave sorrow amid the blooming wine revolution. In 1992, while driving back to La Libertad from one of the Catena vineyards, Hobbs saw an obviously fatal automobile accident. Not thinking much of it, that night he ate dinner with Catena in a local restaurant. Around eleven o'clock Nicolás's bodyguard entered and spoke to Nicolás. When the bodyguard left, Catena remained silent for a long pause and then said he had to leave. The accident Hobbs had seen had been his brother Jorge's car going under a truck. Jorge's son had been killed. Hobbs remembered the hair-raising drive with Jorge across the Andes just a few years before. Now his old friend had met unspeakable tragedy on those same roads. Jorge's grief soon plunged him into a deep, multiyear depression.

CHAPTER 7

# CLIMBING THE ANDES

Nora Favelukes, Paul Hobbs, Elena Catena, and Alfredo Bartholomaus (left to right)
selling Catena wines in Washington DC in 1993. Courtesy of Paul Hobbs.

WHEN FRENCH WINEMAKER Jacques Lurton visited Mendoza in late 1991 to choose the *bodega* where he would produce an Argentine wine for the UK supermarket chain Tesco, he had already spent seven years making international-quality wines around the globe. In 1984, six months after graduating from the oenology program at Bordeaux's Université Victor Segalen, he participated in his first harvest in Australia, at the McWilliams winery in Griffith; he stayed with a winery worker's family and learned how to lawn-bowl and drink beer ("I'd never drunk one before because in my family it was forbidden," he said in a 2010 article). Making wine in exotic destinations quickly became Jacques Lurton's obsession, and since his first trip he says he has participated in sixty vintages in twenty-five regions spread across ten countries. Over twenty of those harvests have been in Australia, leaving him with an accent that renders "perfect timing" as "pearfect toiming" when he speaks in English.

By the time Lurton arrived in Mendoza, he had built up an ample toolbox of tricks and techniques from his years as one of the first "flying winemakers." But Lurton had more to offer Nicolás Catena than a few oenology lessons. The lean, affable Lurton—a man possessing an Abe Lincoln physique, with wavy brown hair and a long, straight, slim nose—represented something far more important: a gateway into French wine aristocracy. A member of the fifth generation of a prominent Bordeaux wine family with connections to more than thirty Bordeaux châteaux, Jacques had struck out for the New World with his brother François because they realized early on that they would not inherit the family properties—Châteaux Bonnet, La Louvière, Couhins Lurton, and others—from their autocratic father André. A wine industry legend who, among other roles, served as mayor of his native village of Grézillac for over forty years, André is the kind of modest *bodeguero* who states on his website, "My name on the label is a guarantee of irreproachable quality, recognized around the world."

For Catena, then, Jacques was the ideal guide into the oenological upper class, a prodigal son who displayed a perfect mix of Old World aristocracy and New World moxie. Catena listened intently to Lurton when he invited the recently arrived Frenchman to an informal tasting at the sprawling "Californiano" house east of Mendoza that had belonged to his father Domingo. As they discussed Jacques's plans for the Tesco wine he would make at one of the Catena wineries, Nicolás brought out his 1990 Cabernet Sauvignon, the first of his new generation. Catena had never before shown his new Napa-style Cabernet to a true member of the international wine aristocracy.

"Nicolás, this makes me think of Languedoc," Lurton said at last. The silence that followed was uncomfortable, if brief. "Argentina is very hot," Lurton added, by way of explanation. "I wanted to die," says Catena.

Lurton had just told the Argentine, in not so many words, that his wine was somewhere between mediocre and blah. While Languedoc might have been French, it represented exactly the kind of French that Catena did not want to be. The Mediterranean-facing Languedoc (or, more technically, Languedoc-Roussillon) is the biggest wine-producing region in the world; at the time of Catena's chat with Lurton, it was bottling far more wine than the entire United States. That wine wasn't good, however—though it has experienced a boom in popularity and quality since, Languedoc was then famous for mediocre table vintages—and it was a big contributor to the European Union's constant glut of cheap vintages, something vividly dubbed "The Wine Lake."

Most dire for Catena was that Lurton's comparison implied that Catena's wine—and by extension that of the whole of Argentina's Andean west—was destined to eternal mediocrity because the grapes were being grown in a bad wine climate. Though Languedoc wasn't a perfect replica of Mendoza, the parallels between the French region and western Argentina were close enough to be scary. Both had hot, sunny, dry summers, and it was just that kind of weather, industry thinking went, that made for Languedoc's mediocre wine.

The major problem was the heat. As grapes mature, the pulps develop the sugar that becomes alcohol, and the skins develop the phenolics and other compounds that give wine its color, flavor, aroma, and mouthfeel. Sugar is a quantity game: more sugar means more alcohol. But the phenolic compounds need time to develop. When immature and young, tannins—the phenolic compounds that define mouthfeel—are simple molecules that give wine a sensation tasters refer to as "green" or aggressive; they make your mouth pucker in an unpleasant way. Over time, tannins combine into longer, more sophisticated chains that are less astringent and lend a wine softness and complexity. Young tannins are more reactive, explains Trapiche chief winemaker Daniel Pi, in the sense that they coagulate a protein in the lubricant that allows a person's tongue to move freely. More mature tannins, however, are less reactive, less apt to thicken your spit.

Grapes grown in hot areas develop lots of sugar quickly and often have to be picked early so that they don't get cooked. Because these early-picked grapes haven't had enough time on the vine to develop mature tannins and other phenolic compounds, the wines they make can be highly astringent creations that lack good color and flavor. The heat also burns off the fruit's acidity. In the end you get wines that are, in Paul Hobbs's words, "insipid, simpler, more monochromatic."

Go to a very cold area like Oregon, which inevitably means a place where the growing season is very short, and you may be faced with the opposite problem: because the grapes need to be picked before the fall frosts arrive, the tannins and other phenolic compounds won't have time to develop in colder years; the sugars may not either.

Adding to the complexity of choosing a location for planting, each varietal responds differently: grapes like Chardonnay and Pinot Noir are "cold" in that they develop fairly quickly and thus can thrive in areas with short, usually colder, seasons; whereas "hot" varietals like Cabernet Sauvignon require more time on the vine. Needless to say, grape growers are always looking for the perfect locations where the length of the growing season exactly matches the length of the varietal's grape maturation process. For a winemaker, finding a good climatic match for the varietal he wants to grow is often as simple as moving closer to or farther from the equator. In France, southerly Bordeaux is famous for blends based on "hot" Cabernet Sauvignon, while 320 miles to the northeast, Burgundy is known for wines made from "cold" Chardonnay and Pinot Noir grapes.

At the time of Lurton's tasting with Catena, grape growers in Mendoza, San Juan, and Salta had yet to embrace this obsession with microclimate. With the Andes cordillera blocking rain clouds from the Pacific Ocean to the west, water was the limiting factor. Without irrigation, Argentine vineyards simply do not exist. For this reason, grape growers planted only in zones that had access to irrigation canals, which tended to be in lower, hotter areas near Mendoza and other cities. Unlike the situation in France, where centuries of trial and error have determined which wine varietal grows best in specific folds of each hill, Argentina's immigrants simply planted their vines where they were closest to water.

When quality was not a top concern, this manner of planting worked, but in the fine-wine game such agriculture by default would not fly. This became an issue early at Catena's wineries, where Paul Hobbs was working with Chardonnay and Cabernet Sauvignon vines that had been planted in the 1980s in the *La Pirámide* Vineyard in Agrelo. The zone is one of the cooler irrigated areas in Mendoza, but it is still fairly warm. Although Hobbs and Galante were turning out top-notch Chardonnays that could be directly and fairly compared with international vintages, some of them were still a bit "hot." The first Chardonnays Hobbs made from the Agrelo grapes were very delicious and successful, of course. But they lacked acidity, and their leading flavors tended toward tropical fruits—a style associated with well-made Chardonnays made in warmer areas; they were great, but not great enough to put them alongside the world's top vintages.

"The fruit was delicious and happy, and the wine worked well with wood because it was sufficiently concentrated, but if you compared it to French wine, we didn't have that," says Pedro Marchevsky.

Catena's crew had, in a sense, been trying to make a Burgundy wine with Bordeaux grapes. To make a truly great Chardonnay or Pinot Noir in Mendoza, they were going to need grapes grown in cooler areas. The question was how to metaphorically shift from Bordeaux to Burgundy without physically moving the whole enterprise hundreds of miles south, away from the equator.

At the time, during the early 1990s, Paul Hobbs was also consulting for Peter Michael Winery, a Sonoma County winery with high mountainside vineyards that printed harvest T-shirts emblazoned with the logo "Wine with Altitude" and the elevation of the plots harvested. Peter Michael was experiencing phenomenal success with his Chardonnays (in 1992, all four of them would receive between 92 and 96 points from Robert Parker Jr.), and Hobbs suggested to Catena that one option might be to experiment with higher altitude. It would offer the cooler temperatures that, as Lurton had told Catena, some grapes seemed to require to develop into greatness; the coolness would slow sugar development and let the agronomists leave the grapes on the vine a bit longer, which in turn would lead to more mature phenolic compounds. Plus, as Peter Michael had shown, altitude wasn't a bad wine-marketing ploy.

Where to go was another question. A possible solution presented itself when the *bodega* made a Chardonnay in 1991 with grapes from Tupungato, a town about thirty miles south of Agrelo in the Uco Valley. The soils of the two areas were somewhat distinct—in Tupungato the soil was sandier and shallower, with more lime—but the most notable difference was altitude. At 3,700 feet, Tupungato was about 600 feet higher than Agrelo, and that meant a cooler climate and a shorter growing season. The wine, which they used in the *bodega*'s 1991 Chardonnay blend, displayed what Hobbs describes as citrus and racy green apple notes that had been missing and that made for a more complex wine. Convinced by Lurton's theories on temperature, Hobbs's experience with Peter Michael, and his own winemakers' praise of the high-elevation grapes, Catena embraced the theory that increasing altitude was the way to improve his wine without changing latitude.

Like all other winery owners in the region, Catena had long been aware of the Uco Valley. When his father Domingo put aside wine for his best friends, it came from grapes grown in the Uco Valley's high-altitude town of La Consulta (at 3,870 feet), so named because it was where General San Martín had "consulted" with local Indians before attacking the Spanish army in Chile (he gave the Indians bad information because he knew they would pass it to his enemy). Grapes from La Consulta, Domingo said, created the region's most intense, dark, and lush wine.

A medley of Italians, Spaniards, Syrians, and Lebanese had settled and planted vineyards in several Uco Valley areas at the turn of the twentieth century, but the long distance from the city of Mendoza (over fifty miles south) made transportation difficult and finding workers nearly impossible. Worse, large swaths of the Uco Valley, especially the high-altitude parts, didn't have rights to use the region's irrigation canals, which effectively had rendered them useless.

But technology was changing that. In the mid-1960s, an Israeli kibbutz had founded the company Netafim to exploit an invention by Polish-born water engineer Simcha Blass. That invention was a tube-and-pump system known as "drip irrigation." In drip irrigation, water is brought up from a well and then pumped through hoses that run down vineyard rows a foot or so above the ground. At each vine, a small "emitter" sprays or drips water directly onto the ground above its roots. For Israel, the invention was born from necessity: without it, the Israeli deserts would desiccate all crops. For *Mendocino* grape growers like Catena, the invention meant they could pull water from an underground aquifer that was fed by the same Andean snowmelt that flowed through the region's irrigation canals. With that water they could spread vineyards into the Uco Valley and up the arid Andean foothills.

Of course, the drip irrigation system wasn't cheap, and with scarce resources, few Argentine *bodegueros* had invested. But, flush with money and eager to improve quality, Nicolás Catena had opened his checkbook and taken the plunge. Pedro Marchevsky had learned of the system while working as an instructor in irrigation at the local university, before his job with Catena. In 1981 he installed drip irrigation in one of the Catena company's bulk-wine vineyards in the hot flats of east Mendoza. They were the first, Marchevsky says, to use the system in Argentina: "We were using it to produce as many grapes as possible. It was like hydroponics: you could get plants as much water as they wanted, whenever they wanted it. Later, we realized it was spectacular because it let you manage the water with precision."

In 1992, after Catena bought land for what is now the company's 85-acre Domingo vineyard in the Tupungato suburb of Villa Bastias, Catena's viticulturists—led by Marchevsky, Carlos Vázquez, and a young American who knew Hobbs, Matt Novak—planted it with a mix of grapes that leaned toward the "cold" varietals of Chardonnay and Pinot Noir (with some Cabernet Sauvignon thrown in). "Nicolás was very committed to trying different things and putting his money where his mouth was," says Novak. "At the time, the ground in Tupungato was a little experimental. Nicolás Catena drove me to Tupungato for my first day, to move my stuff. It was snowing that day, and I thought, 'This place feels like a bleak Siberian town on the steppes of Mongolia.'"

Catena could not have known it then—it takes several years to get from planting to first grapes to finished wine—but the critics' reaction confirmed the wisdom of the high-altitude gamble. While the *Wine Advocate* and the *Wine Spectator* had consistently given Catena Chardonnays from *La Pirámide* B+ ratings—in the upper 80s on a 100-point scale—a 1995 Chardonnay made from grapes grown in the Domingo vineyard pushed the winery to another level, garnering 92 and 91 points, respectively, from the two journals. "Its individualistic character is a synthesis of style between a top-notch white Burgundy and a rich California Chardonnay. The nose offers up intense tropical fruit aromas, as well as a striking minerality similar to that found in high class Chablis," Parker wrote in the *Wine Advocate* in 1997. "Bravo to Nicholas Catena and his consulting oenologist, California's Paul Hobbs."

Nicolás Catena did not wait for the reviews to come in before taking the next step, however. Catena has an academic's natural inclination to push his theories, as well as a marketer's understanding of the attraction of the unique, and the altitude-as-latitude idea was simple enough to push to the extremes and sell to his wine buyers, now that he had drip irrigation technology. He had been convinced of the value of altitude—both viticulturally and from a marketing angle—and he was going to dive in with the passion of the converted. The old winemaking adage that great wines come from the most challenging environments didn't diminish Catena's desire either.

Armed with hoses and emitters, Catena took to the hills. He chose to stake his claim high up the Uco Valley slopes in a place called Gual-tallary. There, in a vineyard no-man's-land about ten miles west of and 1,150 feet higher than the Domingo vineyard, Catena bought 42 acres in 1995. "At the time, there were no other vineyards at that altitude. Nowhere close," says Catena.

Marchevsky was not convinced. He told Catena that at such extreme altitudes, the cold weather would arrive before some of the grape vari-etals—especially Cabernet Sauvignon—could mature. Marchevsky told the *bodeguero* that he could do what he wanted with his money, but slow-growing varietals planted there wouldn't be any good. "We weren't in agreement," says Catena.

Undeterred, Catena had Marchevsky plant the vineyard and then doubled his bet the next year, before the results were in. He had a good reason: the technology of drip irrigation was by then universally avail-able, meaning that anyone could copy what Catena was doing. A success on one small plot would be a gratifying but minimal coup. It would only amount to R & D for other people, Catena told Marchevsky. Anyway, the land was rock-bottom cheap: the most expensive parcel they bought cost $600 per acre, Marchevsky says.

At almost 5,000 feet above sea level, the Adrianna vineyard—named for Nicolás's youngest child—would grow to nearly 300 acres. It boasted soil that was 90 percent sand, the kind of poor earth that, in Nietzschean winemaker parlance, "stresses" vines to grow stronger or die. On the expanded vineyard, Marchevsky and his team planted a smorgasbord: today, the vineyard is home to Malbec, Merlot, Chardonnay, Cabernet Sau-vignon, Pinot Noir, Viognier, Sauvignon Blanc, and Cabernet Franc. "We planted all the varieties there, because we wanted to learn," says Catena.

And then they waited.

It takes at least two years for vines to begin producing and years more before the grapes hit their stride. As Marchevsky had warned, the slow-growing Cabernet Sauvignon planted in the highest areas produced immature grapes with rustic "green" tannins, though the grapes could still be used in blends. But it became clear that shorter-season plants like Chardonnay and Pinot Noir were inspired to greatness by altitude. The theory was correct.

It's worthwhile to note here that higher-altitude vineyards do not necessarily imply better wine. High-altitude wines are in vogue today, and many wineries market the altitude of their vineyards as proof of their wine's quality. But altitude is altitude, nothing more. If a high-altitude vineyard is not properly managed, the soil is wrong, the incorrect varietals are chosen, or the grapes are not well elaborated into wine, the vintage produced will not be good.

As they made their first high-altitude wines, Catena's crew began to notice that the altitude near Mendoza offered two unexpected agricultural advantages, says Alejandro Sejanovich, who worked as an agronomist, winemaker, and vineyard director at Catena from 1994 to 2010.

The first advantage was that the nighttime temperatures plunged much further than in the low-lying flats. Known as "thermal amplitude," the variation between day and night temperatures averages more than an impressive twenty-three degrees Fahrenheit in Gualtallary during the March harvest season. This gap is important because vines have two primary activities: photosynthesis, in which they use sunlight to make glucose (a sugar); and respiration, in which they burn that glucose for energy. Normally, vines have a positive energy balance during the day because they photosynthesize more than they respire, and a negative balance at night because they respire without photosynthesizing. But when night temperatures drop below fifty degrees—a common occurrence at altitude—the vines basically shut down. That is, they stop wasting energy—and acidity. That energy saved is then converted into richer aromas and the phenolic compounds that define tannins, flavor, and color.

The second advantage was that the atmosphere grew thinner at higher altitudes, which meant that the solar radiation—the UV rays—

was stronger. A lot stronger, actually. At 5,000 feet, the sun in Mendoza is some 80 percent more intense than in Bordeaux. While this may not be great news for people with fair skin, it is wonderful news for the grapes.

"The plant produces color molecules to filter the UV rays," says Sejanovich. "If you look at a photo of the leaves, those from high-UV areas are much redder. The same happens in berries, because the skin has to protect the seeds from the UV rays. There's much more color. At high altitude, all the glucose the plant produces doesn't go to form the sugar in the pulp that becomes alcohol. Instead, it forms polyphenols—color and tannins. You get grapes with less alcohol, more acidity, and much more concentration."

In a basic sense, Mendoza's high altitudes offered the advantages of both "hot" and "cold" regions. The cool temperatures slowed sugar maturation down enough that the flavor, color, and tannins could mature before the sugar levels hit the limit, while the intense sunlight made sure everything matured before the frosts arrived.

Just a few years after planting his high-elevation Adrianna vineyard, Catena's high-altitude experiment broke through decisively: Parker's magazine called the 1999 Adrianna Chardonnay "lush, powerful, and extremely well-balanced," and gave it an eye-popping 93 points.

Suddenly, everything was in sync at Catena's empire. José Galante and Paul Hobbs were designing world-class wines, and Marchevsky and his crew were coaxing brilliant grapes from high-altitude soil. As access to drip irrigation and word of the "new" grape zone began to spread, scores of other *bodegueros* joined in an increasingly frantic search for extreme altitude. Between 1997 and 2005, *bodegueros* would plant 22,700 acres of vines in the Uco Valley. The run to the hills had begun.

As his early vintages outperformed his expectations, Catena, like all of Argentina's most quality-obsessed *bodegueros*, faced an important commercial puzzle: how to sell the wine overseas. It was all well and good to create world-class wine, but it wouldn't matter if no one bought the product.

After three harvests with Hobbs, Catena felt that his wine was ready to take the leap. Appropriately, he chose to begin his international campaign in the same country that had inspired him: the United States. But though he knew his wines were ready for North American prime time, he also knew it wouldn't be easy. Many Americans had heard of Chilean wine, but most couldn't find Argentina on a map.

Two decades before, Americans had started to drink wine in earnest. While still paltry compared to the European habit, an average American's annual wine consumption grew by 80 percent between 1970 and 1985. But Americans were peculiar in how they chose wines. Whereas a typical European could be depended on to know something about wine regions and treat historical rankings of French châteaux with the proper respect, Americans thought of themselves as rational, almost mathematical consumers. Wary of being sold a pile of Old World bullshit about the elegance and gentility of overpriced French plonk, America's new wine drinkers were desperate for a straightforward meritocratic way to rank vintages and brands and thereby assure themselves that they were getting a good buy.

Groping for buying tips inside the vague poetry favored by traditional English wine writers left many aspiring oenophiles dissatisfied. While Robert Parker Jr.'s influence as an honest broker was growing in the American market, his *Wine Advocate* was still a journal that circulated largely among the wine cognoscenti. Although wholesalers used Parker's ratings to market their wines to retailers, the bottle tags that retail stores use to flag brands with high "Parker Points"—which today's consumers use as a sort of neutral *Consumer Reports* rating when choosing wines—were not the ubiquitous staple that they are now.

Such a wide-open but undefined market held advantages and pitfalls for Argentine *bodegas*. With their self-image as meritocrats, Americans would be open to anything, as long as it could be proven that it was good and well priced. The downside was that, lacking national liquor stores or widely read wine journals, the US market was so fragmented that it would require a herculean effort just to get the wine in front of a critical mass of consumers. Into this conundrum stepped a Virginia-based wine importer named Alfredo Bartholomaus.

Alfredo Bartholomaus is a big-bellied and gregarious man with a gourmand's aspect, floppy sweep of gray hair, bright green eyes, and bushy, owl-like eyebrows. With a wardrobe than leans toward brass-buttoned blue blazers and gray slacks, Bartholomaus dresses like a wine-drinking yachtsman. And indeed he is: an experienced sailor, he keeps his Ericson 38 docked on the Chesapeake Bay.

After emigrating from his native Chile to the United States in the early 1960s, Bartholomaus became a wine importer almost by accident. While working as a waiter in Washington DC in the 1970s, at a Sheraton Hotel several blocks from the White House, Bartholomaus says he was struck by how *little* wine was drunk by American power brokers at the time. "In the seventies and eighties in the US, people didn't drink wine. You used to see senators, congressmen, and chairmen of the board who'd rather have Scotch on the rocks than a wine," he says. Nevertheless, Bartholomaus decided to dabble in the wine business in 1978 when his brother, an advertising executive back in Santiago, Chile, brought him an interesting proposal: One of his advertising clients had produced a batch of wine and wasn't quite sure what to do with it. Would Alfredo try his hand at unloading it on the US market? Bartholomaus managed to sell the wine, but the business did not flourish; he closed it after four years. "French, Italian, and German wines were the big ones in the 1970s and 1980s," he says. "I was before my time."

But during the company's brief existence, he had fallen in love with wine. There was something about fermented grapes that thrilled him. "When you sell computers, it's cut-and-dried. When you sell wine, you don't just talk about the numbers; you talk about everything else. You talk about family, poetry, other things," he says, in a wine merchant's appropriately unplaceable accent. Plus, the product itself was different. It didn't excite people's material desires like a shirt or a car; instead, it opened them to the beautiful things in life. "I love this business because it turns people into better human beings," he says. "We spend all our time showing what we are not. When we have two or three glasses of wine we lower our defense; we show who we are."

After a stint working for several wine distributors, Bartholomaus decided to strike out on his own, and in 1985 he relaunched as Billington Imports. From his first foray into the importing business, Bartholomaus had learned that he wanted to sell good wine, not discount stuff. So he made his flagship brand a top Chilean Cabernet Sauvignon, Cousiño Macul Antiguas Reservas, and priced it at $6.99 a bottle, about double the usual price for Chilean wines of the era.

Selling the first three thousand cases out of the trunk of his car, Bartholomaus had learned several lessons about the American market. First, Americans were willing to pay a good amount for quality wines from nontraditional regions. An unknown wine didn't have to be dirt cheap to get a foothold, which had been where Chilean wines had aimed before Cousiño Macul; it just had to be a good deal compared to known vintages. Second, Americans wanted to be shown, not told, which wines were the best. They wanted blind taste tests and advice from friends, not anonymous clouds of fluffy praise. During his first year in business, Bartholomaus barely made enough money to cover the cost of gas, but the lessons he learned would pay invaluable dividends.

In 1990, Catena began to discuss his fine-wine project with an industry acquaintance named Nora Favelukes, a Buenos Aires native who had moved to the United States and had recently gone to work for Bartholomaus as national sales manager. On her semiannual trips to Argentina,

Favelukes and Catena would sit in the *bodeguero*'s Buenos Aires office and talk about his modernization project and the work done by his secret weapon, Paul Hobbs. And when she returned to the United States, Favelukes would tell Bartholomaus about the interesting Argentine project. But Alfredo didn't seem interested. His Chilean wines were taking off, for one thing. And he already had one Argentine winery in his portfolio: Valentín Bianchi. It looked like his Argentine quota was filled. "No one wanted Argentine wine. There was no need," says Favelukes. "Plus Chileans and Argentines don't normally get along so well."

After her third chat with Catena, Favelukes got the outgoing Chilean salesman and reserved Argentine economist to set a meeting in early 1992 at a Washington DC restaurant. Catena brought samples of his Chardonnay and Cabernet Sauvignon, and the men discussed Catena's aims. Bartholomaus was impressed by Catena's new wines, of course, but also by the Argentine's passion for research and his desire to prove that a world-class wine could be made in South America. But there was the question of price.

When Bartholomaus asked Catena why he wanted *him* to represent the Catena brand, the Argentine said, "You have been the only one able to sell wines from South America for more than $3.99 a bottle." Catena wanted to go further than the Chilean had in his aggressive pricing of Cousiño Macul, which at that point sold for $7.99. As his would be the first Argentine wine for many Americans, he had an opportunity to create a benchmark for price, and he wanted it to far outpace the trans-Andean competition. In Argentina, he had found that putting high prices on good wine got people's attention. He had also seen how difficult it was for Chilean wines to shed their bargain image and raise prices, and he didn't want to fall into that trap. Plus, prices at Napa wineries had been rising, and there was a lightly contested territory between Chilean bargains and California and French premiums. Catena told Bartholomaus that he wanted to charge between twelve and fifteen dollars a bottle.

In this, Catena was stepping back from one of Argentina's obvious advantages: its dry climate meant less grape mold and disease, which in turn meant lower grape-growing costs. While this gave Argentine producers a price advantage, Catena saw that following the cheap-wine route would be an easy exit, and would offer only short-term gain. "Argentina's climate lets you put slightly lower prices on Argentine wines. But you mustn't put prices too low, because the consumer associates price with quality," says Jean-Pierre Thibaud, the former head of Bodegas Chandon and the current head of Mendoza's Bodega Ruca Malen. "To set the right price is not an easy thing. You have to put a sufficiently high price to show that it's a good wine but not so high that no one buys it."

Bartholomaus was dubious of Catena's price reach, however. He told the economist that it would be a tough sell and require pricey marketing for an unknown Argentine wine to break the ten-dollar barrier. But Catena was insistent: he had made a good-quality wine, and he wanted the prices to reflect that. He said he was prepared to do what was necessary. Bartholomaus still thought pricing in that range was aggressive—perhaps insanely so—but he liked Catena, the wine, and the challenge. A quick decision maker, he said he was willing to give it a try. He agreed to take Catena's wines.

"When I get up in the morning I do not thank God," Bartholomaus says today, "I thank France and California for raising their prices so high that they made my wines look reasonable."

To unveil the new Argentine product, Bartholomaus and Catena's wife Elena—sometimes accompanied by Favelukes or Hobbs—began a barnstorming tour of the top wine-selling stores on the East Coast and the Chicago area, armed with Catena's 1991 Chardonnay and 1990 Cabernet Sauvignon. For the wines to succeed, they needed trusted store owners to recommend the wines as well-priced premium vintages. At each stop, the attractive and lively Elena would tell the Catena story—from its origins, through the Napa epiphany, and to the present day—and then they would taste the wines with the store owner or wine buyer. "We started with small amounts of wine and we did a one-to-one approach, which I believe is one of the best. Open bottles to your accounts so people will feel the quality," says Bartholomaus.

For the Cabernet Sauvignon, the selling process was straightforward: Bartholomaus brought a brown-bagged bottle of Catena's wine and another of a Weinert, the era's Parker-approved benchmark for Argentina, and had the store owners blind-taste them. Although the wine that Weinert produced was good, it couldn't stand up to Catena's understanding of the American palate. "Buying bottles of Weinert was my best investment. Catena won nine out of ten taste tests. Weinert was the old style, and Catena Cabernet had nice fruit and flavor and a good finish," says Bartholomaus. "At the time, for the American consumer, there was one word: fruit. Instant gratification."

The white was another story. No one believed that South America could produce a top-flight Chardonnay and, faced with such low expectations, Catena's risky bet on an Old World white was proven correct. When dubious buyers balked at the Chardonnay's price tag, Elena would purchase an expensive California Chardonnay and challenge them to a comparative tasting. Presented with a fair face-off, the wine buyers were consistently shocked by the quality of the Argentine Chardonnay. "It was the greatest white wine I had ever tasted from South America. It was between California and France in terms of having the ripeness of New World wines plus the balance and acidity of European Chardonnays," says Paul Provost, who bought the wine for the Massachusetts-based Yankee Spirits. "We sold 125 cases of Catena Chardonnay in less than a year. I thought people would think we were bonkers for trying to charge twelve dollars for an Argentina Chardonnay."

Still, other stores wouldn't even consider taking a leap of faith on the high-priced Argentine upstart white, at least at first. Carlo Russo's Wine & Spirit World in Ho-Ho-Kus, New Jersey, was one such store. Carlo Russo was a pharmacist who became interested in wine and, taking advantage of the pharmacy's liquor license, began holding tastings and leading wine tours to Europe. When Alfredo Bartholomaus and Elena Catena arrived in northern New Jersey and showed him their new Chardonnay, Russo said he was impressed but declined the pair, despite their considerable charm. It would be impossible to sell wine from Argentina at twelve dollars a bottle, he told them. As they were leaving, however, he asked if they would leave several bottles for an upcoming tasting. In true meritocratic American style, the bottles would be brown-bagged so that tasters could not be influenced by producer or country of origin.

Bartholomaus had almost forgotten about his visit with the ex-pharmacist from Ho-Ho-Kus when an agitated Russo called him several weeks later demanding to buy fifty cases. At the tasting against a dozen California Chardonnays priced up to almost thirty dollars, the Catena Chardonnay had come in second only to a Kistler Chardonnay more than twice its price, and now Russo had orders to fill. "It created a huge opportunity to have an Argentine wine that came in second to Kistler at half the price," says Nora Favelukes. "In the American market, it's not the price or the quality, but the price-to-quality ratio."

Whether the timing of Catena's American invasion was intentional or merely lucky, it turned out to be impeccable. "At the same time Catena entered the market, the American consumer entered into the market," says Bartholomaus. "They'd go to the wine store, and the store would say we have this great new Argentine wine. And the consumer would say, 'This Argentine wine is good. Why do I have to spend sixty, seventy, eighty dollars for a bottle of wine when I can buy an Argentine Cabernet for under twenty?'"

Within six months, Bartholomaus sold his entire allotment of 2,500 cases of Catena Chardonnay and the same number of the Cabernet Sauvignon. It wasn't a huge amount of wine, but that was good in a way: with small amounts in stock, wine store owners tipped off their top customers to their Argentine find, and Catena's reputation grew among taste makers. The first Chardonnay and Cabernet Sauvignon acted as the wedge that opened America's door to Argentine wine. And once it was open, the race was on.

During these early years of Argentina's wine revolution, Catena's wineries had the vibrant aura of a Silicon Valley start-up, albeit one founded far from the rest of civilization. An evolving mix of long-term locals and short-term foreigners had been brave, crazy, and curious enough to take a chance on Argentina. They worked absurd hours, usually without necessary tools or clearly defined roles. They improvised with what was at hand in order to turn mediocre wine into something great in a place where few thought such a thing was possible. Despite the chaos—or perhaps because of it—things moved forward.

Catena's plans required a creative workforce with unconventional talents. He took chances on untested youth, good ideas, and—to the surprise of many male-dominated wine companies in Argentina—female executives. "For me, women are very capable," he says; then he adds, "If they didn't have to take care of children, they'd beat men in everything."

One of the women Catena hired was Marina Gayan. In 1993, Gayan was twenty-four, a recent graduate in graphic design with plans to move to Milan to study design theory, when a friend asked her to do a favor and interview for a job as marketing assistant. The interviewer ended up being Nicolás Catena and, although Gayan tried to explain that she viewed the job as a temporary assignment before moving abroad, she soon found herself being tutored in basic accounting theory by her new boss, a doctorate in economics. "When I started working for Catena, obviously people assumed I was his lover or a friend of his daughter Laura," says Gayan of the consternation created by her presence in the winery's hierarchy.

The inexperienced Gayan was quickly charged with reinventing the *bodega*'s premium-wine marketing to its domestic clients. With little preparation save Catena's trust, she created a premium-wine sales crew for Saint Felicien, replete with a branded van that traveled around Buenos Aires giving restaurant clients glasses and decanters with the Catena logo. The street team gave lessons in pouring wine and using proper stemware. She hired famous Argentine artist and architect Clorindo Testa to design a label. And she set up a delivery system that got the premium wines to their clients within twenty-four hours—and achieved day-of-use delivery for one particular restaurant that had been flagged for the bad old habit of storing excess wine near the stove. All common practices now, these innovations were revolutionary at the time.

"It's very exhausting working for Catena because he doesn't give you one minute. It was all the time, 'What are we going to do? How do we progress here?' You can never sit down and relax," says Gayan. "They were incredible times."

Now a London-based industry consultant—her years there have left her with a marked British accent and a proper English haircut and mien—Gayan became the first Argentine to earn an "MW" title from London's Institute of Masters of Wine, an advanced wine degree given to those few who are willing to grind through a twelve-hour written exam, correctly assess wines during seven hours of blind tasting, and complete a ten-thousand-word piece of original wine industry study.


Nicolás Catena may not have been an expert in the technical specifics of winemaking, but he did recognize important ideas when they were presented to him. As he produced his first new wines, the academic-minded Catena hungrily absorbed the contemporary winemaking theories that Paul Hobbs brought from California, and poured on concepts gleaned from research and conversations with other winemakers. In his eagerness, Catena demanded that these new and sometimes contradictory theories be put into practice, often simultaneously.

"Sometimes we would complain that Catena listens too much," says Gayan. "You had a whole strategy, and in the middle he would want to change it because someone said something that sounded logical. And you'd say, 'This sounds logical but it doesn't have context.' All the time you had to give arguments. The best argument won. You had to fight all the time."

This mental battle was a thrill for people like Gayan and Susan Balbo, who praised Catena's "extreme intelligence," but for others it caused repeated frustration. Pedro Marchevsky, for example, says he always lost in his role as Nicolás Catena's intellectual sparring partner. "I could never win an argument with Catena. I would get impassioned," says Marchevsky. "He does not have passions. He considers them weaknesses."

Indeed, while Catena veered away from in-person confrontation, his clever skill at creating competitive rivalries between his subordinates earned him the nickname of "Puppet Master," says Scott Peterson, an American consultant who replaced Paul Hobbs in 1998. Catena would regularly give his employees assignments that put them in another colleague's domain, or he would agree to one employee's plan for a project and then change his mind and tell another to change it. Such leadership tactics reminded his subordinates of Machiavelli, an author whom the *bodeguero* avidly read. "Every time he would do that, I would ask, 'Did you have the Black Prince next to your bed last night?'" jokes Gayan. "He used to work by 'divide and conquer.'"

Not surprisingly, such techniques seemed manipulative to some. "He believes in a competition between employees that is harmful for the business because it breaks apart supportive teams," says Marchevsky about Catena. But many thrived, and Catena makes no apologies. Keeping his people working separately and competitively got better results. "More people give you more ideas, and I'm going to like one more than the others," he says. "If you work in a team, one person influences the rest and you lose creativity. If there are three people, you lose two."

Catena was far from exclusively Machiavellian, however. He never forgot his rural roots, and was generous to his wine industry friends. In the 1970s his company began delivering powdered milk to some fifteen rural schools so that every child, no matter how poor, could have a glass of milk in the morning. Today, the Catena family foundation, Fundación Angélica Zapata, annually awards some twenty multiyear scholarships to poor rural children to pay high school tuition. And when the wine consultant Jacques Lurton announced that he was going to be married, Catena shipped enough Argentine beef for a thousand people to the French oenologist's upcoming Bordeaux wedding.

In the end, the presence of a chief with a hard-driving vision and Machia-vellian style inspired the company's top employees to charge forward and take risks. But one unplanned side effect of an environment with such enthusiastic fervor was the occasional goof. In 1995, Gayan was called by Catena's secretary and told that he wanted to see her in the shipping department.

"What can you see, Marina?" Catena asked, pointing at a wall of red, blue, and yellow shipping boxes for his top-selling Valderrobles brand.

"Boxes?" Gayan said, confused. "Did something happen today? Do we have too much stock?"

"Marina, they're in color," he said.

A month earlier, Gayan had noticed that all cases of wine in Buenos Aires supermarkets were displayed in brown or white corrugated card-board boxes, and in a burst of insight she realized that hers should be brightly colored to stand out. The only problem was that Marina had forgotten to tell Catena about her redesign, much less ask his approval. "I turned completely white," she says. "He said, 'Okay, let's see the num-bers at the end of the month.' And it sold well and he said, 'You're for-given, but never do it again.' It was at the point we were going so fast, changing everything."

Similarly, Pedro Marchevsky jumped ahead of the company's plans after learning that the company's aged *toneles* were a main culprit behind the oxidation that was killing their wines. When a traveling scrap buyer visited Bodegas Esmeralda in the early 1990s, Marchevsky made an impulsive decision to sell him the nearly century-old barrels and put an end to the nightmare once and for all. When Catena returned from a trip he had been on in the United States and passed through the *bodega*, he was stunned to find himself walking through empty warehouses that had once housed his *toneles*.

"What have you done to me, Pedro? I'll kill you," Catena said.

"They're vinegar factories. They're not useful anymore," Marchevsky said of the *toneles*. "I sold them to a gypsy."

"What do I do?" said the shocked *bodeguero*.

"Buy steel."

The viticulturist's move and his *bodeguero* boss's shock were both justifiable under the company's modernization drive; it's just that the two men had been focused on two separate points in the future. For Marchevsky, the *toneles* were simply a piece of winemaking evil that had to be excised immediately. Catena agreed in theory—there was no way he would make wine in the old casks again—but he had a longer horizon in mind. He imagined a future in which Argentines would look back at their wine history with nostalgia, and he wanted to start a wine museum where a *toneles* exhibit would show how things had been done in the quaint olden days. But Marchevsky wasn't thinking about looking back from some point in the future; his boss's passion for change had simply overwhelmed him.

"We fell in love with the new style, without wood, without oxidation," says Marchevsky. "The conviction about what we had to do came from Catena, and we fell in love with it."

CHAPTER 8

# "DISCOVERING"
# MALBEC

Alberto Antonini, Carlos Vázquez, Antonio Morescalchi, and Mauricio Parodi (left to right)
walking the land that would become the vineyards for the
Altos Las Hormigas winery. Courtesy of Alberto Antonini.

THE INTERNATIONAL WINE CONSULTANT Alberto Antonini spent much of the first half of 1995 crisscrossing Italy in an Audi A4 with Antonio Morescalchi, scouting vineyard land. The wealthy twenty-seven-year-old Morescalchi had been bitten by the wine bug. A just-graduated electrical engineer, he had already fixed up his family's single-acre Tuscan hobby vineyard, and now he wanted to launch a winery project. His close friend Antonini, a slender man with a swept-back mop of wavy brown hair, made the perfect partner.

Then in his mid-thirties, Antonini was head winemaker at Tuscany's Marchesi Antinori wine company, a Florence-based Chianti Classico powerhouse that traces its history in wine back twenty-six generations, to 1385. In 1924, Niccolò Antinori, the current owner's father, had scandalized the region by introducing a type of Chianti containing Bordeaux grape varieties, a bastard blend that sat outside Chianti tradition. His son and current owner Piero went further soon after he took over the business in 1966. At the time, local appellation regulations held that in order to bear the "Chianti Classico" title, a wine had to contain at least 75 percent Sangiovese, with the rest made up of other local grape varieties; any wine breaking the rules was classified as *vino da tavola* ("table wine"), Italy's least prestigious category.

The problem was that Chianti was seen by many at the time as poor wine, and forward-thinking Tuscan *bodegueros* saw that to improve its reputation—and to compete with Bordeaux—they would have to break the restrictive rules. In the 1970s, Piero shook the industry by creating Tignanello and Solaia, two "Super Tuscans" that contained Bordeaux grape varieties Cabernet Sauvignon and Cabernet Franc (the original Solaia contained *only* Bordeaux grapes); soon his *vino da tavola* was fetching some of the top prices for Italian wine and led wine authorities to modify the restrictive appellation system.

As Antonini and Morescalchi toured rural Italy, however, one downside of Piero's innovation became clear. After a Super Tuscan–led boom in Italian wine, vineyard land had become prohibitively expensive—some $40,000–$50,000 per acre. Unable to pay the price of admission to make wine in their homeland, Antonini remembered a wine he had tasted the year before. While studying oenology at UC Davis in 1994, Antonini, an obsessed fan of 1960s West Coast rock by Janis Joplin, the Grateful Dead, and Jefferson Airplane, had met Patricio Santos, the son of former Bodega Norton owner Ricardo Santos. Out at dinner one night, the younger Santos had described Mendoza and given Antonini a taste of 1968 Norton Malbec. Antonini had not been impressed by the style of the wine—he says it struck him as old-fashioned, "kind of tired, kind of funky oak"—but its "flavor intensity and beautiful structure" had caught his eye. "It was rich and dense, attractive in a way," says Antonini, an avid skier and marathon runner who counts Olympic gold medalist Alberto Tomba among his friends.

Intrigued by his memory of Malbec, Antonini suggested to Morescalchi that they visit Argentina and Chile to see if the burgeoning wine capitals of South America had anything to offer them. They arrived during Antonini's summer vacation in August 1995. Staying in the Hotel San Pedro in the east Mendoza town of San Martín—a quirky, modest lodge where the air conditioner sounded like a 747 taking off and the shower drain was a hole in the center of the bathroom floor into which one squeegeed water—Antonini and Morescalchi toured Mendoza with Patricio Santos in Santos's Ford Escort. The car had worn-out shock absorbers, which made for bone-rattling rides as they visited the Norton, Catena, and Nieto Senetiner wineries. They quickly fell in love with the altitude, the dry climate, and the hot days and cool nights. "We were impressed by the potential of the wines and the beauty of the vineyards, and the *terroir* was impressive," says Antonini. "I thought it must be a very special place to make great red wines."

Equally if not more important to Antonini—a native of Vinci, the Tuscan town that produced the painter Leonardo—was the region's soul. Adriano Senetiner, an Italian immigrant and co-owner of Bodegas Nieto Senetiner, showed special interest in his compatriots, chaperoning the visiting Italians and asking Antonini if he could help create an Argentine Super Tuscan in the mold of the ones the winemaker oversaw at Antonori. Mendoza, with its Italian immigrants and wine culture, felt like home.

"Mendoza was kind of a piece of Europe in the New World, an amazing network of small, family-run vineyards who were selling their fruit to larger wineries: you feel that people are living on that and it's not just temporary. It has been there for over a hundred years and will probably be forever. It's their life and you feel that commitment," says Antonini.

But there was one thing that did seem odd to Antonini and Morescalchi. As the two Italians toured the region's *bodegas*, the winemakers and owners all tried to steer them away from the grape that most intrigued Antonini: Malbec. "It's funny because now they all want to be the 'Pioneers of Malbec,' but when I first got there all the wineries I visited were proudly showing me their Cabernet, Merlot, Chardonnay, and Sauvignon Blanc," says Antonini. "I'd ask where the Malbec was and people got shy. They'd say, 'Yeah, we got some but don't worry about that. Taste our Cab.' No one believed in that grape."

"You can tell what the winery owners wanted then by looking at what they planted," says Morescalchi, stubbled but still baby faced. "What did they plant in the best areas? Cabernet and Chardonnay. The rest is talk."

During the Middle Ages, the powerful, dark wines of Cahors, in the Lot valley of southwestern France, were known as "Black Wine," and they aroused strong passions. In 1225, Henry III of England forbade the authorities of Bordeaux from stopping or taxing the wines sent to him by Cahors merchants under his protection; Pope John XXII used Cahors vintages as sacramental wine; Cahors-born French Renaissance poet Clément Marot sung their praises; and seventeenth-century Russian czar Peter the Great drank Cahors wines. The main ingredient in those heavily ballasted wines from Cahors was a grape known as Côt or Auxerrois. Thin-skinned and difficult to grow—poor at pollination, susceptible to cold and disease—it needed more sun and heat than either Cabernet Sauvignon or Merlot to mature. But when it did mature properly, it offered a wine with deep violet color derived from a high level of anthocyanin pigments and a particular dark fruit aroma of blackberries and plums.

The grape spread through France, picking up names along the way. It was common practice to name grapes after their appearance or after the person who introduced them to an area. Famed French botanist Pierre Galet has catalogued over a thousand monikers for Lot's black grape, from Pressac, Luckens, and Magret to Medoc Noir, Pied Noir, and Costa Rosa. Popular history holds that a Hungarian viticulturist introduced the grape to Bordeaux, where the region's winemakers soon realized that its dark juice would give heft and color to their Clarets. Little is remembered about the mythical Hungarian, save for his last name: Malbec.

Malbec's inky dye earned it a place as one of the six varietals authorized for use in the Bordeaux blend (the others are Cabernet Sauvignon, Cabernet Franc, Merlot, Petit Verdot, and Carménère), and the grape came to occupy large swaths of the region. At top Bordeaux châteaux like Château Latour and Château Cheval Blanc, Malbec eventually accounted for over half the vineyard plantings. But its success was not to last: after the nineteenth-century phylloxera epidemic, many French winemakers abandoned the disease-prone grape. They found that when Malbec was grafted onto American roots that were resistant to phylloxera, its foliage grew too vigorously. On these bushlike vines, winemakers had to deal with thick canopies of leaves that, if not vigilantly trimmed, blocked the fruit from the sun's warm caress and led to grapes that didn't fully mature during the growing season. Then, after a 1956 killer frost wiped out more than 75 percent of the vines in some parts of Bordeaux, those winemakers who had replanted Malbec after phylloxera did not bother to replant the fragile vine again.

Today, Malbec is almost absent from France, except in its old Cahors home, putting Bordeaux winemakers in the curious position of having to depend largely on Argentine imports if they want to taste one of their own six great varietals. In 1999, when Château Cheval Blanc director Pierre Lurton—a cousin of Jacques and François—was searching for a New World winery with which to form a joint venture, he chose the Argentine *bodega* Terrazas de los Andes in part as a way to connect with the Malbec side of his Bordeaux winery's past. Several years later, in 2003, the winemaker at Terrazas, Roberto de la Mota, traveled to Cheval Blanc to present the Argentina-based joint venture's Cheval des Andes Cabernet Sauvignon–Malbec blend. During the visit, château manager Jacques Hébrard—the man whose schnauzer famously had attacked Robert Parker Jr.—introduced himself to De la Mota and thanked the Argentine winemaker. "Here at Cheval Blanc, I've had 5 acres of Malbec for a long time because it's very important to me," Hébrard said. "It's never given me a good wine. Since grafting it for protection from disease, it doesn't give the wines it used to. That's why for me it's so important to have tasted today a Malbec as it was supposed to be."

Had not the crazy French father of Argentine viticulture, Michel

Aimé Pouget, packed cuttings of Malbec when he moved to Mendoza to open the province's model farm in 1853, the varietal might have been condemned to viticultural history. Pouget had brought Malbec cuttings largely because of the grape's importance in Bordeaux—especially in Cheval Blanc's home area of Saint-Émilion—but the soil and climate conditions of Argentina's desert west were so different that it wasn't clear at first that the inky grape would thrive. Malbec has only average acidity in its temperate French setting, which can be a problem in the hotter parts of the Andean desert, where the broiling sun tends to burn off grape acids. Since acidity is a prime component of wine flavor and ageability, Mendozan Malbec often must be balanced with the addition of tartaric acid; otherwise, drinkers can face a combination of flat flavor and a propensity to spoil. Early in the twentieth century, the fact that Malbec occupied 75 percent of vineyard acreage was considered a "transcendental error" because *bodegueros* had to spend millions of pesos every year on acid correctives. Leopoldo Suárez, the director of Mendoza's vitiviniculture school (Escuela Nacional de Vitivinicultura de Mendoza), even suggested that Argentina's winemakers consider swapping Malbec for Tannat—a higher-acidity French grape common in Uruguay—because it would adapt better to the climate and soil of Argentina's hot west.

Nevertheless, the grape flourished. The tender Malbec plant had not been an easy vine to grow in Bordeaux, where it was especially susceptible to diseases. In damp, cool weather, vine rot and a nasty condition called *coulure* (in French) or "shatter" (in English)—in which the flowers do not pollinate or the berries fall off soon after they form—can destroy a crop. But Malbec grew easily in the high Andean desert, where the hot dryness discourages most molds and bugs and lets farmers grow grapes almost organically. Even better for Argentina's quantity-obsessed growers, the long growing season and the ability to irrigate regularly vastly increased yields over what the vine had produced in its French home. While the wines they produced with the grapes may have been rustic, Argentine grape growers, winemakers, and wine drinkers came to treasure Malbec. By the mid-twentieth century, some 120,000 acres had been planted.

But soon the Argentine palate changed.


During the 1970s and '80s, Argentine wine drinkers switched from Argentina's rustic reds to strained off-white wines made from high-volume varietals. With consumption shifting from 75 percent red to 75 percent white, grape growers followed the market's dictates, and the great Malbec pull began. As the number of *criolla*, *cereza*, and *Pedro Giménez* vineyards soared, the acreage planted with the comparatively low-producing Malbec fell. Between 1970 and 1990, Malbec acreage tumbled by 80 percent, to 25,000 acres. It seemed that the black grape of Cahors might just disappear from its Argentine home.

"Around 1990, old Malbec from the best vineyards was worth six centavos per kilo," says Hervé Birnie-Scott, the estate director of Mendoza's Bodegas Chandon. "Old Malbec wasn't profitable then. You grew it because you loved the vine. It didn't even cover your costs."

It didn't help that Malbec's onetime ubiquity meant that it ended up shouldering the rap for Argentina's recent history of poor, unsanitary winemaking techniques. Like all local reds, Argentine Malbecs suffered the harsh, hot pressing that infected it with bitter tannins; the aged *toneles* that killed its fruit flavors; and the leaky pumps, pipes, and bottling lines that oxidized it into sherry.

Malbec's low-quality image was reinforced by poor international reception. A typical review of the period, from the *Wine Spectator*, gave the six-dollar 1985 Malbec from Valentín Bianchi 76 points and dubbed it "a rough-and-ready red wine, with a texture on the coarse side." An eight-dollar 1988 Trapiche Malbec did little better, earning 74 points and the title of a "lean, somewhat hard-edged wine." The joke that went around was that Malbec's name derived from the French *mal bec*, or "bad

beak." "For people of that era," says Ángel Mendoza, former head oenologist at Trapiche, "'Malbec' was a bad word."

Malbec did have its defenders, of course, but they were few. The
1977 Bodega Weinert Malbec, made by Raúl de la Mota, set an early
high-water mark. The French consultant Jacques Lurton got in on the
act in 1992, when he created a £3 Malbec for his "International Winemaker" series that the *Independent* dubbed an "excellent value and
gluggable, with lovely rich fruit." And at Trapiche, Ángel Mendoza's
eight-dollar 1991 Malbec Oak Cask earned 87 points and a "Best Buy"
label from the *Wine Spectator*. "Oodles of ripe black currant flavors are
marked by sweet American oak, lending immense appeal," the magazine wrote. Ricardo Santos, the onetime owner of Bodega Norton, was
one of the biggest supporters. At Norton, Santos and Pancho Giménez
had created what was probably the first Argentine Malbec exported to
the United States, the 1971 Norton Mendoza Malbec. After selling his
company in 1989, Santos went so far as to start a label designed specifically for Malbec (El Malbec de Ricardo Santos). But beyond these
rare cases, Malbec's rejection was universal. "When we planted Malbec
in 1992, everyone thought we were crazy," says Santos's son Patricio.
"'How are you going to plant Malbec when it's a second-tier grape?'
[people asked]."

The visionary Nicolás Catena was one of many who missed the boat
on Malbec. Although he possessed old vines descended from Pouget's
cuttings, when Nicolás Catena entered his 1980s post-Napa Chardonnay and Cabernet Sauvignon fugue, he did so to the exclusion of those
old Malbec vines. It meant little to him that pre-phylloxera Malbec had
once covered huge swaths of Bordeaux and was considered the gem of
that zone. His mind was set: Malbec was at best a second-tier grape. Paul
Hobbs recalls the *bodeguero* pointedly reading aloud to him from French
wine manuals that said Malbec was useful only for adding color and body

to Bordeaux Claret. "He showed me the book [and told me,] 'The French say this is no good,'" says Hobbs.

"The Malbec I knew was an oxidized wine, and as such I didn't like it. Not just oxidized; *very* oxidized. The old Italian and Spanish style," says Catena. "I thought the problem was with Malbec."

Catena's rejection of Malbec fit the Argentine mind-set. While the stereotypical Argentine is famous—or infamous—for his belief that his country and its products are the best in the world, that pride is in part a fig leaf hiding a larger insecurity: that Argentina had a chance to equal or best the Old World, but in the end flubbed it. Other South Americans mock Argentines for their Europhile aspirations, and in a sense that "Europhilia" was behind the Argentine *bodegueros'* rejection of Malbec. The Argentine *bodegueros* wanted their wine to be accepted by the Old World, and the French had, after all, rather convincingly rejected Malbec. Now a low-class exile, for many in the *bodeguero* upper class Malbec signified all that was wrong with Argentina.

But Catena's winemakers, like many technicians in the region, were not as obsessed by international varietals as Catena himself was; perhaps because they had spent less time traveling and absorbing foreign wine norms, they *liked* the grape they had known from birth. "Malbec was the greatest wine of Argentina, the most grown. We always loved it," says Marchevsky. And those who had grown up during Argentina's proud wine-growing heyday also had happier memories of the black grape. Catena's father Domingo had added 30 percent Malbec to his top-of-the-line generic blend, Buenos Aires A, to give it better color and body. Domingo's experience producing blends for Argentina's eastern cities had shown him that old vines in Mendoza's colder high-altitude areas, like La Consulta, produced Malbec grapes with strangely intense color, flavor, and structure.

Domingo told his son he was positive that a Malbec from the right area could one day be the basis of a wine as great as a top Bordeaux. "When my father saw me in this fever to plant Chardonnay and Cabernet, shortly before he died in 1985, he said to me that I was wrong, that Malbec was very good and that, while I wanted to make a great Cabernet, I should also try to make a great Malbec," Catena says. "I must confess that I started a Malbec project only to satisfy my father. It was an emotional question. Nothing rational at all."

While sentimental reasons were enough to convince Catena to try Malbec, they weren't enough to get him to do it quickly. "Use the few barrels we had for Malbec? Never," says Pedro Marchevsky of the early years. "Why use barrels for Malbec if the world wanted Cabernet and Chardonnay?" It was not until 1992 that Galante and Hobbs began making a Malbec in the Bordeaux/Médoc style, concentrated and dark and aged in expensive French oak barrels. And even then, Hobbs says, they used ten barrels he was given as a sample by Seguin Moreau, a 170-year-old French cooperage that was keen on expanding in South America.

The wine showed promise, Hobbs says, intriguing several members of the US wine press whom Bartholomaus brought to visit the next year. But the cautious Catena was unsure that the wine was ready for the international stage—or that the obscure Malbec grape would ever be—and he did not export the oak-aged 1992 or '93 vintages. They remained to be sold in the domestic market, an Argentine grape for an Argentine palate.

In 1992, Paul Hobbs and Nicolás Catena's wife Elena traveled to Tuscany. The wave of Italians who immigrated to Argentina had brought with them a love of Sangiovese, the main component in Chianti. Now a small percentage (7,500 acres) of Argentine vineyards were Sangiovese. Considering the impact that Sangiovese-heavy Super Tuscans had had in the international wine trade, Nicolás was curious if the Italian varietal could amount to anything in the New World. While in Tuscany, Paul and Elena contacted the winemaker Attilio Pagli, whom Paul had met in

California. A sturdy, opinionated man with a pronounced stutter, Pagli resembles a friendly version of actor Michael Chiklis, star of *The Shield* and *The Commish*. A 1983 oenology graduate from the University of Siena, Pagli had studied with the master of Italian Chianti, Giulio Gambelli. Paul and Elena met with Pagli at a restaurant in the Chianti town of San Casciano and explained the project. Over the next few months, they negotiated with Pagli via fax, a process that at the time could take hours to send a single page. Finally, in March 1993 Pagli arrived to see what he could do with Argentine Sangiovese.

Pagli's Sangiovese experiment was short-lived: he quickly discovered that the "Sangiovese" in Argentina either wasn't Sangiovese or was a very ugly stepchild of the proud family line. After examining their huge fruit bunches and pergola-style trellising, Pagli told Catena the vines he saw had no chance of producing good wine. This assessment put both Pagli and his employer in a bind: the Italian had been hired with a fairly substantial consulting contract, and now he had nothing to do. Hoping to salvage something from the trip, Paul Hobbs and Pedro Marchevsky suggested to Pagli that he travel around Catena's vineyards with Carlos Vázquez to see if there was anything he wanted to work with. On that tour, Pagli visited the Angélica vineyard in Lunlunta and fell in love with the old vines of Malbec grown from its own roots.

On the grounds of Catena's La Vendimia country house in 1993, Pagli sat down with Nicolás Catena and his wife Elena, Paul Hobbs, and Marina Gayan to eat a meal cooked by Argentine celebrity chef and Catena friend Francis Mallmann. When the conversation turned to Malbec, Pagli told the others that, after walking Catena's vineyards, he had come to believe that Malbec was the Argentine premium grape variety. In the spirited discussion that followed, he says that all his fellow diners told him he was off target. "The others said I was wrong. No one defended Malbec. Malbec was just color," Pagli says.

But something about the counterintuitive passion Pagli had for Malbec intrigued the *bodeguero*. Catena had enough intellectual curiosity to take a chance on an outsider's contradictory opinion, so although he had been lukewarm in his support for the Malbec experiments that Galante and Hobbs had been doing at Bodegas Esmeralda, Catena set Pagli to work on the varietal at Bodegas Escorihuela, a winery he had bought in 1992.

This master in Tuscan reds brought a unique sensibility to the project, an artist's vision tweaked by an obsession with numbers. At the time, Michel Rolland's influence was blooming, and his characteristic "Parker-approved" style—concentrated wine made from very mature grapes—was sweeping the industry. Pagli had a different take on achieving concentrated fruit flavors and aromas. To avoid some of the heaviness that comes from using superripe fruit, Pagli preferred to pick early and then discard some of the watery juice that comes out during pressing. This process, known in Spanish as a *sangría*, or "bleeding," reduces the ratio of juice to skin, thereby increasing the concentration of the flavors, aromas, colors, and tannins extracted from the skin during fermentation. Combined with an extended maceration, the process whereby new wine is left in contact with the skins for days or weeks before or after fermentation, the Pagli method produced tightly concentrated wines that retained freshness.

The problem was that no one really knew how to make a modern Malbec using these techniques. Pagli told Catena he would like to experiment a little. "What do you mean by 'experiment'?" Catena asked.

"Normally you bleed out no more than 10 percent of the juice, but it seems to me we could do a little more," Pagli answered.

"Okay," said Catena. "Do 20 percent, do 30 percent, do 40 percent."

"It may not work, and we might have to throw it out," Pagli explained.

"Just do it," Catena said. It was just Malbec, after all.

After the 1994 harvest, Pagli made a series of test tanks of the Malbec, each with a unique *sangría*, maceration, fermentation, and signature.

Though he chose something in the usual range of a 10–15 percent bleed, Pagli was surprised to find that some of the more heavily bled Malbec was not nearly as harsh as expected after spending so much time in contact with the skin. In fact, it was downright velvety.

Pagli then set about blending Malbecs to assemble a proper barrel-aged Malbec in the new California/Bordeaux style: concentrated and fruity, explosive and strong. The precision with which he approached his art stunned his Argentine coworkers. "In Argentina, traditionally blends were round numbers—50 percent of this, 20 percent of that, 10 percent of another," says Marchevsky. "But Attilio was sophisticated. We did a blind tasting and he'd say, 'This is with 1.7% from the third barrel from the fourth row.' As a teacher he was amazing. We learned that blending was a delicate art. We learned how to discover the mix."

Later that year, at the office of Bodegas Esmeralda, Nicolás Catena sat down with Pedro Marchevsky and his daughter Laura Catena to taste the newest Malbec. Doubting that an unknown "Argentine" grape would ever be accepted on the world stage, Catena would hold this wine to the highest standards. He wanted the wine to be as good as the best wines of France. Not a twenty-dollar bottle, but one that went for ten times that price.

Now the president of the family's top winery, Bodega Catena Zapata, Catena's daughter is the keeper of the family's business and legacy. A demanding multitasker—she is also a part-time emergency room doctor in San Francisco and the author of a book on her family and Argentine wine—the broad-faced, wavy-haired Laura bears a striking resemblance to her father, albeit with more extroverted confidence. "Nicolás in a skirt," jokes longtime family friend Arnaldo Carosio. At the time of the tasting, she was a twenty-six-year-old student on a break from Stanford University School of Medicine. Although she was not yet terribly involved in the wine business, Laura did know one thing about the wine she had tasted: the 1994 Malbec was really good. "If we don't do it with this vintage we never will," said Laura.

Facing subordinate pressure was one thing, but getting it from his daughter was something else entirely. The wine wasn't bad either—maybe not a top Bordeaux, but better than he had hoped. At last, Catena relented. He would allow the wine to be exported, making it the first Catena Malbec sold overseas. "I think I convinced him with my excitement more than because he thought it was that good," says Laura Catena.

All that was left to do was to fight over semantics. Marchevsky wanted to use the anglicized spelling "Malbeck," while the French-speaking Laura voted for the original "Malbec." The Catena won.

Two years later, points-obsessed Nicolás Catena was relieved when Parker rhapsodized about his 1994 Malbec Lunlunta Vineyard. "Elegant yet rich and flavorful, this medium-bodied, supple, velvety-textured wine exhibits just what heights Malbec can achieve in Argentina," Parker wrote, giving it a respectable 89 points. "Already delicious, it should age well for 5–6 years. Kudos to Catena!"

"It went really well," Catena admits today. "Much better than I'd ever expected."

The next year's vintage further convinced Catena of Malbec's possibilities. Building on their 1994 experience, Galante and Pagli and the rest of Catena's winemaking crew created a Malbec of rare elegance and concentration. "It was the first time I liked a Malbec, so much so that I named it for my mother, Angélica Zapata. In Argentina it was a huge hit," says Catena (the wine was sold only in the domestic market).

It was the 1996 vintage that made Catena a true believer. That year, during the summer preharvest months of February and March, unseasonably cool temperatures settled over the region, with averages as low as sixty-five degrees Fahrenheit in the Angélica vineyard. The grapes on the now seventy-five-year-old Malbec and Cabernet Sauvignon vines there, usually harvested fairly early because of the zone's heat, got to hang on the vine until the twenty-eighth of March. Their colors, flavors, and aromas grew incredibly concentrated.

With the knowledge gleaned from the previous years, Catena's winemakers set to work. Early on, they realized that the wine would be special. The question was how special. In honor of the special wine, Catena purchased "Imperial" bottles for it, glass behemoths that weighed almost three pounds. As the winery staff awaited word from Catena on what to call the wine, it was known internally as "Imperial." The name question was not a small one. Catena was one of the few *bodegueros* not to use his name as a brand in the domestic industry, and for years he had been talking about making a wine good enough to bear it. "I must make my name known," French consultant Jacques Lurton recalls Nicolás Catena telling him.

After 1997 arrived and the wine's release date approached, the question was whether Catena would make the Malbec (blended with 10 percent Cabernet) his first icon wine by dubbing it with the name he had reserved for his flagship: Nicolás Catena Zapata. Proud of what they had made of the iconic Argentine grape, Pedro Marchevsky and other Argentine staff members urged him to do so. So did Susana Balbo, a winemaker who would become Catena's export manager.

"Would you sell that wine with the brand Nicolás Catena Zapata?" Catena asked Balbo after she tasted the wine in 1997. Balbo said she would.

"But I'm not sure Malbec has the ability to age like Cabernet," Catena answered.

"Why not?" Balbo asked. "Raúl de la Mota showed it could."

"But this was a different process. I'm not sure. I think the best wines are Cabernet," said the *bodeguero* with the conservative palate.

"If I were to pick a fine wine for Argentina, it would be Malbec, not Cabernet," Balbo answered. "But you know marketing better than I."

Scared of making a misstep, the Europhile Catena blinked: his first eponymous icon wine, which would end up being released both domestically and internationally with the 1997 vintage, would be a Cabernet-dominant blend (with just a 5 percent touch of Malbec) elaborated by José Galante. Catena compromised, though: the 1996 Malbec would be promoted to Catena Alta ("High Catena") for exports, and he would continue to risk his mother's name, Angélica Zapata, on it in Argentina.

"It was extraordinary," Balbo says today. Reviewers agreed. The *Wine Spectator* bestowed 92 points on this newly discovered grape. "This vivid, concentrated red shows how brightly Malbec can shine in Argentina," it said of the 1996 Catena Alta Malbec. "It has the lush oak and polished texture of the best international-style reds, married to the meaty, smoky, plummy flavors characteristic of this obscure variety."

It was the pronouncement from Robert Parker Jr. that made Catena celebrate, however. Parker gave it 94 points, a ranking usually reserved for great French and Californian bottles. "This Malbec gushes with jammy black fruits that have soaked up its aging in 100% new oak casks. Although extremely intense and rich, it comes across the palate as elegant, with no sense of heaviness, rather remarkable in view of its exceptional intensity and length," the American reviewer wrote in October 1997, employing his characteristic mix of clear and purple prose. "To this day, the 1977 Bodega Weinert Malbec remains one of the great mature red wines from this beautiful country. Catena's 1996 Malbec should give Weinert's 1977 plenty of competition."

With the success of these Malbecs, Catena was forced to admit that he had made a mistake by marrying his business solely to Bordeaux's top varietals. For one thing, Chardonnay and Cabernet Sauvignon weren't specifically identified with Argentina in consumers' minds. Concentrating on them put Argentina at risk of becoming another Chile, a country that produced dependable wines but didn't have much of an identity. More important, Chardonnay and Cabernet Sauvignon weren't what necessarily worked best in Argentina's soil. "I forgot about climate, or *terroir*," he later told *Decanter* magazine of his attempt to re-create Napa and Bordeaux. "My conclusion was superficial, premature."

Catena's experiments, like those at Weinert and Norton before, showed beyond a doubt that Malbec thrived in Argentina's arid, high-altitude valleys as it never had in France. "Here, Malbec is in its home. It does well by itself. Other places, you need to work on it," says Pagli. "You can make good Cabernet Sauvignon here, but Malbec has a unique personality in Argentina. It's like in Burgundy you could make a good Cabernet, but the Pinot Noir has a unique personality."

Finally convinced that Argentine Malbec deserved a spot on the world stage, Catena began searching for the best version of the grape with the same scientific rigor and ample resources he applied to the rest of his business experiments. When planting one of France's noble varietals like Chardonnay or Cabernet Sauvignon, the planting process was reasonably straightforward: you bought cuttings or seedlings of the most appropriate "clones" from a local nursery or one in Europe or California. Unlike most crops, grapevines are not reproduced sexually; that is, they are not grown from seeds. That's because vines grown from seeds do not necessarily inherit the varietal characteristics of the plant the seeds came from: a son of a good Chardonnay may not be good; it may not even be a Chardonnay.

Prizing uniformity and consistency above all else, growers have avoided this problem by propagating grapes asexually since vines were domesticated some eight thousand years ago. A branch of a good vine is cut from the trunk and then either planted or grafted onto an existing root system (as was done to combine American and European vines during the phylloxera scourge). That way, a grape grower can produce an infinite number of exact copies; he can, in effect, xerox his vineyard. But that doesn't mean all Chardonnays worldwide are the same. Inside each varietal is a rainbow of different versions, or clones, each subtly different from the next. For example, the "Wente" Chardonnay clone was brought to California from the University of Montpellier in the early twentieth century and worked well there. But when it failed to ripen in colder Oregon, growers there brought in early-ripening Dijon clones from the chilly Burgundy region. Even among the Dijon clones there are differences: clone 277 is known for higher production than clone 76, while clone 95 is said to have more white peach flavors than the mineral-noted clone 96.

The problem with Malbec was that no nursery offered the best clones. No one in Argentina had ever bothered to perform a clonal selection to isolate and identify which clone worked in heat or cold, what kind produced more plum flavors, and so on. And as it had essentially been eliminated from its native France, there simply was no Old World clonal selection to choose from. Even if there had been, it might have been irrelevant: some local *bodegueros* and winemakers felt that the Malbec that had been brought to Argentine in the mid-nineteenth century had an advantage over its French brethren because it had evolved, ever so slightly, to thrive in the local soil.

All this meant that Catena's viticultural staff would have to do the genetic lifting themselves. They would have to isolate and audition local Malbec clones to find the top ones. That would not be easy. To start with, many Argentine "Malbec" vineyards were actually varietal hodgepodges known locally by the generic name of *uva francesa* ("French grape"); that is, they were a preponderance of Malbec peppered with Merlot, Petit Verdot, Tannat, and others. "My vineyard is a potpourri. It was a mosaic when we bought it, a botanical garden," says Ángel Mendoza, the former Trapiche winemaker who today farms ninety-five-year-old Malbec vineyards at his family-owned Domaine St. Diego winery.

Marchevsky and his team embarked on their own clonal classification. With little information to go on, save some vine classification work done at INTA and general word of mouth, Marchevsky and his crew fell back on the one resource they possessed: the 195-acre old-vine vineyard in Lunlunta. "We couldn't bring better clones than what we had," Marchevsky says. They walked the rows of vines in the Lunlunta vineyard, searching for the healthiest-looking Malbec vines, those with the small grapes and small bunches that produced wine with the most concentrated flavor. "We chose the ones that looked most like Cabernet," says Catena, always partial to the world's great varietals. They took clippings of the hundred best, along with some twenty clones from INTA and another fifteen from the local university's agronomy school, and replicated them all until they had enough to plant a row of each (some fifty-seven plants) in the 260-acre *La Pirámide* Vineyard in Agrelo in 1995. And then they waited.

Vines take two years to enter into full production, and even then their fruit is considered young and imperfect. When the vines began to produce grapes, Marchevsky and his team performed a phenotypic study of the outward appearance of the plants and grapes. After tossing several for not pollinating well or for growing too much foliage, they put the remaining clones through a database census of every possible grape and foliage attribute. "Imagine what it was like to walk those vineyards, count the number of bunches, the size of each bunch, the size of the grapes of each clone," says Marchevsky in a voice that suggests he is still exhausted by the thought. "We took samples on three separate dates on each clone of its sugar, acidity, and color."

Then they gave each attribute a ten-point ranking and eliminated the clones that didn't have the most important qualities. They ruled out those that scored below a certain level for color, grape size, and so on. After whittling the contestants down to 17, they fermented small samples of each of the finalists in 1997. Then they held a taste test and decided there were 10 worth testing further. And then they engaged in the second step of the great Malbec classification: they planted the top clones in Catena vineyards of various altitudes and soil compositions to see where each achieved its best expression.

Wine is a business of the long term, and Nicolás Catena's willingness to embark on a rigorous academic study of Argentine Malbec not only showed intellectual curiosity, but also evinced the patience of Job. In the process of choosing the plants, growing the clones, selecting the best of those clones, and replicating the best clones in other vineyards to the point that they bore fruit, some five years passed. Catena exhibited similar patience when he planted the Adrianna vineyard in a place where no one looked for wine—much less, premium wine—before. Good grapes and the good wine they make come many years later, so determining an experiment's success or failure can take decades. "We haven't pulled any vines, because an experiment like that lasts thirty years," says Catena. "Five years to get real grapes. At least ten years to best production, maybe fifteen."

"Planting Adrianna is something that now may not seem like a big deal, but putting in all that money and waiting twenty years in a place where everybody thought, 'Forget it'? It *was* a big deal," says Catena's daughter Laura.

Though Nicolás Catena was far from the first *bodeguero* to believe in Malbec, he was the first to have the resources and patience to delve into its possibilities. And the experiment his company performed changed the Argentine wine industry. Not only did it show which clones worked best; it also delivered an encyclopedia of the flavors produced by Malbec at different altitudes. "Malbec varies with the climate where it's planted," says Pedro Marchevsky. "High up in Gualtallary, where the Adrianna vineyard is, it has the aroma of violets. Lower, you get the flavor of black cherries. Even lower, there's blackberry. Then as you keep going down you get plum, then red cherries, then strawberry."

The Catena study still stands as a landmark moment. Suddenly Argentina's *bodegas* had a whole new palate, and Catena had the clones to prove it.

Poetic words may be spoken about wine, but the beverage will always be a product that needs a buyer. Happily for Malbec, it found those buyers in one of the world's greatest untapped wine markets: the United States. Since Norton shipped off its first export Malbec in 1971, the grape has found a special home in the United States, where imports of the stuff exploded from about 900,000 twelve-bottle cases in 2006 to 1.3 million in 2007 and 2.1 million in 2008. Just as Malbec the grape adopted Argentina, Malbec the wine adopted the United States.

When Malbec broke into the American market, it was a beginner's wine for a country of new oenophiles, a straightforward, fruity beverage that could be enjoyed without pretension. "The Argentine style of Malbec is very consistent with today's American consumer," says Nick Dokoozlian, the vice president of viticulture at E.&J. Gallo Winery. "Fruit forward, concentrated, dark fruits (cherries, raspberries, blueberries, plums), but not overextracted or tannic or astringent." In other words, it's the perfect variety for a young country that's new to wine; great for drinking with a steak, Argentine Malbec is yummy, fruity, and dark and, though sometimes powerful in the booze department, low on the pucker that turns your mouth into a frown. And Malbec is fun in a most unrefined way that fits with American informality: the wine stains a drinker's mouth purple, like ink. Indeed, it is so dark that it sometimes seems to blacken the glass that holds it.

Since that first meeting of the two New World children—Malbec and America—they have matured alongside one another. Both maker and drinker have learned to appreciate complexity, uniqueness, and elegance. "The American consumer and Argentine producer grew up together. The producers have been working to provide better-quality fruits and wines. At the same time, the American consumer is not the same consumer as twenty years ago. He's much more sophisticated today, more open to new things," says Nora Favelukes, now owner of the Manhattan-based QW Wine Experts brand and marketing consultancy. "Malbec (and Argentina) has entered the subconscious of the American consumer. It's not weird anymore. Which means that it's here to stay."

For those who bet early on the grape, Malbec's ascent was sweet vindication. A few months after their first visit to Argentina, in 1995, Antonini and Morescalchi spent $100,000 for 535 isolated acres to launch a winery they named Altos Las Hormigas (after the swarms of ants—*hormigas*—that tried to eat their vineyard's first tender shoots). Catena Malbec adviser Attilio Pagli joined them the next year. "The idea was to develop a 100 percent Malbec project. It was considered impossible. People would say you won't last two years," Antonini says. "It's funny thinking about people saying we wouldn't survive. Now we're close to 1.5 million bottles a year, and about 90 percent of that is Malbec."

Rarely has the battle between New World and Old so clearly gone in the direction of the child. After suffering extensive damage to its vineyards in the 1956 frost, Cahors slowly replanted, and by 1971 there were 1,100 acres of vineyards in the Cahors appellation, mostly of Côt, or Auxerrois (Malbec). That number has risen to a little over 10,000 acres today. In Argentina, however, there are over 70,000 acres of Malbec, including more than 60,000 acres in Mendoza alone. In the 2009 version of the biennial Vinexpo trade show in Bordeaux, the booths for Argentina and the Cahors trade association were immediately adjacent to one another. It was a direct challenge, of course, but not in the traditional form of child to parent; it went the other way. The French booth did not pump itself as the home of Côt or Auxerrois. Instead the region's slogan was a simple aspirational claim meant to steal a little of Argentina's glitter: "Cahors, The Original Malbec."

The winemakers of Cahors have reason to want to gather a little of the fairy dust. In a 2004 article in *Food & Wine*, Robert Parker Jr. offered twelve predictions about the future of wine. Number seven was, "Malbec will make it big." Parker wrote, "By the year 2015, the greatness of Argentinean wines made from the Malbec grape will be understood as a given. This French varietal, which failed so miserably on its home soil in Bordeaux, has reached startling heights of quality in Argentina. Both inexpensive, delicious Malbecs and majestic, profoundly complex ones from high-elevation vineyards are already being produced, and by 2015 this long-ignored grape's place in the pantheon of noble wines will be guaranteed."

# CHAPTER 9

# THE VALLEY
# OF THE KINGS

Nicolás Catena (left) and Baron Eric de Rothschild at the 2001 inauguration
party of Bodega Catena Zapata. Courtesy of Nicolás Catena.

ON APRIL 1, 2001, a Sunday, more than 140 invited guests—industry bigwigs, press, politicians, and friends—made their way from the city of Mendoza to the winegrowing district of Agrelo, about thirty minutes south. The guests turned off the packed dirt of Calle Cobos ("Cobos Street") and crested a small ridge before heading down a vineyard-bordered gravel road. And, for a moment at least, each of them paused to gape at what they saw in front them. In the midst of the 260 acres of his Agrelo vineyard, the unassuming Nicolás Catena had built an enormous, futuristic Maya-style pyramid. The shy professor had rebuilt Tikal.

Constructed of local stone and wood and topped with a pyramidal skylight that bathed the interior in sunshine, the beige pyramid (a $12 million investment, according to the local *Los Andes* newspaper) was marketed as a statement of Mendoza's New World identity. Instead of pledging fealty to France or Italy with some sort of tile-roofed pseudo-château, Catena told those who asked that he had decided on the eye-catching pyramid to honor the Mayans, the authors of the New World's most impressive pre-Columbian culture and monuments.

While lovely, the Mayan design choice baffled some observers with its seemingly arbitrary motif. "Even by the flamboyant standards of modern winemaking, few know how to grab the public's attention better than Argentina's Nicolás Catena," a *Businessweek* writer later noted. "Never mind that the Mayans were hooked on cacao, or that their empire never stretched beyond Central America." Some on the inside chalked it up to internal Catena family dynamics. "[Nicolás's son] Ernesto went to Guatemala and fell in love with the Mayans and came back and drilled his father with how great the civilization was," says Marina Gayan. No matter its inspiration, the pyramid was an unforgettable attention grabber, and it gave Catena's company an iconoclastic edge. And, with a gravity-fed vinification system designed to treat the grapes and wine with utmost gentleness, not to mention room to store 2.25 million liters of wine in steel tanks along with five thousand barrels, the building gave Catena the right to greet his party guests with the simple, proud phrase, "Welcome to one of the most modern *bodegas* in the world."

The pyramid was the final piece in Catena's coming out as a major international *bodeguero*, and a look around the grounds showed that he had definitely arrived. Local *bodega* owners Michael Halstrick, Carlos Pulenta, Roberto Arizu, and Carlos López were there to honor the pioneering *bodeguero*. His five-months-pregnant daughter Laura, who was gradually taking over management of the business—ensuring a fourth generation of Catena control—was dancing tango with Alfredo Bartholomaus, the Chilean importer who had turned Catena from an unknown into an American hit. Also dancing with Laura was Baron Eric de Rothschild, manager of the famous Château Lafite Rothschild, one of Bordeaux's five Premier Cru (or "first growth," the top ranking) vineyards.

Catena and Rothschild had formed a joint venture in 1998, and in 2000 they had produced the first vintage of a Mendoza Cabernet Sauvignon–Malbec blend called "Caro." Their partnership was an obvious echo of the famous Opus One partnership between Catena idol Robert Mondavi and Baron Philippe de Rothschild, Baron Eric's neighbor, cousin, and rival, who owned the equally famous Premier Cru Château Mouton Rothschild. The Caro partnership was so baptized for the first letters of the Catena and Rothschild names but, perhaps coincidentally, *caro* is also the Spanish word for "expensive."

Starting in the early 1990s, investors, especially foreign ones, poured staggering sums of money into Argentine wine country. Catena's burgeoning success became the inspiration for scads of other *bodegueros* who wanted a piece of the vineyard at the end of the world. As Corie Brown noted in a 2006 *Los Angeles Times* article, "Catena introduced his new wines just as the government opened the country to international trade for the first time since World War II. Suddenly, it was easy to export wines. And each year, as the wines improved, the international demand increased. By 1997, the Mendoza countryside was crawling with oenological carpetbaggers." By the end of the decade, between forty and fifty Argentine *bodegas* had upgraded their equipment to a level that equaled the most cutting-edge wineries in the world. As international wine consultant Sophie Jump told University of Miami professor Steve Stein in a 2008 industry study, "Most of them have got facilities that the French would die for."

Foreign investment in Argentina's wine region goes back to 1959, when Moët & Chandon's aristocratic, blue-eyed leader Count Robert-Jean de Vogüé traveled to Buenos Aires to visit Baron Bertrand de Ladoucette, a fellow aristocrat and owner of a Loire valley winery who had married the count's niece and moved to Argentina in 1950. The count had sent Moët & Chandon winemaker Renaud Poirier on a South American tour to find the best *terroir* for growing sparkling-wine grapes, and in 1958 the oenologist had fallen in love with the land of Agrelo, then an isolated desert patch twenty miles from Mendoza, over dirt roads, with no running water or electricity. The count told the baron that he had decided to open a branch in Argentina and he wanted the baron to run it.

It was a curious choice. The baron knew the country: he had bought ranching and agricultural land in the Argentine pampas near Buenos Aires during post–World War II paranoia when people believed that the Soviet Union would invade France. But he had a comfortable life, with a personal fortune, a castle, an important French winery, and a wife who was part of one of Europe's most important Champagne dynasties. He wasn't the first person one would expect to start a *bodega* in the middle of a high-altitude desert.

And yet de Ladoucette agreed. The baron, the winemaker Poirier, and twenty-four workers soon bought 10 acres and, working against nature and their ignorance of the local *terroir*, in September 1960 launched Bodegas Chandon. "When we settled here, we were in the middle of a raw desert," Baron de Ladoucette said. "I set the first brick in the heat and the dust of a desert. That's how this business was born."

"It was a challenge developing a *bodega* in the middle of a desert seventy-two hundred miles from headquarters. Discovering a *terroir*. Developing foreign varietals here. Mastering local ones. Building in an earthquake zone. And doing it all with very few people," says Bodegas Chandon estate director Hervé Birnie-Scott. "And the bottles they bought locally exploded because they couldn't handle the pressure from the bubbles. Everything was difficult."

After Chandon, foreigners stayed away for decades. Save for the Brazilian transportation executive Bernardo Weinert's opening of Bodega y Cavas de Weinert in 1975, and Austrian crystal magnate Gernot Langes-Swarovski's purchase of the financially battered Bodega Norton from Ricardo Santos in 1989, it was not until the late 1990s that the Mendoza land rush really began. The capital then flowed with righteous intensity, in part because the price was right: excellent Argentine vineyard land was selling for half of what it cost in Chile, a third of the land price in Australia, and a tenth of the cost in Napa or France. But there was something else: Argentina offered Old World winemakers New World freedoms. In countries like France and Italy, each area's appellation laws—created over centuries of winemaking—regulated what grapes may be grown, their maximum yields, the legality of irrigation, acceptable alcohol levels, and so on. But Argentina, with its shorter history, was refreshingly unbureaucratic. The country had never introduced strict appellation laws, so a winemaker could use all available tools and ideas, as long as the wine he made was safe to drink.

"We look to the Old World, to the conception of wine that the French, Italians, and Spaniards have. But we're part of the New World of wine, in the sense that we don't have a lot of regulation," says Familia Zuccardi *bodega* head José Alberto Zuccardi. "Here we have liberty. Our only regulation is that wine is a natural product."

Upon arriving, international moneymen and consultants fell in love with Argentina's *terroir*, potential, people, and prices, donned the gaucho pants known as *bombachas*, picked up a *mate* gourd, and put together investment groups to launch wineries, usually in the recently "discovered" high-altitude land of the Uco Valley. Between 1991 and 2001, an estimated $1.5 billion was invested in the Argentine wine industry, with a shocking $1 billion of that coming from overseas. Once as economically isolated as North Korea, Argentina became Hong Kong, an international frontier hub.

Alberto Antonini, the Italian wine consultant who co-owns Mendoza's Altos Las Hormigas winery, says, "Mendoza today can be considered the most international wine region in the world."

To better explain the scale of this land rush, it's worth noting just a few of the investments that came into Argentina in the early years, as compiled by researchers for the UN's Comisión Económica para América Latina y el Caribe (CEPAL): In 1992, beverage industry giant Pernod Ricard paid $5 million for half of Arnaldo Etchart's Bodegas Etchart and then bought the rest four years later. The Spanish firm Marqués de Grignon paid $22 million for Bodegas Norte in 1995. Then, in 1996, the UK beverage giant Allied Domecq bought Bodegas Balbi-Maison Calvet for $25 million, and Chilean *bodega* Santa Carolina bought the majority of Santa Ana for $22 million. The same year another Chilean wine giant, Concha y Toro, bought the small *bodega* Premier for $1 million. Also in 1996, a subsidiary of Diageo bought the Navarro Correas and Rodas brands for $15 million. Portugal's Sogrape Vinhos paid $12 million for 60 percent of Finca Flichman in 1997. And in 1998, the American investment firm Donaldson, Lufkin & Jenrette (DLJ) spent $40 million on a minority share of Peñaflor. And this list represents just a small portion of the deals in a period spanning a mere six years.

But it was the seal of approval from Michel Rolland that made it truly okay for skittish foreigners to move their millions to the Uco Valley. The original "flying winemaker" had made a slight miscalculation when he first arrived in Argentina. When he signed up to work with Arnaldo Etchart in the northwestern province of Salta, he agreed to an exclusive contract. The problem with the agreement wasn't that Salta was a bad wine zone—it produces brilliant vintages—but that Rolland couldn't work in Mendoza. The world's most famous winemaker didn't start working in the center of Argentina's wine revolution until 1996, after the party was already under way.

Once Rolland reached the end of his exclusive deal, Trapiche president Carlos Pulenta immediately hired the Frenchman to consult for the label, his family's fine-wine brand. At the time, Trapiche winemaker Ángel Mendoza was perfecting the mix for Trapiche Milenium, a Cabernet-Malbec blend meant to celebrate the arrival of the twenty-first century. The Argentine economy was in nouveau riche ascent after President Menem's pro-US free-market reforms, and the whole project had an end-of-days madness to it: sold in advance for the unheard-of price of $1,000 each, only two thousand six-liter bottles would be made, packed into coffinlike individual wood boxes and delivered for Christmas 1999. Ángel Mendoza was understandably anxious that the wine be done right. He worried that an Argentine Malbec wouldn't be able to age for five years, so as he prepared the Milenium blend he asked Rolland, a master blender, for advice. Rolland begged off—the wine had been harvested and fermented before his arrival, so he didn't want to comment—but he did want to taste the unblended parts.

"Where did you get this Malbec?" Rolland asked, his curiosity piqued by the inky color, generous fruit and soft tannins that were the calling cards of the high-altitude Malbec. "We bought the grapes from some friends in the Uco Valley," Mendoza replied. "The Uco Valley?" Rolland asked. "Yes," Mendoza answered. "In Vista Flores."

A few months later during harvest season, Mendoza took Rolland and the Frenchman's ever-present retinue to visit the vineyard in Vista Flores that had produced the Malbec grapes for the Milenium blend. As they walked through the vineyards, the short Argentine winemaker grew visibly agitated. "Look what happens when you make a grape-grower famous," Ángel Mendoza said. "Look how fat those grapes are. When we bought them last year they were tiny. He must have put tons of water on it to make more money this time around." Rolland did not commiserate. Instead, he offered Mendoza a simple piece of advice. "There's no need to get angry," Rolland told him. "What you have to do is buy the vineyard." But Ángel Mendoza, like most Argentine *bodegueros* and winemakers, didn't have money. While President Menem's economic liberalization had brought Argentina back into the world community, the country's collapses had been so frequent that banks were loath to lend to local businesses. Even today, as Laura Catena says, "Argentina is a country without credit."

Mendoza may not have been able to buy the vineyard, but Rolland could. And after learning of the area's perfect combination of high altitude, intense sun, ample "thermal amplitude," and relatively low prices, he did just that. In 2001, Michel and Dany Rolland and an associate of theirs, a gaucho pant–wearing Algeria-born Frenchman named Philippe Schell, bought the 22-acre vineyard of sixty-year-old Malbec vines and began to elaborate Val de Flores, a wine that so astounded Robert Parker Jr. that he referred to its inaugural 2002 vintage as "a wine of great intensity, sumptuous richness, gorgeous freshness, and a vigorous personality" and gave it 95 points, thus showing once again the access to Parker's palate for which Rolland's consulting clients paid so dearly.

It was not this small purchase that turbocharged Argentina's wine industry, however, but a bigger deal Rolland put together in the same era. As he reconnoitered the Uco Valley, Rolland used his connections with France's oenological royalty to put together an investment group of Bordeaux winery owners that would make most anyone in the wine world blush. Besides the trio of Rolland, the late Bordeaux vintner Jean-Michel Arcaute, and Philippe Schell, the group had six other partners: Catherine Péré-Vergé, owner of several châteaux in and around Bordeaux, including Pomerol's Château Montviel; the d'Aulan family, former owners of Piper-Heidsick Champagne and current owner of Château Sansonnet, in Bordeaux's Saint-Émilion region; Baroness Nadine de Rothschild, owner of Château Clarke, and her son Benjamin de Rothschild, owner and CEO of LCF Rothschild Group; the Cuvelier family, well-known Bordeaux *negociants* ("wine merchants") and owners of Château Léoville-Poyferré and Château Le Crock; the Bonnie family, who own Bordeaux's Grand Cru Classé–level Château Malartic-Lagravière; and Laurent Dassault, whose family owns Saint-Émilion's Grand Cru Classé–ranked Chateau Dassault and Dassault Aviation, maker of the Mirage fighter aircraft. (The d'Aulan family left the partnership in 2002.)

After deciding on a property in Vista Flores in late 1998, the seven partners formed what would be one of the most ambitious and spectacular winemaking complexes in the world: Clos de los Siete—literally,

"Enclave of the Seven." With its 2,100 acres, Clos de los Siete would be as large as the entire Pomerol appellation of Bordeaux—home of the famed Château Petrus winery—where Rolland had been raised.

And an enclave it was: each partner was not only to plant his own huge vineyard, but also to build his own huge *bodega* inside the walled compound, like some overgrown McMansion development. Rolland would consult at each *bodega*, and in a slick marketing move designed to build the Clos de los Siete brand, the partners pledged about half of their production to the Clos de los Siete blend, a mix of Malbec, Merlot, Syrah, Cabernet Sauvignon, and Petit Verdot made under Rolland's supervision. The group now produces 650,000 bottles a year of the blend, an under-twenty-dollar wine that *Bloomberg News* wine writer John Mariani called, "a serious red wine to rival cult wines 10 times the price."

To enter the Clos de los Siete complex is to experience the pharaonic extreme of the Argentine boom. After driving down a dusty-pan road and being checked through a guarded security checkpoint, you cross Avenue Michel Rolland. As wine writer Matt Kramer aptly noted in the *Wall Street Journal*, "Modesty, you quickly realize, is not the order of the imperial day here." Bouncing up the vineyard roads inside the compound, sloping up toward the breathtaking Andean blue screen, one gets the impression that the founders wanted to re-create the gardens of Versailles rather than a working vineyard. Indeed, it is a place of privilege and perfection, but not for people. "Plant equilibrium" and "low production" are watchwords of today's premium-wine movement, and in Clos de los Siete, the plants are treated better than many children: they are the Wagyu Kobe beef cattle of the wine world.

The vines are densely snuggled some 2,200 plants to the acre, and each 4- to 8-acre parcel gets its own watering schedule and hand fertilization. Led by Carlos Tizio, now the general manager of Clos de los Siete, the staff prunes, tweaks, and loves the vines to botanical perfection: during the period of pollination and first growth, Tizio says, the vines are deprived of water in order to make smaller grapes with a higher concentration of phenolic compounds, and afterward the greenery is trimmed to fourteen to sixteen leaves per grape bunch to create perfect equilibrium between deprivation and lushness. In the orderly beauty of this plant spa, the vines are allowed to produce a maximum of only three tons of grapes per acre; many produce less than two. Compared to the yields squeezed out of vineyards during Argentina's bulk-wine era, it's almost as if they're on vacation.

The *bodegas* that Rolland's partners have built are gargantuan. In a sense they have to be if they are to compete with the majesty of the looming Andean mountain range. Marooned in the midst of their horticulturally perfect vineyards, the lonely beasts have the thickset presence of reinforced cement, the prime building material in seismically active Mendoza. But they are beautiful in a monumental way. The first one built, Catherine Péré-Vergé's Monteviejo, is winningly tucked into the land, with vineyards covering half of its sloping 2-acre roof. Guests at the 2010 opening of the newest, the Bonnie family's minimalist Diam-Andes (a wordplay on "diamonds" and "Andes"), were drawn to ogle at its centerpiece, a two-story metal-armature diamond.

Compared to the others, Rolland's recently built Mariflor *bodega* is all business, as befits a man who began his winemaking career in the laboratory. Cement gray, boxy, and topped with high, industrial tin ceilings, it is a cross between a hospital and an aircraft hangar. Inside, the human scale is dwarfed by wide, spotless hallways that run between unbroken rows of 10,000-liter cement tanks. The colors are variations on gray, white, and stainless steel, and everything shines wet with recent cleaning. In keeping with the perfection so evident in the vines, the grapes are delicately hand-harvested in boxes that hold no more than thirty pounds. Once inside the *bodega*, they go through a four-part selection process. After being mechanically destemmed, they are denuded by hand of any remaining leaves. They are then sent down a vibrating table meant to shake off impurities, and workers (mostly women) arrayed in a row on both sides of a conveyor belt pick out underripe grapes to avoid lending the final wine a "green" taste.

At the end of the belt these coddled grapes tip into an inverted conical container, akin to a giant wheeled, stainless steel martini glass, which, when full, is lifted via crane (no brutish pumps to move the grapes here) and then emptied through a porthole in the cone's nether point into the top hatch of one of the cement tanks. The grapes repose in the translucent swirl of a horror movie fog, the product of the pellets of dry ice mixed into the stew. The dry ice performs a double role: by keeping the temperature down during a prefermentation maceration called a "cold soak," it lets the wine develop bright fruit flavors, more aroma, and deep color without the harshly astringent tannins that heat can bring out; in addition, because dry ice is carbon dioxide in solid form, its gas "melt" pushes out oxygen and thereby avoids oxidation.

Leaving the grounds, what one remembers most about Clos de los Siete is the silence. Even during harvest season, save for the quiet chatter of the line of women sorting grapes in Rolland's *bodega*, the walled compound is blanketed with a reverential hush. These *bodegas* have neither the casual domesticity of the artisanal wineries of Argentina's early years nor the bustling industry of the wine factories that sprang up in the middle of the twentieth century. They feel more like an especially beautiful collection of royal mausoleums, places that their superrich masters can visit several times per year to revel in their amazing wealth before they pass to the beyond.

Much of this colossal "Mendoza look" can be traced to a single couple: Eliana Bórmida and Mario Yanzón. Completed in 2000, Bodegas Salentein was the first *bodega* they built from scratch; all told, the pair's Mendoza studio, Bórmida y Yanzón Arquitectos, has designed or remodeled more than thirty *bodegas*, including DiamAndes and Mariflor. In the process, their architectural philosophy has come to define Argentine wine country's aesthetic. Even many of the Argentine west's new *bodegas* that weren't designed by the pair feel as if they were. While each *bodega* is, by definition, customized to the landscape and the owner's needs, wallet, and ego, Mendoza's modern *bodegas* share enough common DNA that the Bórmida y Yanzón style seems pervasive. Imagine what Napa would look like if all its wineries shared the undulating curves of Frank Gehry and you will have an idea of these architects' aesthetic ubiquity. Whether that is a good or a bad thing depends on the observer. Bórmida and Yanzón's reliance on thick concrete and hard angles strikes many as beautiful and regionally appropriate; for others, however, their style is Mussolini's architecture, Brutalist and cold.

The two architects form an interesting first couple of *bodega* architecture, in no small part because they continued to work together after divorcing seven years ago, following thirty-two years of marriage. A typical Mendozan descendant of Piedmontese Italian immigrants—her grandfather arrived in the early twentieth century to import Fiat autos—Eliana Bórmida is the articulate presenter of the two: elegant, well coifed, and with an eye for weighty necklaces, a beautiful woman of a certain age. Mario Yanzón is more down-to-earth. His big friendly mug gives him the look of a character actor, perhaps a kindly, design-savvy member of the *Sopranos* family. He says his family came from places unknown—the name Janson was Hispanicized to Yanzón at some point—before settling in the northern desert province of San Juan. The pair came into the wine industry almost accidentally, when the Trapiche winery asked them to design an event for visiting journalists in the mid-1980s. They immediately realized the advantage to be gained by playing up the romantic side of winemaking.

"The *bodegas* then were very ugly and industrial, covered inside with light blue tiles, something that was neither aesthetic nor correct," says Bórmida. "We said the dinner we can do in the cellar but with all the lights out, in total darkness, so you can't see anything except we'll light the fronts of the *toneles*. And the next day we'll do the lunch in the aisles of the vineyard simply so people can walk on the earth and smell the grapes. And we'll put out big tables with big baskets of homemade bread and *empanadas*, and cover it all with rough fabric, the most rustic we could do."

After the success of the event and ones like it, Argentina's *bodegueros* began to see the advantage in selling consumers and journalists on local icons—the gaucho, the *empanada* meat pie, the *asado* barbecue, the vineyard—and the need to upgrade their *bodegas* to do so. The Italianate wine palaces of the early twentieth century were too old-fashioned (not to mention out-of-date), and the industrial factories that came later were aesthetic horror shows. Bórmida and Yanzón began offering local *bodegueros* something neo-*Mendocino*—a blend of industrial functionality, regional identity, and Hollywood science fiction that played to their desire to appear both historically rooted and technologically progressive.

As with the use of irrigation and antihail netting in Mendoza's vineyards, a good deal of the aesthetic was defined by Mother Nature. The reinforced concrete is a reflection of antiearthquake construction codes. The near complete lack of windows and doors—their blank-faced *bodegas*, while monumentally lovely, often exhibit the open-armed friendliness of a supermax prison—reflect the blistering sun of the Argentine desert. Thick walls with few windows offer strong "thermal lag," lowering energy bills.

"Architecture has to be sustainable, something that works with the climate without expending too much energy," says Bórmida. "A glass box wouldn't work at all in our climate. One must protect oneself from the sun." Bórmida notes that the aesthetic fits into Critical Regionalism, the rubric used by UK architectural critic Kenneth Frampton to describe buildings that have an identifiable regional style and take into account the local needs but do not have the folkloric aim of re-creating the past. "The *bodegas* have to have something in common, an intimate relationship with the location, the climate, and landscape," says Bórmida. "But each *bodega* has to be different, because they represent a brand. And every owner has to feel that his *bodega* is the best, something exclusive that represents his vision of wine."

That final product generally involves a lot of abstract geometry and a good dash of the theatrical. Bórmida and Yanzón's sprawling design for the 1.5-million-liter-capacity Bodegas Salentein, which has art-collecting Dutch owners, comes replete with a Dutch-Argentine art museum and an epic barrel-aging cavern full of repeated arches, a glass-domed rotunda, and a sunken center stage decorated with an inlaid Greek cross. With its "climate of eternity, silence, the temple," in Bórmida's words, it is somewhere between a Renaissance church and the egg room in *The Matrix*.

Down at the southern reaches of the Uco Valley, Spanish *bodeguero* José Manuel Ortega Gil-Fournier has taken this to the extreme. His $3 million O. Fournier *bodega* follows the precept of gravity winemaking, which means that the product is never moved mechanically. At O. Fournier, two sweeping cement ramps bring grape trucks to the roof level, where they start the gravity-fed process that ends in a cool, subterranean barrel and bottle cellar. With the pincerlike ramps playing the role of the mandibles, the 124,000-square-foot *bodega* bears an eerie resemblance to an extraterrestrial scarab beetle intent on ingesting the nearby Andes. "I only gave them two rules," says owner Ortega. "One, always do what the winemaker tells you. And two, once you've completed rule number one, do whatever you please. This had to be a flagship winery, something that has never been done. That's how they came up with the whole sort of spaceship, underground cellar, the whole thing."

Looking at the O. Fournier spaceship, one could be forgiven for thinking Argentine wine country was being colonized again, this time by a new generation of couture-clad, check-writing extraterrestrials. But the new colonization has certainly not been as bad for the locals as the original colonization had been for the Huarpe. "The foreigners have been great ambassadors, and they brought know-how and money," says Laura Catena.

It did not always work out for the colonists, though. Latin Europeans like Antonini and Rolland, who built up personal contacts and cultural knowledge, maneuvered fairly ably through local norms. But new arrivals who did not understand Argentina's long history often were lulled into complacency by the country's seeming familiarity, only to painfully discover that Argentina operates by a far different code. "It's typical for Westerners to think that because Argentines look like us, the society's the same," says English wine consultant Sophie Jump. "But Argentina is like nineteenth-century Europe."

The Waterloo for many new arrivals was grape contracting. Almost all Argentine *bodegueros* contract fruit from third-party grape growers. Early in the growing season, the *bodeguero* and the grower will come to a general oral agreement on quantity and price, with the fine print to be determined at harvest time. This system is necessitated by Argentina's system of landownership. Unlike the situation in Chile and Australia, where a handful of corporations control huge swaths of vineyard land and can therefore dictate exactly how their grapes will be grown, Argentina's vineyard land is owned by a quilt of small farmers spread over the Andean west. Of the twenty-six thousand vineyards in Argentina today, 80 percent are smaller than 25 acres.

When Argentina's newly arrived foreign winemakers joined this system, they often were in for a shock. They would visit what they thought were "their" grapes on the day of harvest, only to find that the grapes had been picked and sold to someone else. "I had a contract with a Señor Rollo, who had nice Cabernet. We went by the day before we were going to pick it up, and it had already been picked. I said, 'What the hell, Señor Rollo?' Señor Rollo said, 'Somebody came by after you and made me a better offer. But my wife made some nice tomato sauce, so why don't you stay for dinner?'" says California winemaker Patrick Campbell, who began making wine in Argentina in 1998 and importing it to the United States to bottle and sell under his Laurel Glen brand. "They can screw you with the greatest aplomb and ingenuity. They won't stick a knife in you; they'll screw you and no hard feelings."

Argentina's reliance on oral agreements and personal relationships made what seemed to the foreigners an amoral practice perfectly acceptable to the home team. In a precarious society prone to crisis, the economic system was necessarily based less on legal niceties than on trust between longtime friends. Such a system would collapse if people ignored promises made to friends and clients of twenty years. But it was something else entirely—barely a venial sin—to break an agreement with someone you didn't know when a better deal came around. Life was too short and the world too unstable to act otherwise.

While foreign winemakers like Campbell learned from their early missteps and built successful Argentine businesses, not every overseas investor deciphered the Argentine system in time. Some were sent packing with far less money than they had had when they arrived. The most spectacular example of those was California's famous Kendall-Jackson Wine Estates.

Kendall-Jackson was founded in 1982 when a grape glut hit California wine country and Jess Jackson, a San Francisco lawyer who owned an 80-acre vineyard in Lakeport, just north of Napa, couldn't find a buyer for his fruit. The Chardonnay he made from his unsold grapes was sweeter than normal, and American wine drinkers loved it. Kendall-Jackson Vintner's Reserve Chardonnay became a sensation, and today some 2 million cases of it are sold each year.

Now a surfing, thoroughbred-owning billionaire, Jackson began to look overseas for growth as he built his wine company into a colossus. As part of his overseas expansion, in 1993 Jackson hired winemaker Randy Ullom to launch and run Viña Calina, his operation in Chile. The tall, rangy Ullom had spent time in Chile in the early seventies during college, in order to take advantage of South America's opposite ski seasons. Despite being a native of Ann Arbor, Michigan, Ullom gives off the western vibe of a Marlboro man, replete with a Sam Elliot–style walrus mustache. With his frontiersman's drive, knowledge of South America, and ability to speak Spanish, he was well positioned to oversee the Chilean project.

Almost from the moment of the launch of Viña Calina, Jackson and Ullom began salivating over what was on the other side of the Andes in Argentina: thousands of acres of cheap, unexploited, high-quality vineyard land. In 1994, Jess Jackson suggested to Ullom that it was time to start Argentine operations. But Ullom put him off: they needed to wait until the long unstable Argentine economy calmed down a bit, he said. About a year later, though, when Ullom informed Jackson that things were looking better, the American wine mogul decided it was time to move.

With the grand dreams of a real American entrepreneur, Jess Jackson went in big. After Randy Ullom sent his winemaker and vineyard manager from Chile to scout for land in 1996, they bought an 1,100-acre chunk of unplanted high-elevation land above the Uco Valley town of Tupungato, well beyond the vineyard frontier at the time. Later they would buy another 1,350 acres in Agrelo, not far from Catena's *La Pirámide* Vineyard, and two other 200-acre parcels. In the meantime, with no planted vineyards of their own, they bought third-party grapes and turned them into wine at a *bodega* they had rented from Hervé Joyaux Fabre, a Frenchman prone to wearing ascots and gaucho pants who had come to Mendoza several years before and founded the winery Fabre Montmayou. The name for their Argentine wine was Mariposa—or "butterfly"—a word that, like the animal it described, somehow managed to be beautiful in every language.

"They wanted to buy land and plant vineyards and find winery sites in a manner of months. I've never seen a company so aggressive," says Greg Adams, an American viticulturist who worked in Argentina from

1992 to 1998 and spent his last year there as the Kendall-Jackson vineyard manager.

While the speed was admirable, the plan began to go sideways early on. When Ullom was given a huge promotion to "winemaster" for the entire Kendall-Jackson empire in March 1997, he decided he would need to bring in a replacement to run day-to-day winemaking in Argentina. An intern named Brenda Lynch—now the owner and winemaker of Sonoma County's Mutt Lynch Winery—had been watching over things, and the work was beginning to overwhelm her. To help Lynch keep her head above water, Ullom called Lynda Hanson, a thirty-five-year-old who was making Pinot Noir for Kendall-Jackson's Hartford Court business. "How's your Spanish?" he asked. "I know *cerveza* and *baño*, in that order," Hanson answered. Three days later, Hanson boarded a plane to Mendoza and immediately found herself sucked into the maelstrom of a speeding overseas start-up. "I was supposed to be there for a few months, and I was there for three years," she says.

Hanson's appointment was a symbol of the missteps that would come: to be its winemaker in beef-mad, macho Argentina, Kendall-Jackson had chosen a vegetarian female who didn't speak Spanish. Cultural slips began to pile up. Hanson discovered that the name they had chosen for the wine didn't, in fact, mean what they thought: a few days after her arrival the office assistant at Fabre Montmayou asked her why they had picked "Mariposa." "It means 'homosexual,' you know," he said. (The company changed the brand to "Tapiz," or "tapestry.") Then, irrigating the huge expanse of isolated Uco Valley land they had optimistically chosen caused problems. Kendall-Jackson had to drill expensive, deep wells, several of which produced less than they hoped. Their desire to use American plants was another issue: after an agricultural inspector found mold on one of the shipping pallets, the operation had to burn the shipping materials and give each vine what Adams calls a, "highly supervised, fungicidal 'dip' before the agent would allow us to bring the material to the field."

To top it off, the winery the company built in Agrelo at a cost of $2 million, according to a 2000 *USA Today* article, stood out like a sore thumb because Kendall-Jackson demanded an American-style gable-roofed barn design. "They didn't try to understand or entertain the local vernacular," says Laurence Odfjell, the Norwegian architect of Kendall-Jackson's wineries in Chile and Argentina (and the chairman of his family's giant shipping conglomerate). "It's a terrible-looking building; it's a shed. But we were not given any options. They wanted a gabled roof. That's what they wanted." The building worked fine, but its design was emblematic of the company's general deafness to local mores. Kendall-Jackson's leaders expected that they could act as they would in the United States and that, as had happened in Chile, Argentina would accept them as they were. But they soon learned that Argentina and Chile were almost diametrically opposed cultures. "Randy was very familiar with Chile, but Argentina was a very different world. Chile is open to outsiders and helping them do business. Argentina is who you know, and family and corruption and time," says Greg Adams, an American of Greek ethnicity who wears gaucho pants and could almost pass for Argentine. In the face of this reality, Kendall-Jackson dug in and refused to adapt.

"The reason we had non-Argentines there was because we wanted to instill a culture as we did in Chile or elsewhere. There was a way we wanted things done. How to make wine, how to grow grapes, how to account for things, how to do the financial records. We're very strict and have some very focused plans. It's our way or the highway," says Ullom. "There were a lot of roadblocks because in Argentina there is this expectation of how to get things done. And we don't do that. If it costs $2,000 and is to be delivered on Friday, we expect that. If they say, 'Well, you know, it's $2,000 and will be delivered in two months, or if you can pay this extra it will be ready in five days,' we don't do that. We're proud of it."

Noble as its principles might have been, Kendall-Jackson's ethical rigidity put obstacles in the path of company growth. And that made it vulnerable. In 2002, Argentina defaulted on its international debt, and the peso was delinked from the American dollar. With the devaluation, the local currency lost almost three-fourths of its value. Exhausted after years of struggle—fighting against the Argentine way, paying to change the brand name, facing a terrible El Niño–soaked harvest in 1998 (the worst in recent memory), and then suffering the economic collapse— Jess Jackson decided that Argentina wasn't worth the trouble. He sold the venture in 2003 to a Buenos Aires couple for a reported $2.5 million— a $5.5 million loss on his reported $8 million investment, according to the *Wine Spectator.* "With no economic assurances from the government anymore, and having thirty-five years of experience with South American governments, it was clear that the financial future and economic state of this country were nebulous," Ullom told *Wine Business Monthly* in 2007. "We had a tremendous degree of commitment up until the government failed with its commitment."

Kendall-Jackson's sudden exit was a great disappointment to many of those who had worked with them in Argentina. The Americans were supposed to point the local *bodegas* toward innovative and more corporate, professional ways of running a winery—the methods that had made California great. Kendall-Jackson had broken long-standing traditions by, for example, buying very-high-altitude land, stressing its vines with the bare minimum of water, and filling its *bodega* with small (2,000- to 8,000-liter) stainless steel tanks so that it could ferment each vineyard parcel separately to determine its *terroir*'s unique characteristics. The company was ahead of its time. These are the protocols that many of Argentina's top wineries today follow in their search for the best *terroir.*

"Go to high elevations, have a lot of little lots, don't water a lot, have a lot of good barrels, and keep everything separate. Everybody thought we were nuts for isolating each block with its own tank," says Randy Ullom. "In those days they said you're totally off your rocker."

In the end, Kendall-Jackson was forced out of town by its refusal to meet the local culture halfway. It was a sad day for the industry—the failure and departure of the first big American investment in Argentine wine country. It would also turn out to be the last. No other notable American winery has opened an Argentine branch since.

"Working down there as an American, trying to do things an American way . . . It's all connections," says Hanson. "If you notice, now most of the Argentine wineries with foreign money partner with Argentines. That's a smart thing to do because you can figure out how the system runs."

It was a different story in the new Tikal, where the years of effort were paying off for Nicolás Catena's fine-wine company, Bodega Catena Zapata. His wine business was pulling in a reported $100 million a year, according to a 2001 *Los Andes* article by Darío Gallardo about the opening of his pyramid, making Catena, "one of the few local survivors of a sector that has gone through a phenomenal process of consolidation and foreign takeover." His yearning for international recognition was also being fulfilled. In August 2001, the legendary *New York Times* writer R. W. Apple lathered him with this praise: "Dr. Nicolás Catena is changing things; not single-handedly, exactly, any more than Michael Jordan single-handedly won pro basketball championships for the Chicago Bulls," Apple wrote. "But he has shown customers in North America, as well as friendly rivals here, what Mendoza can do at every price level. At 61, slight, soft-spoken and studious-looking in rimless glasses, he is the acknowledged star, the pacemaker, the public face of the Argentine wine industry."

But it was the 2000 release of the first wine to bear his full name—the 1997 Nicolás Catena Zapata Cabernet-Malbec blend elaborated by José Galante—that offered Catena the icon status he so long had cherished. "Unevolved and supple, with enormous concentration and richness in addition to a funky, grilled meat flavor, this huge, full-bodied wine is surprisingly well-balanced and symmetrical for its size," wrote Robert Parker Jr. in a June 2000 note giving it a 95-point rating.

To convince the world that he deserved a permanent place among the wine elite, three weeks after his pyramid winery opening, Catena sent his first eponymous wine on a seven-stop blind-tasting tour. After passing through top hotels and restaurants in Boston, New York, and four other US cities, the tour would land in London's Dorchester Hotel, where, at a $13,000 lunch attended by UK wine press luminaries like Jancis Robinson and Oz Clarke, it would go up against giant wines from Château Haut-Brion, Château Latour, Opus One, and Caymus. The plan was to re-create the 1976 Judgment of Paris tasting that had shocked the wine-drinking world and launched American wine. There were differences between the two events, of course. While the original tasting could be framed as a spontaneous and friendly Franco-American taste test, this one was tailored to use the objectivity of blind tasting to showcase Catena's top wine alongside the established greats.

In choosing the 1997 vintage for his first Nicolás Catena Zapata blend, Catena had a stroke of luck. In order to compare apples to apples, all the wines in the test would be from the same year. Nineteen ninety-seven had been an outstanding year for Argentine *bodegueros*, but the harvest had not been a great one for many of the industry's leaders. Robert Parker Jr. gave the 1997 vintages of both Latour and Haut-Brion 89 points—respectable but unimpressive ratings for wines that cost well north of a hundred dollars a bottle—and the Opus One got 88 points and the label of "a disappointment." The Caymus Special Selection fared even worse: the *Wine Spectator* gave it a miserly 86.

Whether the Argentines did a great job picking the competition or just got lucky with the vintage year, the tasting definitely succeeded. Shocking many, the 1997 Nicolás Catena Zapata came in first place five times and second twice. "It was one of the most gratifying moments of my wine career when I saw the faces of those so-called experts when they realized they'd selected an Argentine wine," says Catena's then US importer Alfredo Bartholomaus.

...

As the Catena empire grew and took a leading role in the industry, much of the original crew departed to make their own mark. After seven years at the company, Marina Gayan left in 2000. "I was very much part of the family, but not really. I wasn't going to inherit the winery, and I was killing myself. I respected them all and loved working for Catena, but it was not mine. And I did not have a life. I had 1.5 million miles on United," Gayan says. Nicolás and his brother Jorge, who had lost one of his sons in the horrific 1992 car accident, also fought about the role of their children in the company. Jorge thought his daughter should have a position in the business. But even though his own daughter Laura was involved, Nicolás told his brother no. After an acrimonious fight, Jorge left with an old family vineyard in La Consulta that had been their father Domingo's favorite property. (There, with his son and daughter, he produces wines called Ricominciare—Italian for "to begin again.") And Pedro Marchevsky left in 2002 to join his then-wife Susana Balbo, who had managed Catena's exports and the construction of the pyramid, at their own Dominio del Plata Winery.

Marchevsky and Balbo made for a combustible pair. Now considered one of Argentina's top winemakers, Balbo says she was only the second woman licensed in enology in Argentina when she graduated in Mendoza in 1981, and the first to work as a winemaker in the country. "Women were not considered to be able to be in charge of anything," says the blonde, weathered Balbo. As a woman, the only winemaking job she could find was outside of Mendoza, at Sucesión Michel Torino in Salta, where she stayed for nine years. The first owner had a heart attack; the second lost the winery during a bout of hyper-inflation; and the third didn't pay her salary for a year. Still one of the few female winemakers in the male-dominated business, the strong-willed Balbo is, not surprisingly, often described as difficult. Like her ex-husband Marchevsky, she is unafraid to speak her mind.

After returning to Mendoza in early 1990, Balbo launched the Lovaglio-Balbo winery. Faced with an inflationary spiral (prices rose 20,000 percent between March 1989 and March 1990), she performed the kind of absurd financial juggling that is taken for granted in Argentina. With prices changing daily, each Monday morning (and on some Wednesdays) she woke at 5 a.m., called her cork and bottle suppliers for the day's prices, marked up her own list, and then at 8 a.m. called her customers for their orders—which in turn required payment by noon so she could pay the suppliers. It was a dangerous game.

Balbo nearly lost everything in 1994 when a new client came with a dream offer: a $350,000 purchase of 25,000 cases of wine, or over three months of normal sales. Suspicious, she said she needed collateral before she invested in making the wine. After turning down the deed on a meat-processing plant—"I said, 'We're not a real estate company,'" Balbo recalls—she agreed to accept an insurance policy that guaranteed payment. But then the client's checks began to bounce, and the insurance company claimed that the policy forms had been stolen. "Imagine the desperation," says Balbo, now fifty-five. Only when she talked with one of the insurance company's former executives, whom she'd met while in Salta, did she manage to extract a 70 percent payout to pay her bank and suppliers. Six months later, she sold the *bodega* and took to spending as much time as possible working in U.S. wineries. "I couldn't deal with the unstable business environment in Argentina while I was raising two kids," she says.

But it was the departure of Paul Hobbs that signaled the true break between the *bodega*'s start-up stage and the new era of entrenched power. The *bodeguero* and Hobbs had developed an almost familial bond. "He was actually like a father to me, and I think he saw me as a son as well," Hobbs says. They were united in the struggle to redefine Argentine wine; it was them against the world. "Paul Hobbs had worked for Opus One and Simi, but he wasn't the Paul you know now, who gets three pages in the *Wine Spectator* and is considered some sort of pope," says Marina Gayan. "He was not famous at all. That's why it worked. He and Catena grew together." But as they became the leaders of the local wine world and their international reputations grew, so did the friction over who should get the credit. In the early years, Hobbs had been the public face for the retiring Catena, the smooth voice that enticed the American wine press— and collected the Argentine's accolades. So much so that a 1996 article by Tom Stockley in the *Seattle Times* about Argentine wines referred to the *bodega*'s entry-level Malbec, Cabernet Sauvignon, and Chardonnay export line, Alamos Ridge, as "an affordable line actually made by an American, Paul Hobbs," without mentioning the Catena name.

But now that the business had taken off, the *bodeguero* Catena wanted rightful credit for the transformation he had conceived, financed, and led. Hobbs had already taught Catena's winemakers almost every technique he could, and the American's continued presence was confusing matters. "Paul left in a certain moment because I didn't need him anymore," Catena says today. "There came a moment in which his name was very associated with the business—too associated—and I considered that that wasn't good for me. He understood perfectly." Hobbs, however, remembers the end somewhat differently. Though he agrees that Catena wanted to be known for pioneering Argentine wine and Malbec—"I don't blame him," he says—he contends that the major issue was money. Hobbs worked as the original importer for the entry-level brand Alamos on the oral agreement, he says, that if the importing went well, Catena would allow him to import the rest of the company's brands.

Whatever the reason, the 1997 harvest was Hobbs's last. Once he left, the family made sure that no foreign consultant would again get such an outsized piece of the glory. "After Paul they got really kind of stung because most of the credit for the styles and the caliber of their wine went to him," says Scott Peterson, the owner of Sonoma's S.P. Drummer Wines and a consultant who worked for Catena for several years after Hobbs left. "There was like a memorandum that you do not promote the American consultant, you do not promote Scott Peterson. 'This is an Argentine wine made by Argentines.'"

The *bodeguero* and the consultant go out of their way to say that they continue to be friends, and they still work together—they're partners in Sonoma County's Paul Hobbs Winery, and Hobbs consults for some Catena properties—but they compete mightily over credit for Argentina's boom.

In the company history on the Bodega Catena Zapata website, Paul Hobbs—arguably the man behind the wines that first propelled the firm onto the international stage—is not mentioned. In person, Nicolás Catena is equally clear about Hobbs's role in the development of the wine that has come to define Argentina: Malbec. "Paul? He had nothing to do with Malbec. Absolutely nothing," he says.

Hobbs feels quite the opposite. "I'm proud of my work on the Chardonnay and helping Nicolás get that started, but I'm more proud of the work I did to kind of uncover Malbec," he says. Hobbs says he worked heartily on Malbec early on, experimenting on premium elaborations of the varietal despite Catena's lack of interest. For the American, Catena stories like that of his father's end-of-life exhortation to look into Malbec are more mythmaking than strict reality. "Nicolás has romanticized the thing, and it sounds wonderful," says Hobbs. "But I'm sorry to say Nicolás was a stick-in-the-mud when I wanted to make Malbec." It is clear that their breakup troubles Hobbs to this day.


In the end, even though Hobbs and Catena's tight friendship finally chilled, the relationship between the foreign consultants and their Argentine clients continued to be symbiotic in the mutual beneficial way of the clown-fish and the sea anemone. The consulting winemakers helped Argentina's *bodegueros* mend their ways and turn this South American outpost into a wine power, and the international visibility the *bodegueros* provided them gave them renown and access to capital that they in turn used to turbo-charge their own careers. "They enriched us a lot," says former Trapiche winemaker Ángel Mendoza, "and we enriched them too."

# CHAPTER 10

## THE NEW PRINCES OF
## ARGENTINE WINE

Achával-Ferrer partners Santiago Achával Becú and Manuel Ferrer Minetti, and winery
operations manager Diego Rosso (left to right), in their recently purchased
Finca Altamira vineyard in 1999. Courtesy of Santiago Achával.

S ANTIAGO ACHÁVAL BECÚ looked at the 20-acre vineyard that Italian winemaker Roberto Cipresso had just convinced him to buy, sight unseen, for some $120,000 in cash. It was unkempt and full of weeds and trash, the head posts of its rows so broken that vine trellises lay flat on the ground. The vineyard's only nod to respectability was a ramshackle caretaker's adobe house. The exact words Achával then spoke on that Monday in March 1999 have been lost to history, but they more or less boiled down to a carefully chosen question: "Are you out of your fucking mind?"

The thing was, Achával was already familiar with the property. The previous week he and Cipresso had been driving in the high-altitude Uco Valley near the town of La Consulta, scouting locations for a high-tech vineyard. The idea was to start from scratch with top varietal clones; install a weather station, drip irrigation, and neutron probe sensors (for measuring soil moisture); and run everything from a computer—the whole thing as space age as a satellite. But they found nothing worth buying. On the way back they had passed a miserable-looking vineyard—*this* grungy patch, their new $120,000 dump—and Achával had turned to Cipresso and said, "How much better *our* vineyard will be." A few days later, after Achával had returned to spend the weekend with his family at their home in the city of Córdoba, Argentina, some 375 miles east of Mendoza, Cipresso had called. He had asked Achával meaningfully and repeatedly if Achával trusted him. Because, Cipresso said, he had found land that was producing grapes with the potential to make a world-class wine—wine that had a sense of place, of *terroir*—and he needed to sign immediately to stave off a competing bidder. Imagining greatness, Achával had acquiesced. And this was what Cipresso brought him?

Three days after questioning Cipresso's sanity, Achával was out in his new vineyard—named Finca Altamira—overseeing the picking of the dilapidated vines. The vineyard's grape yield was so low that the seller had sold Achával and his partners the property for the price of empty land. "The assumption was that we were going to pull it out and plant some young, vigorous Chardonnay or whatever," Achával says. "At that point nobody was interested in old-vine Malbec." Two-thirds of the seventy-five-year-old vines weren't producing grapes, and the average production was less than one pound per plant. Because pickers were paid by volume and at a typical high-volume overhead-canopy vineyard a worker could pick more than sixty pounds from each plant, no one wanted to work Achával's vineyard. So Achával and his partners began paying the pickers by the day instead of by weight, and for good measure they overhired to get picking done by eleven o'clock in the morning, before the day got hot.

"We paid for an expensive harvest," Achával says. Expensive, but the start of something great.

If Catena and his contemporaries had started a trend, a new generation of risk-taking oenological entrepreneurs like Santiago Achával, some homegrown and some from abroad, would build a fine-wine movement. They came from *bodegas* like Achával-Ferrer, Paul Hobbs's Viña Cobos, the Chilean-owned Renacer, the Susana Balbo–Pedro Marchevsky project Dominio del Plata, Roberto de la Mota's Mendel Wines, José Alberto Zuccardi's Familia Zuccardi, the Spanish-owned O. Fournier, and Swiss *bodeguero* Donald Hess's Colomé. These new pioneers took the precepts of Argentine fine wine that their predecessors had perceived—Malbec (preferably from old vines), high altitudes, low yields, and the use of new technology—and amplified them. They delved deep into Malbec's DNA, climbed even higher up Argentina's dizzying mountainsides, cut yields to infinitesimal amounts, and turned their vineyards into MIT-level laboratories. And in doing so, these new princes of Argentine wine launched a wave of icon vintages—often with wallet-wrenching hundred-plus-dollar price tags—that solidified Argentina's reputation as a producer comparable to the best in the world, even France. Sales followed: after five years of exports in the range of $150 million, Argentine foreign wine sales jumped to $231 million in 2004 and $379 million in 2006. It was a great time to be exporting Argentine wine, in part because the 2002 devaluation of the peso had lowered the wine industry's costs and made winemaking incredibly lucrative. An Argentine winery's expenses—labor, grapes, and the like—were now mostly in weak pesos, which had lost 70 percent of their value against the US dollar. But the wineries still sold their exported wine in dollars, which left them with extraordinary profits.

This is not to say that it was easy. After leaving Catena in 1997, Hobbs launched a winery with local friends: winemaker Luis Barraud and his wife, Andrea Marchiori, a viticulturist whose family owned an eighty-year-old Malbec vineyard. He put in $40,000 to match $40,000 from Marchiori and Barraud, and the partners named the venture Viña Cobos, after the neighboring Agrelo road that also passes Catena's pyramid.

The first years brought disaster after disaster. In 1998, abnormally wet weather caused by one of the strongest El Niño patterns ever recorded led to twenty days of rain during the March harvest season, resulting in Argentina's worst wines in recent memory (despite the greatness of the 1997 vintage, Catena didn't even bother to produce a Nicolás Catena Zapata blend in 1998). In 1999, Hobbs tried to make up lost ground by contracting fruit from another grape grower. But after overseeing the vineyard all year, Hobbs was crestfallen to learn that the owner had sold the crop to another buyer just before the harvest. "What are you going to do?" Hobbs told a *Los Angeles Times* reporter in a 2006 article. "Contracts in Argentina mean nothing." In the summer of 2000, just days before antihail netting was supposed to be delivered, the random fury of Andean hailstorms slammed the Marchiori land, stripping the vineyards of grapes and leaves.

And then at the end of 2001, Argentina's economy collapsed. The country defaulted on $95 billion in loans, and the official one-to-one peg between the US dollar and the peso was removed. Freed from its mooring, the peso lost 70 percent of its value, impoverishing most Argentines and causing a violent wave of citizen revolt that cycled the country through five presidents in three weeks. While the devaluation made the wine industry more profitable, it killed those who had money in the country. When Hobbs finally got back into Viña Cobos's Argentine bank accounts, he found that they had been converted from dollars to pesos, eviscerating their value overnight. "The money was just gone," Hobbs said.

Swiss-born wine magnate Donald Hess (owner of Napa's Hess Collection) had a similarly difficult time getting into the Argentine wine business. After visiting the high desert of Salta with his sister and great aunt in 1996 and being blown away by a Malbec-Cabernet blend from a super-high-altitude winery called Colomé (founded in 1831), he fell in love with the idea of pressing the altitude limit and buying that *bodega*. "When I tasted it in a restaurant, I just thought, this is a raw diamond," he told British wine writer Jancis Robinson. At 7,500 feet above sea level, some 2,600 feet higher than Catena's Adrianna vineyard, Hess thought that Colomé's extreme elevation would offer all the advantages of altitude in spades.

"The UV radiation causes the skin to become thicker, and as they do that they get more phenolics, more tannins, more anthocyanin pigments, which gives the wines very dark colors. And if you let them hang on the vine, which is easy to do because we have little risk of rain, you get big but round and velvety wines," says Randle Johnson, Hess's chief winemaker. "You have good concentration and a great color and wonderful mouthfeel and tannins that are age worthy. With all that combined, you get rocket fuel wines."

But the location was so remote that overflowing rivers kept Hess from actually visiting Colomé for two years. When he finally did manage to buy the land in 2001, two years after buying a smaller plot nearby, he encountered enormous problems getting electricity up to the site, which lies three hours up a dirt road. Hess ended up spending $350,000 to install a 260-kilowatt electric plant, including an Italian hydroelectric turbine and two diesel generators, to power the winery and hotel on his 96,000-acre property. (The four hundred residents of the village that came with the property are responsible for their own power; some have solar power, some have small generators, and some go without electricity.) He planted 150 acres to go along with the 25 acres of fifty- to one-hundred-year-old vines already growing there—pushing the desert water levels to their limit—and then he pressed higher still. In 2004, at a ranch he had bought a few months before Colomé near a tiny town called Payogasta, Hess planted an experimental vineyard called Altura Máxima ("maximum altitude"), whose Malbec and Pinot Noir vines, at 10,000 feet, qualify as the highest in the world, Johnson says.

Like Hess, another foreign-born *bodeguero*—Spaniard José Manuel Ortega Gil-Fournier—made the quixotic decision to grow grapes in a corner of Argentine wine country that seemed perfectly happy without him. A rumpled forty-three-year-old with a black beard that runs from his upper cheek to middle neck, Ortega comes from a family whose

Heraclio Fournier S.A. playing-card company (founded in 1832) was the biggest in Europe when it was sold to the United States Playing Card Company in 1986. While working as a banker for Goldman Sachs in London in the mid-nineties, Ortega noticed that whereas the prices of top Bordeaux reds were rising handily, equally good wines from his country weren't even present at wine auctions. Figuring there was a great arbitrage opportunity in this, he began to buy and warehouse top Spanish reds, hoping to make a smart profit when Sotheby's and Christie's realized their mistake. "I decided to invest in bottles. I always said worse comes to worst I can always drink it," says Ortega, who earned a double political science and economics degree at the University of Pennsylvania.

As he spent more time speaking with *bodegueros* whose wines he wanted to buy, Ortega started to think about launching his own venture. A few years later, in 1999, while starting an investment fund for Banco Santander in Latin America, a friend in Buenos Aires called him about a bankrupt Mendoza *bodega* that was looking for a buyer. When he came to kick the tires in December of that year, Ortega decided not to buy, but four months later he did pull the trigger on the purchase of a tomato farm at the desolate southern end of the Uco Valley. Adding two other farms to bring the total to 750 acres (about 250 of which are planted, some with forty-year-old vines of Tempranillo, a favorite Spanish varietal), Ortega jumped into the wine industry with the confidence of a neophyte who had overcome every other obstacle he'd faced in his life. "I started with liquidity at 5 percent interest and ended with liquidity at 14 percent alcohol," he jokes.

That confidence would prove necessary as Ortega faced a series of setbacks, some born of his own innocence and others beyond his control. The cold nights of Ortega's high-altitude vineyard were the catalyst for amazing grapes, but they brought both spring frosts that ruined the fruit before harvest and *zonda* winds, ferocious hot gusts that tear down the eastern slope of the Andes and lay waste to germinating crops. He still buys half of his grapes from outside farmers, in part to plug the gap caused by natural disasters. Ortega also had to switch construction companies in the midst of building his Bórmida y Yanzón–designed winery, losing a year in the process. And he got roughed up in the market the first few years when he tried to concentrate on blends and the Spanish varietal of Tempranillo instead of Argentina's increasingly popular Malbec.

But as exhausting as this sounds, the first thing one learns about the Spanish banker-cum-*bodeguero* is that he seems to enjoy the flagellating difficulty of becoming a winemaker. "I learned from Michel Rolland that exceptional wines are always made in borderline areas, in areas prone to disaster," Ortega says, shrugging off his weather problems.

One part marketer, one part wide-eyed wine enthusiast, Ortega travels the world selling his wines to anyone who will listen. By his own count, he spent 282 days away from home in 2009, a number that explains why Hobbs jokingly refers to this frenetic traveling salesman as the "Fuller Brush Man." Ortega had to travel, though: coming from outside the business, he had no distribution network when he started, and he had to sell every bottle himself the first few years. "The hardest part is to get the first snowflake to move. And then it goes faster and faster. Our importers may buy one pallet the first year, two the second, and a container the third," Ortega says. "My grandfather was a workaholic, and I work. I believe in work. Talent is God given, but work we decide."

But Ortega is no mere huckster or coiner of pithy phrases. Talking to him, one realizes that he has been infected by a passion for great wine, economics be damned. He has spent some $3 million on his Argentine *bodega*—not to mention the two others he has in Spain and Chile—and taken an 80 percent cut in his banker's salary, all to follow his dream of producing vintages with timeless elegance. It's a noble aim, but considering that the few wineries known for timeless elegance have been making wine for centuries in France, it seems borderline deranged to bet the farm on a product meant to be judged in twenty years, especially when the bills are due today.

"Even though we get great reviews, I think we get hurt by that style because our wines aren't that exuberant and big when they start. But as time goes on and those other wines lose their exuberance, our wines are still kicking," says Ortega. "I've always believed if you seriously want to be part of the aristocracy of wine you have to make wines that in twenty years are still incredible."

Finally, the family owners of Familia Zuccardi—Argentina's third biggest wine exporter—are nontraditional *bodegueros* who came to winemaking from the cement industry. In the early 1960s, Alberto Zuccardi, a civil engineer of Italian descent, owned a Mendoza factory that sold cement pipes and other prefabricated cement construction products. Eager to expand his pipe sales, in 1963 he planted a vineyard in Mendoza's desert east side, in an area not known for grapes, and, using his prefabricated pipes, installed an early irrigation system called Cimalco. The idea was that grape growers would see how easy it was for Cimalco to turn a desert into a vineyard—to use it, one split up a vineyard into quarter-acre plots and flooded them every seven to ten days with water pumped from a well—and snap up his prefab pipes. Cimalco never really caught on, but something more important happened: Alberto Zuccardi fell in love with wine, and five years later he began to build a *bodega*.

Now run by the founder's son José Alberto Zuccardi, who joined the business in 1976, the pipe magnate's company grew in a way that wouldn't normally mark it for wine industry greatness. From vineyards planted in the dismissed pergola style in Mendoza's broiling east, the company harvested grapes that it fermented and sold as bulk wine for the first decade of its existence. It was only in the eighties, after José Alberto began to convert the vineyards to fine-wine varietals, that it began to sell its own bottled wine; in the 1990s it began to export. And even then, it sold its wines in a more "Chilean" manner than that followed by Catena and others: instead of creating a reputation higher up and using that reputation to sell wine further down, it started at the bottom of the price scale.

But while the Zuccardi family was selling ever-increasing amounts of inexpensive wine, that wasn't all they were doing. Without a wine industry background to constrain their ideas, the Zuccardis grew obsessed with experimenting with grapes that weren't considered fine-wine material to see if they could find the country's next great grape. In the 1960s and '70s, Alberto and José Alberto planted the Spanish grape Tempranillo, a variety that had been grown in the country since the eighteenth century but had not generally been used for fine wine. They also planted Bonarda. Called Charbono in the United States and Corbeau in France, Bonarda is the second-most-planted grape in Argentina and produces a dark, fruity, easy-drinking wine; but it, too, was long thought to be good only for bulk vintages. In 1997, José Alberto made Zuccardi Q Tempranillo, what he calls the country's first premium Tempranillo, and followed with attempts at high-end Bonarda.

"My father said he had a piece of luck: he didn't have a tradition to follow. He had to discover everything. He didn't have a dogma," says José Alberto, a voluble man with a close-cropped gray beard. "People said you can't make quality Bonarda, quality Tempranillo. But we did. I think you need to wake up every day and find what to do that day, not think about the previous day."

Bonarda turned out to be a prescient choice for an up-and-coming *bodeguero*: Between 2002 and 2008, the amount of Bonarda exported from Argentina grew 261 percent, from $1.5 million to $5.6 million, according to the Mendoza wine consultancy Caucasia Wine Thinking. The price of each case of wine sold—a representation of the value given to the grape—also grew, by 24 percent.

Quickly entranced by experimentation, Familia Zuccardi started bottling increasingly obscure grapes. Today, one wing of the vast Zuccardi *bodega* is filled with small (3,000- to 8,000-liter) tanks filled with more than thirty-five rarely seen varieties like Caladoc, Ancellotta, Marselan, and Touriga Nacional. There are other experiments too, such as a port-like Malbec called Malamado (whose name, roughly meaning "badly loved," is laden with Argentina's tango-fed nostalgia). What is also unique about the Zuccardi *bodega* is how its meticulous self-presentation manages to stand out in an industry famous for its image grooming. The charismatic and friendly José Alberto is known among wine writers for his willingness to answer any question, anytime, with thought and detail. (*Washington Post* wine columnist Dave McIntyre aptly writes that Zuccardi is "one of the easiest interviews ever. All you have to do is say 'Hello.'") And during my visit to the *bodega*, when I asked why several employees were wrapping new oak barrels in a large roll of plastic wrap, José Alberto's son Sebastián told me they didn't like the barrels to get dirty. "Because if we don't, when we put them in the barrel room they'll be very stained," said Sebastián. This was pretty far from the adobe huts of Mendoza's colonial era.

But while José Alberto Zuccardi may be known for his eccentric wine experiments, unfashionable *bodega* location, and curious irrigation system, it was an old-fashioned business decision—to concentrate on inexpensive and dependable before trying to go too high on the price scale—that made his *bodega* very successful (and angered others in the industry, who worried that he would cheapen the Argentine brand). Critics did not always celebrate the Familia Zuccardi wines; for the first decade, *Wine Spectator* scores for the "Q" premium Tempranillo wavered between the upper 70s and mid-80s. But José Alberto's dedication to providing a solid product for a reasonable price—a good value—set him apart from his artistic Old World industry and helped to build a loyal clientele. While other *bodegueros* talk about the *bodega* founded by their great grandfather, José Alberto has posted in his winery signs that read, in part, "Who is the boss? . . . the boss is always the same, The Customer . . . He doesn't think about whether our business is one hundred years old."

At times, this customer-focused mentality brought success with such speed—and from such unexpected quarters—that it was almost funny. In 2004 the company began to export an entry-level Malbec-Syrah blend called Fuzion—named for Argentina's fusing of grapes, cultures, and climates, with a "z" from Zuccardi—to the European market. As it did so, it applied to sell Fuzion in several Canadian provinces with state liquor monopolies. The wine achieved modest success in Europe, but when Zuccardi managed to place it in the Canadian state stores, sales immediately, and almost inexplicably, took off. There had been no advertising, no splashy introduction, but the C$7.45 price (about US$6.75 at the time) grabbed the fancy of Canadian drinkers and wine reviewers.

"Producers of $15 Australian shiraz and $20 California merlot should be afraid of Familia Zuccardi Fuzion Shiraz Malbec 2007 . . . Very afraid," wrote Beppi Crosariol, a wine writer at Toronto's *Globe and Mail* newspaper, in an article titled "Run, Don't Walk, to Taste This under-$8 Treasure." "Based on quality versus price—admittedly a metric wine consumers with lots of California cabernet and red Bordeaux in their cellars will consider irrelevant—this Argentine red is off the charts."

In 2009, Fuzion was the top seller for the Liquor Control Board of Ontario—the first time in the liquor board's eighty-two-year history that a wine topped the charts. Government-controlled stores sold the absurd amount of 419,000 cases of the stuff in the province (population: 13.1 million), more than the total sales of all thirteen Yellow Tail products, the bargain Australian line that had, until then, dominated the wine category in Canada. More than a beverage, Fuzion was Canada's first great Internet wine sensation. "People were talking about it on blogs and at parties, on Facebook, via text messaging, on BlackBerrys and in chat rooms," Shari Mogk-Edwards, vice president of merchandising for the liquor control board, said in a *Toronto Star* article.

In 2010, Zuccardi exported $40 million of wine, including 900,000 cases of Fuzion.

Despite the difficulties they faced, frontier winemakers like Hess, Hobbs, and Ortega would be rewarded for their persistence. The only wine Hobbs managed to release before 2002, the 1,000 cases of his 1999 Cobos Malbec, got 95 points in the *Wine Advocate* and 92 from the *Wine Spectator*; and the *Wine Advocate* gave his "near perfect" 2006 version a rare 99-point score (it was apparently lust at first taste: "A glass-coating, saturated opaque purple/black in color, the wine offers up a sexy/kinky bouquet of pain grille, Asian spices, pencil lead, mineral, lavender, blueberry, and black cherry"). Perhaps more important, after pouring almost $1.5 million of his own money down what must have seemed an ever-swirling drain, Hobbs must be gratified that his iconic wines go for up to $200 dollars a bottle and Viña Cobos pulls in some $4.5 million a year.

Similarly, Hess's limited vintage of 250 cases of the ninety-dollar 2003 Bodega Colomé Reserva collected 93 points from both magazines ("a wine to spread on toast," the *Wine Spectator* said in curious praise of the "extreme" Malbec–Cabernet Sauvignon blend that "smells and looks like Port, with molasses and blueberry aromas and inky color"). And the quixotic Spaniard Ortega proved that his twenty-year dream was not absurd. In a review giving it 91 points, the *Wine Advocate* described the 2006 vintage of his top wine, Alfa Crux Malbec, as follows: "Dense, concentrated, and structured on the palate, it has layers of succulent fruit, spicy flavors, and enough structure to evolve for 4–6 years. This impeccably balanced wine will offer a drinking window extending from 2014 to 2026." Ortega is finally making some money too: a decade after launching, his Argentine *bodega* sold $4.5 million in wine in 2010. Even Zuccardi got in on the high-end act: the "fleshy and supple" 2005 Familia Zuccardi Zeta, a Malbec-Tempranillo blend that goes for around forty dollars, got 93 points from the *Wine Advocate*.

But it was Achával and his partners who came to personify the risk-taking mentality of the new generation of winemakers. Starting with their first vintage, Achával-Ferrer's Malbecs and blends turned heads for being very Argentine and simultaneously very different from their kin. (The *Wine Spectator* gave 91 points to their eighty-five-dollar Finca Altamira 1999 Malbec and curiously described it as something akin to a torched fruit cannery: "This inky wine smells like raspberry ganache, with lots of toast and smoke laying over superripe blackberry and cassis fruit.") Achával and his partners Cipresso and Ferrer questioned every procedure, no matter how basic. Today the iconoclastic *bodega* has become a figurehead for Argentina, and a 2010 *Wine Spectator* profile of Santiago Achával was titled "The Master of Malbec."

A short, open, friendly man with a squinty smile and a puff of black hair parted on the side, Achával is an interloper in Argentina's wine world. For one thing, his voice is completely miscast. An Argentine born in Minnesota, he sounds less like an impassioned winemaker than an extra from the movie *Fargo* when he says things like, "We don't have a coolin' system or air conditionin' or any of that." His career path doesn't fit, either: a self-described "wine enthusiast"—not an oenologist or *bodeguero* with a family history—Achával, like Alberto Zuccardi, made his way in the world tending the finances of a cement company.

Achával was getting an MBA at Stanford University, paid for by the Córdoba-based cement manufacturer he worked for, when he, like Catena before him, fell in love with the fine wines of northern California. Unlike Catena's epiphany, however, the less wealthy Achával's wine enlightenment didn't come in a wine bottle, but rather from the culture of the industry. "There was no epiphany wine, because I didn't have the money for epiphany wines. My budget was five dollars for everyday wines and fifteen dollars for parties or Sundays," he says. "I started enjoying the vineyards and cellars more than the tasting rooms, and by the end of the semester I realized that I was hooked and this is what I wanted to do."

Once back in Córdoba, he plotted his course to the *bodeguero* life. He gave the cement firm the five years he had promised in exchange for his MBA, and then he set about making money by developing gated communities near Córdoba. He bought and tasted tons of wines and read insatiably, from books about oenology and viticulture to journals from the American Society for Enology and Viticulture. And then through his winery partner Manuel Ferrer Minetti, a shareholder in the cement company, he met Roberto Cipresso, a consultant and winemaker famed for his work in Montalcino, Italy, who later created a special cuvée for Pope John Paul II to mark the 2000 papal jubilee. At the feet of the crooner-attractive Cipresso, who would soon become a partner in the Achával-Ferrer *bodega*, the *Fargo*-accented Argentine learned the tenets that would come to guide the company: that wine is shaped in the vineyard and not just manipulated to greatness by the winemaker, and that vineyard *terroirs* are all unique, even if they're only fifty yards apart.

Cipresso believes that the winemaker's job is to uncover the beauty inherent in a parcel of land, echoing Michelangelo's statement that "every block of stone has a statue inside it and it is the task of the sculptor to discover it." This philosophy explains why, after finding that beauty in the grapes he tasted in the tumbledown Finca Altamira vineyard in 1999, he was driven to buy the land immediately, by tricking his partner if necessary.

The usual goal of New World winemaking is to bring out as much of a grape's fruit flavor as possible—to make a Malbec seem as "Malbec-y" as possible. Conventional wisdom holds that winemakers should take concentrated late-harvest grapes and, after a cool fermentation, engage in extended maceration to suck out every last iota of color, flavor, aroma, and tannin. Though they did not set themselves up in opposition to this prevailing "hedonistic fruit bomb" style identified with Michel Rolland and Robert Parker Jr., Achával and Cipresso had goals that veered sharply from it. Their desires were low alcohol, high acidity, and subtle fruit flavors. Cipresso and Achával wanted something unique.

"In the end I think the consumer craves originality. Merlot that tastes like Merlot from anywhere can't be original. Uniqueness comes from a unique plot of land that gives identity to grapes," says Achával. "The way to be original is not to say, 'Here's my Merlot,' but, 'Here's my vineyard.'"

To get the strongest expression of the local *terroir* in each grape, Achával and Cipresso decided to use very old Malbec vineyards—vines with history—and prune heavily to create low yields, sometimes less than one ton per acre. Getting the yields down to the extreme bottom of the scale had the added bonus of speeding the maturing process of the grapes, which let them harvest about three weeks earlier than everyone else. This early ripening modified the character of the wines produced. Because the grapes weren't in the sun as long, which meant less sugar developed and less acid respired out, the ensuing wines were less boozy and had higher acidity. (In 2010, Achával-Ferrer's average alcohol level was 13.5 percent, a few points below the most "hedonistic" Malbecs.) It also meant that the varietal fruit flavors hadn't morphed into intense stewed fruit tastes that obscured the delicate mineral notes beneath. But having great fruit was one thing; getting to great wine would mean inventing a new kind of winery.

Their first step was deciding not to build one yet. When the Argentine economy imploded in 2001 and 2002, the partners' initial investment, intended for winery construction, was in US dollars. With their suddenly powerful savings the partners decided to put off the winery and acquire land. "I said, we're leasing all these vineyards that we know are terrific; let's buy them," Achával says.

This decision bought them time to think, and what they built shows what they learned. In the Achával-Ferrer *bodega* that finally opened in 2006 in Pedriel, just north of Agrelo, they created a winery that is a rejection of almost every other one in Argentina—neither a traditional *bodega* nor a colossal modernist monument. If it has any architectural root in Argentina's winemaking past, it is in the wine factories built during the mid-twentieth-century bulk-wine boom. A rather ugly structure, the winery is a functional brick warehouse box with a wriggly tin roof that sits hard up against a parched stretch of the Río Mendoza.

"We didn't even hire an architect. We said architects like to do two things: one, make statements, sometimes extravagant and, two, spend your money, because they normally earn a percentage. And we don't want to make statements or have our ego flaunted in newspapers. We want to make wine," says Achával. "So we drew the blueprints ourselves and gave them to an engineer and said, 'Make sure this doesn't fall down.'"

The structure shows how Cipresso's romanticism and Achával's pragmatism have merged. Much of the building is made of recycled scrap collected from an obsolete factory. The *bodega*'s builder was demolishing another site while constructing the winery, so he rescued railway ties and used them for windowsills. Achával's *lapacho* wood office door comes from a sixty-year-old railroad scale, the inch-thick steel center axle of the spiral staircase was once a compressed air pipe, and the roof trusses served the same function in the demolished factory. Unlike in most *bodegas*, the floors are painted cream to show stains, and there are no drains running along the hallway between the cement fermentation tanks. Such drains are considered sanitary norms at most *bodegas*, but during the six years they worked in an old winery rented from the Furlotti family, Achával and his partners discovered that most damaging microorganism blooms emanated from the culverts and exit pipe. When it comes time to clean, the workers at Achával-Ferrer simply spray down the floor and squeegee the water right out the door.

The true heart of Achával-Ferrer's philosophy sits hidden behind the walls of the *bodega*'s cement tanks. To get good acidity, lower sugar, and fewer overpowering fruit flavors, they decided to pick early. Hand in glove with this move, they reasoned that the best way to burn off any overwhelming fruitiness that remained was to ferment warm, at temperatures up to some ninety-three degrees Fahrenheit. But because they picked early, the grapes' seeds were still green, and fermenting them hot would leave the wine with a ruinous and overpowering "green" vegetal flavor. Unripe seeds weren't the only problem. Fermenting hot is dangerous because if the *sombrero*—the cap of skins and pulp that sits atop the juice—gets too hot or too dry, it takes on a rotten-egg stink that ruins the wine beneath. "Most winemakers on a salary stay away from warm fermentation like the plague," says Achával. "They don't get any extra for one more ratings point, but they do get killed if they ruin a tank of wine."

Achával and his partners solved these problems with low-tech ingenuity. To remove the seeds, they designed concrete tanks with bottoms that sloped toward the front, which causes precipitating grape seeds to congregate at the front valve. This, in turn, makes them shoot out first when the valve is opened. And to lower the dangers inherent in developing a hot, dry *sombrero*, Achával incessantly "pumps over"—a process whereby the juice is removed from the bottom of the tank and poured over the top of the *sombrero* in order to extract more color and flavor from the skins while simultaneously keeping them relatively cool and moist.

Done this way, Achával-Ferrer's transmutation of grape to wine feels rough-and-ready, more like two dogs rutting in an alley than the sweet caress implicit in typical winemaking. Instead of leaving the grapes' juice relaxing with the skins and pulp in extended maceration for three weeks after a cool fermentation, Achával hot-ferments for a mere week or eight days before pressing out the wine and tossing the solids. He keeps the liquid churning for a nearly continuous nineteen to twenty hours per day, cooling the pumping wine by directing a fan at the stream. (This fanning, which Achával says offers the side benefit of blowing off up to 1.5 percent of the alcohol level, would cause oxidation in a finished wine but is not a danger during fermentation.) And whereas most winemakers barrel-age their varietals for some six to nine months before mixing them into a blend, Achával combines the parts once the wine has been fermented, or sometimes even a bit earlier, and barrel-ages them premixed. This, he claims, offers more "seamless integration" between the components and makes the ensuing blends less "schizophrenic." (Like many winemakers, Achával is a bit of an amateur psychologist.) "I think the proof is in the bottle," says Achával. "There's no lack of fruit in our wines. And on top we have mineral notes, we have graphite, we have spices, we have tobacco, we have loam. We have notes that aren't just simple fruit."

It would seem that Achával and Cipresso have tapped into an unfulfilled need of Argentine-wine fanatics, at least the wealthy ones. Their wines, especially the three single-vineyard *terroir*-focused Malbecs made from low-yield old vines, have become Argentina's first real cult wines. They ask for—and often get—prices up to $120 per bottle, and in 2009, the *Wine Spectator* ranked Achával-Ferrer's three single-vineyard Malbecs among the top five coming out of Argentina (the much larger Bodega Catena Zapata was responsible for the other two). Perhaps most important, wine critics rhapsodize about the very quality Achával and Cipresso were hoping to achieve: their unique expression of *terroir*.

"The results are stunning, especially the showcase single-vineyard wines. These are Malbecs a Burgundian could love, as each is distinctively, even dramatically, different. Finca Altamira . . . displays rich, intense wild cherry-with-a tang fruit," wrote *Wine Spectator* contributor Matt Kramer in the "Master of Malbec" profile. "Its opposite is the more delicate Finca Bella Vista, which is flowery, with pronounced mineral notes—a Chambolle-Musigny among Malbecs. Finca Mirador, also in Luján de Cuyo, is rich and chocolaty, with hints of minerality, tobacco, dried cherry and spices."

While Argentina's fine-wine explosion trimmed Nicolás Catena's image as the country's only player on the international stage, the crowding of the field did not change the fact that he still led it. With the arrival of the twenty-first century, Catena brought in a new young team. When longtime vineyard director Pedro Marchevsky left to work with then-wife Susana Balbo on their Dominio del Plata Winery in 2002, Catena replaced him with Alejandro Sejanovich. Now in his early forties, Sejanovich had earned degrees in vineyard management and winemaking at the École Nationale Supérieure Agronomique de Montpellier, where he wrote theses on how irrigation is used in Mendoza to improve fruit quality and on the development of Malbec in Mendoza. With red-blond hair and a more guarded conversational style than a prototypical Italian Argentine has, Sejanovich—whose Russian Jewish ancestors escaped the pogroms and arrived in Argentina in 1900—caught Catena's eye for the academic depth of his work under Marchevsky on the clonal selection process in the *La Pirámide* Vineyard and the Adrianna vineyard planting.

Laura Catena also took a larger role in the family business. Nicolás's daughter fell in love with the wine industry in a trip to France when, invited by Jacques Lurton, she and her father met Jacques's father André, who was "always in his mud-covered plastic boots, the essence of the traditional French vigneron," in her words. "I fell in love with French wine and the history and traditions behind it," she says. She took her initial steps into the family business in the mid-1990s—first in vineyard research, where she delved into the effects of the heightened luminosity at high altitudes, then in US exports. In 1998 she cut her work in medicine to half-time and began to spend more time in Argentina. Today she is the president of the family fine-wine *bodega*, Bodega Catena Zapata, poised to be the fourth generation of Catenas to run the show.

But it is Bodega Catena Zapata's current head winemaker, Alejandro Vigil, who most clearly served as a vivid break from the past.


In an anonymous concrete-block warehouse tucked behind Bodega Catena Zapata's Mayan pyramid *bodega*, some one hundred square, white, plastic bins are lined up in aisles. There are almost no windows—light comes in through a sliding garage door—and the floor is demarcated by the yellow lines of a parking lot. Covered with sheets of black trash-bag plastic, the bins look like improvised caskets. The palatable funk of fermentation fills the air.

Vigil pulls the top off one of the bins to reveal the *sombrero* of skins and pulp that top the microfermentation of wine inside. With his fist he shoves the *sombrero* into the wine to keep it wet and to keep the liquid in contact with the flavor-rich skins. After thoroughly submerging the *sombrero*, Vigil pulls his hand free, replaces the plastic cover, and, oblivious to the purple-black juice coursing down his arm and dripping onto his jeans, walks to the next bin. These are Vigil's fermentation experiments: two hundred 500-liter boxes of fermenting grapes from parcels he has selected in the hope that one might be the basis of the next great Catena wine. Vigil is in his late thirties and has a crazed but friendly air. He has an Einsteinian flame of black curly hair, a triangular soul patch of beard, and sleep-deprived eyes. Vigil listens to punk rock by bands like Masacre 68 and Ataque 77 in his pickup, keeps nine dogs (he used to have a cow, but he gave it away), and sleeps as little as three hours between the end of one long workday and the start of the next.

Vigil discovered wine early, when he dropped out of school at age fourteen to work for a cooperative that was yanking excess vineyards to make way for vacation homes, and then went to wash cement wine pools in a *bodega* that offered him an entry-level job on the condition that he return to school. After taking over the soil analysis department of the Mendoza office of the National Agricultural Technology Institute (INTA), the rebellious Vigil came to Bodega Catena Zapata in 2002 at the age of twenty-eight, when he got into trouble at the INTA for performing his own winemaking experiments on grapes from the institute's research vineyards.

As Vigil labored in the company's research department, his personal audacity and odd fermentations caught Catena's eye—Sejanovich showed Nicolás some of the curious wines Vigil was making—and soon the quiet academic mogul grew enamored with the willful and intellectu-

288

ally curious Vigil. In July 2007, Catena promoted Vigil into José Galante's old job, and Vigil has brought his intensity and freneticism to a wine-making crew that was calmly professional after decades under Galante (not that the talented senior winemaker's skills weren't in demand; he currently is the head winemaker at the huge Dutch-owned Bodegas Salentein). The number of hours Vigil spends daily driving from vineyard to *bodega* to vineyard, tasting grapes and wines, is shocking, as is the intense relationship he has with the wines he makes. "I don't believe in flying winemakers," he says, laughing. "I don't know how you stay away from something you love for so long."

The influx of new blood invigorated Catena's already surging wine empire, and it preserved its preeminence despite hordes of new competition. In the *Wine Spectator*'s 2009 Argentine tasting guide, of the seventeen wines singled out as the best, three came from Achával-Ferrer, two from Paul Hobbs's Viña Cobos, and eight from the Catena empire. According to data on the twenty most exported Argentine wines from the Caucasia Wine Thinking consultancy, in the first 11 months of 2010 Catena's top brands brought in more than $51 million in exports alone.

Still, the glory was far from exclusively Catena's. Argentina was quickly becoming one of the world's wine powers. No longer a curiosity, Argentine wine is as easily bought in an American wine store as is a bottle from France, Italy, California, Spain, Australia, or Chile. According to Daniel Pi, the chief winemaker at Trapiche—the fine-wine brand of Argentina's second-biggest wine exporter, Peñaflor—his company's exports quintupled between 2003 and 2010, from 300,000 to 1.5 million cases; domestic sales doubled over the same period, from 700,000 to 1.4 million cases. Overall Argentine wine exports, which jumped from $230 million in 2004 to $379 million in 2006, continued to climb, to $631 million in 2008 and $734 million in 2010.

As exports climbed, Argentina caught up to its once dominant

Andean neighbor. During 2010, Argentina exported $222 million in cases of wine to the United States, $12 million more than Chile. René Merino, president of Wines of Chile, tried to dismiss the success of his country's estranged wine sibling as little more than a blip. "Today, Malbec is a fad in the United States," he said. "And once the fad has passed, Malbec consumption will decrease and we'll have to see how Argentina responds."

But for industry observers like Jay Miller, the chubby, goateed sixty-six-year-old clinical psychologist who reviews both Argentine and Chilean wines for the *Wine Advocate*, such views don't jibe with reality. "Malbec is not a fad. Right now and for the foreseeable future, Malbec looks great. I don't think Malbec will disappear," he says. "Chile has nothing to be ashamed about; their wines are doing great," he adds, chalking the competition up to "a certain enmity between the two countries, same as Spain and France."

Argentine wine has become, at last, a big international business. Inevitably, along the way it became more multinational, competitive, and corporate. Wineries are thought of and marketed as family artisanal affairs that sell handcrafted products of passion, but the business is dominated by a few conglomerates with the marketing and sales muscle to move lots of bottles of booze. According to a study from California's Marin Institute, seven companies control 82 percent of the US wine market, and big beverage companies got very interested in South America's awakening wine capital. Based in Victor, New York, Constellation Brands, the world's largest wine company, saw an opportunity in Argentina's mega-*bodega* construction boom and, in 2007, signed deals with O. Fournier and Carlos Pulenta's Bodega Vistalba to use their unused capacity to produce Diseño, an under-ten-dollar mass-market Malbec. Beverage giants Pernod Ricard, Allied Domecq, and Diageo all bought Argentine wineries. Catena got in on the act in 2007 and 2008, signing deals with E.&J. Gallo Winery to distribute several of his brands in the United States. Included was the most exported Argentine label, Alamos, which, after the deal, was quickly nicknamed "Gallamos." And in April 2011, SPI Group, the spirits company that owns Stolichnaya vodka, bought a majority share in Achával-Ferrer.

Inevitably, there were losers. Powered by Nicolás Catena's wines, Alfredo Bartholomaus's South American wine import business grew from 3,000 cases in 1985 to almost 400,000 in 2008. When Robert Parker Jr. named Bartholomaus one of the Wine Personalities of the Year of 2005, he wrote, "His dogged determination to expose the American market to not only many terrific wine values but also the potential greatness of the best Malbecs of Argentina and the up and coming wines of Chile has paid extraordinary dividends, and he is largely responsible for the enormous success and acceptance the wines of Chile and Argentina have had in this country." But when Bartholomaus's banks cut Billington Imports' credit line during the 2008–09 recession, Bartholomaus found himself overextended. The loss of Alamos didn't help. Billington closed in May 2009. An original pioneer had fallen.

In 2009, Nicolás Catena finally achieved the recognition that would put his name alongside the greats of France, Italy, and California. In its April issue, England's prestigious *Decanter* magazine announced that Nicolás Catena would be its twenty-sixth Man of the Year, joining a list that includes Robert Mondavi, Émile Peynaud, and Marchese Piero Antinori. He would be just the fourth from the Americas—joining Mondavi, André Tchelistcheff, and Paul Draper—and the only one of those not from California.

A celebratory dinner was held at the Argentine ambassador's residence in London that September, and industry stars like Michael Broadbent, Baron Eric de Rothschild, Hugh Johnson, and Oz Clarke turned out to honor Catena. The one question that lingered was whether the preternaturally shy Catena could bring himself to get up in front of a group of fifty people and give a speech at all, much less in English. But after the foie gras soup and sautéed scallops segued into lamb, ox cheek, and black olives, and then dessert, Catena stood and told the story of his *bodeguero* life, from his Napa epiphany to the search for altitude and defining Argentine *terroir*.

Catena accepted the award in the name of Mendoza, his family, and those who had worked in his family's vineyard in the era of change. After the speech, he passed by Marina Gayan, who was shocked at the implausible sight of the quiet economist standing to talk about himself. Catena had always told her that while the American public might buy his products, British wine critics—the group of people who had made France internationally famous—would never recognize Argentina. Not in a million years. And yet, on this night, here he stood. "Can you believe it?" he said, laughing. Whether he meant the speech, the award, or what he—and his country—had achieved, he did not say.

# EPILOGUE

An aerial view of the Vines of Mendoza vineyards, in the Uco Valley.

Photo by Mario Cardama, Aerotec S.A.

*The Vineyard at the End of the World* is structured as a traditional narrative telling of Argentina's wine history, from the sixteenth-century arrival of the Spaniards in the Andean west through the immigrant boom of the late 1800s, the industry's collapse in the 1970s, and the country's rebirth and boom over the last twenty years. Because of the exigencies of the narrative form, much of the contemporary part of the book is built around the story of Nicolás Catena, the winery owner whose company and winemakers played the largest role in the expansion of the last two decades. It would be absurd, however, to suggest that Argentina's boom was owed to one man alone, and I have tried wherever possible to give credit where it is due. For similar reasons, the book also focuses on the Mendoza region and the Malbec grape, but it would do a great disservice to the diversity of Argentina and its wines to ignore the excellent vintages turned out in other provinces or based on other varietals.

Argentina's wine region, and the international industry in which it sits, are far different places than they were just ten or fifteen years ago. As recently as 1996, Argentina exported a mere $7.1 million in bottled wine to the United States, putting it in ninth place on the US export list, just behind Brazil (a country not known for its wines, to put it gently). Today, Argentina is in a dead heat with Spain and Chile for fourth. As it sells ever-increasing amounts, more of its regions and varietals are receiving international recognition for their quality.

In the Patagonian desert some 435 miles south of Mendoza, the chilly Río Negro valley is truly at the end of the world. Here, in 2004, Piero Incisa della Rochetta bought a ragged vineyard that had been planted with Pinot Noir by Neapolitan immigrants in 1932 and abandoned in more recent times. The grandson of a founder of Italy's "Super Tuscan" movement, Incisa turned grapes from the gnarled old Pinot Noir vines into vintages that put Patagonia on the fine-wine map; the *Wine Spectator* gave his $120 *Treinta y Dos* ("Thirty-Two" in English) between 91 and 93 points every year from 2004 to 2009, and writer and *Wall Street Journal* wine critic Jay McInerney dedicated a column titled "Pioneering Wine in Patagonia" to Incisa's wines and their "piercing intensity." (The "It" varietal after *Sideways*, the cool-climate Pinot Noir grape is one of the hardest to cultivate and make into good wine.) Similarly, in the *Wine Spectator*'s 2010 Argentine tasting report, the highest-scoring wine (95 points) was a 2008 Malbec from Bodega Noemía, a fellow Río Negro valley winery. Two Malbecs from Donald Hess's Bodega Colomé, in the northern province of Salta, also scored in the 90s.

Similarly, previously unsung varietals like Bonarda and Torrontés have started to thrill the wine world's palate. Exports of the white Torrontés—citrusy but not sweet—grew 692 percent, to $18.7 million, between 2002 and 2010, and the average price also rose 65 percent, according to data from Caucasia Wine Thinking. For its part, the fruity, easy-drinking Bonarda sported nearly as impressive numbers, with exports growing 158 percent to $4 million and the average price rising 59 percent.

Showing the Argentine wine industry's maturity, interesting projects outside the mainstream have sprung up among the traditional *bodegas*. In

2005, Gabriela Furlotti, the great granddaughter of industry titan Ángel Furlotti, cofounded Soluna Wines, a fair-trade nonprofit that works with nineteen small Mendoza grape growers and sells about 80,000 bottles of the wine each year through Sam's Club, under the label Neu Direction. And Dieter Meier, the Swiss cofounder of the electronic band Yello (the band's big hit is a song called "Oh Yeah"), farms 150 acres of vines at Mendoza's 800-acre organic Ojo de Agua *bodega*. When he began, Meier says, farmers grew organic grapes only in marginal areas, in the hope that it would give them a marketing edge. "People thought, 'Why is this guy doing this in a place where you can make premium wines?'" says Meier, an art-world dandy with his slicked-back gray hair, mustache, and ascot. Today, however, he produces and sells about 500,000 bottles of wine made from organic grapes each year.

The simple physical and human landscape of Argentine wine country has changed along with the industry. Vineyard planting has continued at a ferocious pace. The Vines of Mendoza has sold ninety-five turnkey vineyard plots, planted 650 acres of vines, bought another 1,000 acres, and built the first wing of a Bórmida y Yanzón–designed winery. They are far from alone. Trapiche chief winemaker Daniel Pi says his *bodega* is planting 125 acres a year, two-thirds of that Malbec, in a 750-acre five-year plan, and Catena's Alejandro Vigil says his employer is planting some 200–250 acres a year. Tourism is booming as well: during the first half of 2010—the high season—769,000 visitors toured Argentine wineries, up almost 58 percent from the previous year, according to the trade group Bodegas de Argentina.

Growth has brought its pains, however. The spoils of the wine boom have not always been shared equally, and Mendoza continues to have pockets of grinding poverty. As well-heeled foreign wine tourists flock to the region, they have provided easy targets for pickpockets and others looking to relieve them of their wealth, and Mendoza's new luxury hotels and restaurants have suffered a spate of invasions by armed gangs. In January 2010, Philadelphia gastroenterologist David Goldberg and his parents were visiting Mendoza when, as they returned from dinner to their luxury in-vineyard lodge, a group of robbers pulled a gun on them, slapped David's mother, stole their money, and shoved them into their *cabaña* closet. "I have no intention to go back to Argentina," says Goldberg. "It's still South America. It's still third world-ish there."

More worrisome for the larger industry, however, are changes in the industry's economics. Inflation has been running some 25 percent per year in Argentina. For some products, it's even higher: between 2009 and 2010, the prices that *bodegas* paid to buy grapes and wine rose between 40 and 100 percent, according to *WineSur*. Inflation has taken what had been a high-profit business—wine exporting—and returned it into the near-break-even enterprise it was when the peso was pegged to the US dollar before the 2001–02 crisis. "Why do we do well in the foreign markets? Because we have a great relationship between price and quality. But the inflation rate means that margins are always shrinking," says Bodegas Nieto Senetiner cofounder Adriano Senetiner, the *bodeguero* who recently sold his second winery, Bodega Viniterra, to a large Argentine beverage company named Cepas Argentinas.

The problem is that Argentine wineries rarely can transfer higher costs to international consumers from countries accustomed to stable prices. "With some wines, we're taking them out of the market because our costs are greater than the sale prices and the external markets won't accept that much inflation," Senetiner says. Being a wine-drinking country itself, Argentina has the advantage of selling some 75 percent of its wine inside the country, but a large number of wineries depend on the export market for growth and see it as the key to the future. "The biggest problem is that we're wasting all the effort that we at the *bodegas* have been making for years to increase the sector's exports," Michael Halstrick, the CEO of Bodegas Norton, told the Argentine newspaper *La Nación* in April 2011.

Shrinking margins on midlevel mass exports have in turn led some *bodegueros* to raise prices on their top "icon" wines to try to make up the difference. "The number of wines with triple-digit prices is growing at an alarming rate. There are 18 such wines in this year's report, one more than in all previous years combined," James Molesworth wrote in the *Wine Spectator*'s 2008 Argentina tasting report (the number of hundred-plus-dollar wines was similar in 2009 and 2010). But with an economic crisis gripping prime wine-buying markets in the United States and Europe—especially hitting financial-industry workers who used to splurge on top wines—the timing for such a move isn't great. These attempts at gaining international icon status and charging accordingly haven't always worked. Today, some of Argentina's top wines, including examples from Catena Zapata and Achával-Ferrer, can be found at online wine merchants selling for significantly less than their release price—something that in consumers' eyes hurts the reputations of both the *bodegas* that make the wines and the reviewers who give them astronomical scores.

But while there are some clouds in the sky, Argentina, like Chile and Australia before it, seems to have achieved escape velocity. The two decades of work put in by Argentina's *bodegueros*, winemakers, and viticulturists, and the "flying winemakers" they hired, have so radically improved the industry that it would require extreme maliciousness to send it crashing back to earth. And after its four-hundred-year journey, it's unlikely that Argentina's wine industry would settle for what it had before. As Gustavo Choren writes in his 2003 book, *El gran libro del Malbec argentino*, "A vine condemned to eradication and obscurity in its native France, Malbec found its place more than 6,000 miles away. But not before passing through 150 years of crisis and glory in its new home."

For Malbec, as for all of Argentina, it has been a long trip.

# ACKNOWLEDGMENTS

This book could not have been written without the scores of people (listed below) who gave generously of their time to answer questions and, perhaps equally as importantly, to tell me who else I should *really* interview. Argentina, especially its western part, has a generous culture, and in the midst of many a chat my interviewee would call a friend in the industry to verify a fact or set up my next interview. I am especially indebted to Nicolás Catena, Paul Hobbs, and Pedro Marchevsky, who gave me many hours of their time over multiple interviews, answering questions, correcting misconceptions, and explaining the business of Argentine wine. I would also like to thank Marcos Etchart, Gabriela Furlotti, and Carlos Tizio Mayer, who were especially generous with their time and invitations.

I spent many weeks in Mendoza, and several people there offered indispensable help in opening doors and meeting sources. Two journalists, Carlos Campana at *Los Andes* and Jaime Correas at *Diario UNO*, were especially helpful in tracking down historical materials, as was historian Pablo Lacoste, who knows the past of Argentine wine as well as anyone on the planet. Local tour agency owner Charlie O'Malley knew all the best scandals and tall tales; Sean Maddox helped me track down

301

images when I wasn't there; and Exequiel Barros of Caucasia Wine Thinking provided valuable statistical help. I also must thank Michael Evans and David Garrett of the Vines of Mendoza, who introduced me to many characters in this tale and fed me a serious amount of steak and wine at their vineyard *asados* while doing so.

Although it can be very lonely, writing is a collaborative art. I would have been lost without the insightful and thoughtful editing of Tom Mayer at W. W. Norton. I'd also like to thank my agent Alanna Ramirez at Trident Media Group for taking this project from idea to reality; Denise Scarfi at W. W. Norton for making sure the trains ran on time; and my copy editor, Stephanie Hiebert, who saved me from many a linguistic error and awkward phrase. Finally, my two main readers here in Argentina, Matt Chesterton and Alejandro Audisio, made indispensable comments and suggestions.

Most of all, I thank my family. My mother, Joan Mount, offered support and always believed that publication day would arrive, even when I didn't. My wife, Cintra Scott, gamely handled my disappearances into Winelandia; offered amazing help with the selling, planning, and writing of this book; provided love and support during the long days of First Draft Hell; and in other ways deserves more thanks than I can give here. And last, but not least, there is our son, Henry Emiliano Mount, whose perpetual smile and giddy, bilingual chatter make it all worthwhile.

In alphabetical order, my interviewees were Santiago Achával Becú, Greg Adams, Alberto Antonini, Alberto Arizu, Lee Asbell, Susana Balbo, Exequiel Barros, Alfredo Bartholomaus, William Beezley, Giorgio Benedetti, Carlos Benito, Raúl Bianchi, Hervé Birnie-Scott, Eliana Bórmida, Gerald Boyd, Federico Boxaca, Miguel Brascó, Carlos Campana, Patrick Campbell, Juan José Canay, Arnaldo Carosio, Jorge Catena, Laura Catena, Nicolás Catena, Elisabeth Checa, Enrique Chrabolowsky, Tyler Colman, Jaime Correas, Roberto de la Mota, Mariano Di Paola, Cecilia

Díaz Chuit, Nick Dokoozlian, Palo Domingo, David English, Arnaldo Etchart Sr., Arnaldo Etchart Jr., Marcos Etchart, Michael Evans, Nora Favelukes, Dereck Foster, Daniel Friel, Gabriela Furlotti, José Galante, Carlos García, Guillermo García, David Garrett, Marina Gayan, Carlos Gei Berra, Brian Gillespie, Alejandra Giol, David Goldberg, Joshua Greene, Lynda Hanson, Paul Hobbs, Bernhard Horstmann, Tomás Hughes, Randle Johnson, Sophie Jump, Peter Kay, Marcelo Kogan Alterman, Ralph Kunkee, Pablo Lacoste, James Lapsley, Jorge Liloy, Mauricio Llaver, Leonardo LoCascio, Eduardo López Laurenz, Leandro Lowi, François Lurton, Jaques Lurton, Pedro Marchevsky, Tom Matthews, Jeff Mausbach, Mike McGrath, Ángel Mendoza, Jay Miller, Michael Mondavi, Tim Mondavi, José Morales, Antonio Morescalchi, Matt Novak, Laurence Odfjell, José Orfila, José Manuel Ortega Gil-Fournier, Attilio Pagli, Alicia Palacio, Carmelo Patti, Robert Pepi, Scott Peterson, Daniel Pi, Daniel Posner, Paul Provost, Carlos Pulenta, Steve Rasmussen, Patricio Reich, Jorge Riccitelli, Martín Rigal, Jancis Robinson, Norm Roby, Gabriel Roitman, Michel Rolland, Pierre-Antoine Rovani, Guy Ruhland, Chuck Russo, Patricio Santos, Ricardo Santos, Tom Schmeisser, Alejandro Sejanovich, Adriano Senetiner, Alejandro Shaw, Jeffrey Stambor, Steve Stein, Luis Steindl, Jean-Pierre Thibaud, Carlos Tizio, Randy Ullom, Fabián Valenzuela, Carlos Vázquez, Ángel Vespa, Juan Viciana, Alejandro Vigil, Larry Walker, Bernardo Weinert, Mario Yanzón, José Alberto Zuccardi, Sebastián Zuccardi, and several others who asked to remain anonymous.

# NOTES

## PREFACE

Descriptions of Argentina and its wine history come from Catena, 2010, p. 22; Lubow, 2007; Mount, 2008; and interviews with Alberto Antonini, Michael Evans, David Garrett, Brian Gillespie, Pedro Marchevsky, Ricardo Santos, and José Alberto Zuccardi. ■ The Hess quote comes from Lubow, 2007. ■ Other details of the international wine trade are drawn from Frank, 2010; Frank and Macle, 2007; Matthews, 2007; Mustacich, 2011; Smith, 2007; and Stein, 2008, p. 15.

## INTRODUCTION

Details for the story of San Martín's lunch with Olazábal, Mosquera, and Arcos come from Busaniche, 1995, esp. pp. 146–147 and 258–259; and Correas, 1971, esp. p. 4. The translation of "Cuyo" comes from Diaz Araujo, 2006, p. 9. ■ Other information about San Martín's early life, his return to Argentina, and the death of his wife comes from Pigna, "José de San Martín"; Pigna (2004), esp. pp. 15–23 and 56; Santos Martínez, 1994, esp. pp. 51–61; and the Instituto Nacional Sanmartiniano website (http://www.sanmartiniano.gov.ar).

## CHAPTER 1

Jaime Correas's words come from a speech he made at the Universidad de Congreso in 2004; Correas provided the author a transcript of the speech. ■ Sarmiento's words come from Sarmiento, 2005, p. xl. ■ Details about the arrival of the first Spaniards and Mendoza's early colonial years, including some information about the Huarpe Indians, were drawn from Diaz Araujo,

2006, pp. 9–10; Diaz Araujo, 1989, p. 17; Santos Martínez, 1979, esp. pp. 19–25; and Scalvini, 1965, esp. pp. 19–45.

Additional information about the Huarpe comes from Godoy, 1999, esp. pp. 54–55; Labrador R., 1999, esp. the introduction and pp. 1–29; Morales Guiñazu, 1938, esp. pp. 4–12; and Ponte, 1987, p. 24.

Details on the origins of winemaking come from González, 2003, esp. pp. 13–14; and Hotz, 2011. ▪ Early colonial winemaking details were drawn from Diaz Araujo, 1989, esp. pp. 21–26 (the Padre Alonso de Ovalle quote can be found on p. 23); González, 2003, esp. pp. 14–15; Graham-Yooll, 1999, esp. pp. 13–14; Queyrat, 1974, esp. pp. 22–23; Santos Martínez, 1979, p. 24; and an interview with Alberto Arizu Sr.

The Puebla y Reinoso and Arizmendi stories are told in Lacoste, 2006, and Lacoste, 2007, respectively.

The descriptions of seventeenth- and eighteenth-century Argentine culture and winemaking are drawn from Coria López, 1994, p. 328; Diaz Araujo, 1989, esp. pp. 53–55, 60–65, 76–80, and 88 (the Videla quote comes from p. 80); Diaz Araujo, 2006, p. 10; Reina Rutini, 1985, p. 8; and Santos Martínez, 1979, p. 29. ▪ Details for the biographies of the Spanish kings come from Campbell, 2004; Harsanyi, 2006; and P., 2004.

Travelers' descriptions of Mendoza during the early nineteenth century come from Darwin, 2010, p. 350; and Head, 1826, pp. 69–71.

The story of Pouget and his era in Mendoza is told in Catena, 2010, p. 56; Diaz Araujo, 1989, p. 121; Draghi Lucero, 1991, esp. pp. 27–63; Gargiulo and Borzi, 2004, esp. pp. 64–70; Mateu, 2008, p. 36; Micale, 2001, p. 34; Ponte, 1987, p. 15; and Richard-Jorba, 2005.

CHAPTER 2

The story of the Mendoza earthquake comes from Čermák and Kozák, 2010, pp. 167–168; Correas, 1997, esp. pp. 141–146; "González Videla," 2003; Ponte, 1987, p. 159; Santos Martínez, 1979, esp. pp. 139 and 246; Schávelzon, 2007, esp. pp. 32–36, 45–47, 64, 69–71, and 104; Suárez, 1938, esp. pp. 121–133; and an interview with Alicia Palacio. ▪ The Clereaux quote about the looting comes from Suárez, 1938, p. 161.

The descriptions of Britain's involvement in Argentina and the effects of the railroads are drawn from *An Authentic Narrative*, 1808; Caddick-Adams, 2006; Castlereagh and Vane, 1851, 314–324; Criscenti, 1993, p. 80; Diaz Araujo, 1989, p. 82; Gott, 2007; Graham-Yooll, 1999, esp. pp. 26–42, 225, 231, and 268; Lacoste, 1995, p. 28; Mateu, 2008, esp. pp. 15 and 18; and Richard-

Jorba, 2005; 2006, p. 81; 2009. ■ The *Times* quote about Britain's success in La Plata and the Holland quote about the rabble come from Graham-Yooll, 1999, pp. 28 and 36. ■ The Castlereagh memorandum is quoted from Castlereagh and Vane, 1851, p. 319.

Details for the stories of Ortega, Benegas, Cipolletti, and their era come from Correas, 1997, esp. pp. 218–225; Lacoste, 1994, p. 29; Mateu, 2008, esp. pp. 195–213; Silanes et al., 2007, esp. pp. 33–53, 72, 80, 92, 101–102, 107–123, and 293–295; and Richard-Jorba, 1994, esp. pp. 4–5 and 8; 2005; 2008; 2009. ■ Ortega's quote about serving human meat as barbecue comes from Correas, 1997, p. 223. ■ The Orrego quote and the other critic of Ortega are drawn from Lacoste, 1994, p. 29. ■ The quote from the Ortega immigrant law is from Correas, 1997, p. 221. ■ Ortega's quote about the economic need for immigrants comes from Richard-Jorba, 2009. ■ The Bergman quote is drawn from Richard Jorba, 1994, p. 4. ■ The Cipolletti quote about hydroelectric energy; the Benegas quote about the similarity of land in Mendoza, Italy, and Spain; and the letter from Villanueva to Benegas come from Silanes et al., 2007, pp. 53, 102, and 103. ■ The Civit letters to Benegas are drawn from Mateu and Stein, 2008, p. 247, and Richard Jorba, 1998, p. 267.

The story of phylloxera is drawn from Banerjee et al., 2007; Campbell, 2005, esp. pp. 43–45, 49–50, 74, 184, 200, 215, and 241; Gargiulo and Borzi, 2004, p. 24; "Phylloxera Ravages Italy," 1895; and Robinson, 2006. ■ The quote from *Le Temps* comes from Campbell, 2005, p. 195.

The history of Argentine immigration and the early *bodegueros* comes from *Álbum argentino*, 1910; Collado, 2006, p. 24; Correas, 1997, esp. pp. 123–132; Gargiulo and Borzi, 2004, p. 73; Gatti, 2003, esp. pp. 14–15; Girini, 2007, esp. pp. 2–9; Lacoste, 1994, esp. pp. 27 and 53; 2003, esp. pp. 33–41 and 53–65; Mateu, 2008, esp. pp. 11, 26, 32, 60, and 134; "Nieta de Giol," 2009; Pérez Ferrando and Tartarini, 2005, esp. pp. 15–17; Santos Martínez, 1979, p. 125; *Viti-vinicultura Argentina*, 1910, p. 102; and interviews with Nora Favelukes, Alejandra Giol, and Pablo Lacoste.

The stories of fraud in the Argentine wine industry come from Barrio de Villanueva, 2007; Edmundo Correas, 1971, esp. pp. 8 and 12; Jaime Correas, 1997, esp. 257–263; Mateu, 2008, esp. pp. 29, 32, 239, 331, and 336–337; Richard-Jorba, 2008; and *Viti-vinicultura Argentina*, 1910, esp. pp. 41–42. ■ The Arata quotes are drawn from Correas, 1971, p. 8, and Mateu, 2008, p. 32. ■ The Simois and Ortíz quote comes from *Viti-vinicultura Argentina*, 1910, p. xix.

Details of the Great Depression and the era of Perón are drawn from "Argentina: Boss," 1944; Catena, 2010, p. 22; Correas, 1971, esp. pp. 27–28; Eloy Martínez, 1997; 2007; González, 2003, p. 19; Mateu, 2008, esp. pp. 38,

42, and 346; Pigna, 2006, p. 284; Queyrat, 1974, esp. pp. 28 and 109; Reina Rutini, 1985, p. 13; Winn, 2006, p. 152; and interviews with Ángel Mendoza and Carlos Pulenta.

CHAPTER 3

Details for the story of the Greco rise and fall come from Bustos Herrera, 2007; 2009; Falanga, 2001, esp. pp. 31, 42, 78–84, and 89; Mateu, 2008, esp. pp. 346–348 and 356; Montes de Oca, 1996, esp. pp. 8–20; Morán, 1997; Precilla, 2005, p. 98; Zlotogwiazda, 2007; and interviews with Arnaldo Carosio, Nicolás Catena, Ángel Pedro Falanga, Pedro Marchevsky, and Adriano Senetiner. ■ The Greco quote about the golden egg comes from Montes de Oca, 1996, p. 11.

The history of Grupo Catena and its era is drawn from Aspe Armella et al., 1983, esp. pp. 199–200; Bustos Herrera, 2007; Mateu, 2008, p. 359; Montes de Oca, 1996, p. 18; and interviews with Miguel Brascó, Nicolás Catena, Gabriela Furlotti, and Adriano Senetiner.

The biography of Nicolás Catena comes from Reina Rutini, 1985, esp. p. 31; Rose, 2009; and interviews with Carlos Benito, Arnaldo Carosio, Nicolás Catena, Marina Gayan, Ralph Kunkee, Jacques Lurton, Jeff Mausbach, Steve Rasmussen, Guy Ruhland, Carlos Vásquez, Juan Viciana, and Alejandro Vigil.

CHAPTER 4

The story of the "Judgment of Paris" tasting comes from "Modern Living," 1976; and Taber, 2006, esp. pp. 17, 22, 159–161, 202–205, and 214. ■ Details of the history of UC Davis, Nicolás Catena's early visits to California, and Guy Ruhland's 1981 trip to Argentina are drawn from O'Neill, 1998; Rose, 2009; the UC Davis Viticulture and Enology website (http://wineserver.ucdavis.edu); and interviews with Greg Adams, Nicolás Catena, José Galante, Paul Hobbs, Ralph Kunkee, Pedro Marchevsky, Steve Rasmussen, and Guy Ruhland.

The tale of Nicolás Catena's period at UC Berkeley comes from Apple, 2001; Flynn Siler, 2007, esp. pp. 84–86; Howe, 2005; the French Laundry (http://www.frenchlaundry.com) and Robert Mondavi Wines (http://www.robertmondavi.com) websites; and interviews with Carlos Benito, Nicolás Catena, José Galante, Michael Mondavi, and Tim Mondavi. ■ Catena's *New York Times* quote comparing the speed of American and European wine development comes from Apple, 2001. ■ Pulenta's quote about the necessity of exporting is taken from Schumacher, 1984.

The description of the situation of Argentina's wine industry in the 1980s is drawn from Apple, 2001; Catena, 2010, p. 22; Mateu, 2008, p. 361; Schumacher, 1984; data from the Instituto Nacional de Vitivinicultura (http://www.inv.gov.ar); and interviews with Greg Adams, Nicolás Catena, José Galante, Pedro Marchevsky, Michael Mondavi, and Ricardo Santos.

Biographies of other early Argentine fine-wine pioneers come from Morelli, 2007; Cuculiansky, 2007; and interviews with Juan José Canay, Roberto de la Mota, Carlos Pulenta, Ricardo Santos, and Bernardo Weinert. ▪ De la Mota's quote about fighting with accountants comes from Cuculiansky, 2007.

### CHAPTER 5

Details of Michel Rolland's 1998 visit to Argentina and the tale of his and Robert Parker Jr.'s early years in the industry are drawn from Chrabolowsky, 2008; Echikson, 2004, esp. pp. 89–100 and 173–177; Langewiesche, 2000; *Mondovino*, 2004; Shapin, 2005; and interviews with Tyler Colman, Arnaldo Etchart Jr., Arnaldo Etchart Sr., Marcos Etchart, Jorge Riccitelli, Michel Rolland, Pierre-Antoine Rovani, and Ricardo Santos. ▪ The Rolland telephone conversation with Etchart is drawn from Chrabolowsky, 2008.

The story of Paul Hobbs's 1988 visit to Mendoza comes from Briley, 2005; Brown, 2006; Luxner, 2000; Molesworth, 2006; the Paul Hobbs Winery website (http://www.paulhobbswinery.com); and interviews with Alberto Antonini, Jorge Catena, Nicolás Catena, Marina Gayan, Paul Hobbs, Marcelo Kogan, Ralph Kunkee, François Lurton, Jacques Lurton, and Norm Roby.

### CHAPTER 6

Details for the Argentine group's California visit and Mondavi lunch come from interviews with Pedro Marchevsky, Michael Mondavi, Steve Rasmussen, Carlos Tizio Mayer, and Juan Viciana.

The story of Paul Hobbs's first consulting visits is drawn from Azpiazu and Basualdo, 2000; Bonné, 2008; Brown, 2006; and interviews with Greg Adams, Raúl Bianchi, Miguel Brascó, Laura Catena, Nicolás Catena, Mariano Di Paola, José Galante, Marina Gayan, Carlos Gei Berra, Paul Hobbs, Jacques Lurton, Pedro Marchevsky, and Scott Peterson. ▪ Marchevsky's quote about measuring oxygen comes from Brown, 2006.

Descriptions of the experiences of and roles played by foreign consultants come from interviews with Susana Balbo, Laura Catena, Paul Hobbs, Jacques Lurton, Pedro Marchevsky, Ángel Mendoza, Daniel Pi, Steve Rasmussen, Ricardo Santos, Jeffrey Stambor, and José Alberto Zuccardi.

The state of Argentina's economy in the 1980s and 1990s, descriptions of the first successful wines, and the story of the death of Jorge Catena's son come from Stockley, 1996; data from the Instituto Nacional de Vitivinicultura (http://www.inv.gov.ar); and interviews with Alberto Arizu Sr., Hervé Birnie-Scott, Nicolás Catena, Paul Hobbs, Ángel Mendoza, Ricardo Santos, and Carlos Tizio Mayer.

CHAPTER 7

Details for the tale of Jacques Lurton's arrival in Argentina and his tasting with Nicolás Catena are drawn from Madigan, 2010; McWhirter, 1993; Rose, 2009; and interviews with Nicolás Catena, Paul Hobbs, and Jacques Lurton. ■ The Lurton quote about drinking beer comes from Madigan, 2010.

The story of the search for altitude comes from Catena, 2010, esp. p. 113; the Bodega Catena Zapata website (http://www.catenawines.com); data from Area del Vino (http://www.areadelvino.com); and interviews with Nicolás Catena, José Galante, Paul Hobbs, Jacques Lurton, Pedro Marchevsky, Matt Novak, Daniel Pi, Alejandro Sejanovich, and Carlos Vázquez.

The retelling of the first export sales in the United States is drawn from McIntyre, 2009; "Record High," 2011; statistics from the Wine Institute website (http://www.wineinstitute.org); and interviews with Alfredo Bartholomaus, Nicolás Catena, Nora Favelukes, Paul Hobbs, Paul Provost, Chuck Russo, and Jean-Pierre Thibaud.

The description of life at the Catena businesses is drawn from interviews with Nicolás Catena, Marina Gayan, Paul Hobbs, Jacques Lurton, Pedro Marchevsky, and Scott Peterson.

CHAPTER 8

Details about Alberto Antonini and Antonio Morescalchi's trip to Argentina are drawn from interviews with Alberto Antonini, Antonio Morescalchi, Patricio Santos, and Adriano Senetiner; and the Antinori website (http://www.antinori.it).

The history of Malbec and its reception in Argentina comes from Catena, 2010, p. 26; Grimshaw, 2010; McWhirter, 1993; Robinson, 2006; *La vitivinicultura Argentina*, 1910, p. XVIII; the Cahors Malbec website (http://www.cahorsmalbec.com); data from the Instituto Nacional de Vitivinicultura (http://www.inv.gov.ar); and interviews with Hervé Birnie-Scott, Roberto de la Mota, Ángel Mendoza, Patricio Santos, and Ricardo Santos. ■ The

Jacques Hébrard quote about Malbec comes from an interview with Roberto de la Mota.

The description of Nicolás Catena's early views on and experience with Malbec is drawn from Rose, 2009; and interviews with Susana Balbo, Arnaldo Carosio, Laura Catena, Nicolás Catena, Marina Gayan, Paul Hobbs, Jacques Lurton, Pedro Marchevsky, Antonio Morescalchi, and Attilio Pagli. ■ Catena's quote about forgetting about Argentina's terroir comes from Rose, 2009.

Details for the story of the Malbec clonal study and the start of Malbec's U.S. boom come from Koppel, 2009; McIntyre, 2010; Parker, 2004; Wade, 2011; the Bodega Catena Zapata website (http://www.catenawines.com); and interviews with Alberto Antonini, Laura Catena, Nicolás Catena, Nick Dokoozlian, Nora Favelukes, Pedro Marchevsky, Ángel Mendoza, and Alejandro Sejanovich. ■ The Parker quote about Malbec's future greatness is drawn from Parker, 2004.

CHAPTER 9

The description of the Bodega Catena Zapata pyramid and its opening party is drawn from Apple, 2001; Gallardo, 2001; the Bodega Catena Zapata website (http://www.catenawines.com); and interviews with Alfredo Bartholomaus, Gerald Boyd, Laura Catena, Nicolás Catena, and Marina Gayan. ■ The *Businessweek* comment on the pyramid comes from Goodman, 2002.

Details about the arrival of foreign winemakers come from *50 años de historia*, 2010; Azpiazu and Basualdo, 2000; Bianchi, 1999; Brown, 2006; Catena, 2010, esp. pp. 161–162; Correa, 1996; Lubow, 2007; Nimo, 2003; Robinson, 2003; Shriver, 2008; "Socma Sells Shares," 2001; Stein, 2008, esp. pp. 15–16; and interviews with Alberto Antonini, Hervé Birnie-Scott, Sophie Jump, and José Alberto Zuccardi. ■ The *Los Angles Times* quote about oenological carpetbaggers is drawn from Brown, 2006. ■ The Sophie Jump quote comes from Stein, 2008, p. 16. ■ Baron de Ladoucette's words come from *50 años de historia*, 2010.

The recounting of Michel Rolland's arrival in Mendoza and the story of Clos de los Siete come from Aznarez, 2001; Bigongiari, 2005, p. 217; Kingsbury, 2002; Kramer, "Two Worlds," 2010; Llorens, 2002; Mariani, 2010; Quiroga, 2002; and interviews with Laura Catena, Ángel Mendoza, Daniel Pi, Michel Rolland, and Carlos Tizio Mayer.

Details for the story of Eliana Bórmida and Mario Yanzón come from the Bórmida y Yanzón Arquitectos website (http://www.bormidayanzon .com .ar);

visits to the *bodegas*; and interviews with Eliana Bórmida, José Manuel Ortega Gil-Fournier, and Mario Yanzón.

The experiences of foreign winemakers in Argentina and the Kendall-Jackson story are drawn from Appleson, 1999; Colman, 2007; Knap, 1999; Sax, 2003; Shriver, 2000; Whitley, 1997; and interviews with Greg Adams, Patrick Campbell, Laura Catena, Lynda Hanson, Sophie Jump, Laurence Odfjell, and Randy Ullom. ▪ The Ullom *Wine Business Monthly* quote comes from Colman, 2007. ▪ The $2 million price for the Agrelo *bodega* comes from Shriver, 2000.

Details about Catena Zapata's boom period and international taste test come from Apple, 2001; Gallardo, 2001; and interviews with Alfredo Bartholomaus, Nicolás Catena, and Jancis Robinson. ▪ The stories of departing Catena employees come from the Bodega Catena Zapata website (http://www .catenawines.com); and interviews with Susana Balbo, Jorge Catena, Nicolás Catena, Arnaldo Carosio, Marina Gayan, Paul Hobbs, Ángel Mendoza, and Scott Peterson. ▪ The *Seattle Times* article that praised Alamos Ridge without mentioning Catena is Stockley, 2006.

CHAPTER 10

Details about Santiago Achával Becú's purchase of his Alta Mira vineyard come from Kramer, "Master of Malbec," 2010; and interviews with Santiago Achával. ▪ The tales of export growth and the newer winemakers who helped engineer it come from Aveling, 2009; Brown, 2006; Catena, 2010, esp. p. 161; Crosariol, 2008; Kramer, "Two Worlds," 2010; McIntyre, 2010; Mount, 2007; Pachner, 2010; Robinson, 2003; Stimmell, 2009; data from the Instituto Nacional de Vitivinicultura (http://www.inv.gov.ar); the Familia Zuccardi website (http://www.familiazuccardi.com); and interviews with Santiago Achával Becú, Paul Hobbs, Randle Johnson, Andrea Marchiori, José Manuel Ortega Gil-Fournier, José Alberto Zuccardi, and Sebastián Zuccardi. ▪ Hobbs's quote about the meaninglessness of Argentine contracts comes from Brown, 2006. ▪ Hess's quote to Robinson about Colomé is from Robinson, 2003. ▪ Beppi Crosariol's quote about Fuzion is drawn from Crosariol, 2008. ▪ Shari Mogk-Edwards's quote about the spread of Fuzion via technology is from Aveling, 2009.

Details about Argentina's rising sales, the arrival of international beverage companies, and Catena's current status and new employees come from Catena, 2010, esp. pp. 103–104; "Gallo Named," 2008; Koppel, 2009; McIntyre, 2009; Saieg, 2010; Schachner, 2010; Wesley, 2011; "Myth of the Family Winery," 2009; data from the Instituto Nacional de Vitivinicultura (http://www.inv

.gov.ar); the Bodega Catena Zapata website (http://www.catenawines.com); and interviews with Laura Catena, Nicolás Catena, Jay Miller, Daniel Pi, Alejandro Sejanovich, and Alejandro Vigil. ▪ The Merino quote about Malbec is from González, 2011. ▪ The Parker quote about Bartholomaus comes from Parker, 2005.

The description of Nicolás Catena's *Decanter* award is drawn from Rose, 2009; Rosen, 2009; and interviews with Alfredo Bartholomaus, Nicolás Catena, and Marina Gayan.

EPILOGUE

US wine import figures for Argentina and other countries come from the US International Trade Commission (http://www.usitc.gov). ▪ The description of Chacra winery owner Piero Incisa della Rochetta comes from McInerney, 2010, and the Bodega Chacra website (http://www.bodegachacra.com). ▪ Data about increasing Bonarda and Torrontés sales come from Caucasia Wine Thinking (http://www.caucasia.com.ar). ▪ The descriptions of Gabriela Furlotti and Dieter Meier are drawn from interviews with Furlotti and Meier and the Soluna (http://www.solunawines.com) and Ojo de Agua (http://www ..ojodeagua.ch) websites. ▪ The data about Trapiche and Catena plantings come from interviews with Daniel Pi and Alejandro Vigil; and the tourism data, from "Creció 68%," 2010. ▪ Details about the downside of the boom come from Malizia, August 11, 2010, and from interviews with David Goldberg and Adriano Senetiner. ▪ The Halstrick quote comes from Sainz, 2011. ▪ The quote about the increasing number of hundred-plus-dollar Argentine wines comes from Molesworth, 2008. ▪ The final quote about Malbec's journey comes from Choren, 2003.

# SELECTED BIBLIOGRAPHY

Note: The wine reviews from the *Wine Advocate* and the *Wine Spectator* were accessed through their subscription websites, where readers can search by name, vintage, and varietal. Depending on the type of wine and how much aging it is expected to need, the reviews may appear from several months to several years after bottling.

*50 años de historia: Bodegas Chandon*. Mendoza: Bodegas Chandon, 2010.

*Álbum argentino. Número extraordinario dedicado al Sr. Gobernador Dr. Emilio Civit*. Mendoza: Gloriandus, 1910.

Apple, R. W., Jr. "New Heights for Andean Wine." *New York Times*, August 22, 2001. http://www.nytimes.com.

Appleson, Gail (Reuters). "Vintner Defies Norm in Argentina." *Chicago Tribune*, August 25, 1999, northwest edition.

"Argentina: Boss of the GOU," *Time*, November 27, 1944. http://www.time.com.

Asimov, Eric. "Satan or Savior: Setting the Grape Standard." *New York Times*, October 11, 2006. http://www.nytimes.com.

Aspe Armella, Pedro, Rudiger Dornbusch, and Maurice Obstfeld, eds. *Financial Policies and the World Capital Market: The Problem of Latin American Countries*. Chicago: University of Chicago Press, 1983.

*An Authentic Narrative of the Proceedings of the Expedition under the Command of Brigadier-Gen. Craufurd, until Its Arrival at Monte Video; with an Account of the Operations against Buenos Ayres under the Command of Lieut.-Gen. White-locke*. London: G. E. Miles, 1808.

Aveling, Nick. "Fuzion Wine Goes Viral." *Toronto Star*, May 10, 2009. http://www.thestar.com.

Aznarez, Juan. "Empresarios famosos de Francia construyen bodegas en Mendoza." *La Nación*, February 2, 2001. http://www.lanacion.com.ar.

Azpiazu, Daniel, and Eduardo Basualdo. *El complejo vitivinícola argentino en los noventa: Potencialidades y estricciones*. Santiago, Chile: Comision Economica para America Latina y el Caribe (CEPAL), 2000.

Banerjee, Abhijit, Esther Duflo, Gilles Postel-Vinay, and Timothy Watts. *Long Run Health Impacts of Income Shocks: Wine and Phylloxera in 19th Century France*. NBER Working Paper, no. W12895. Cambridge, Mass.: National Bureau of Economic Research, 2007.

Barrio de Villanueva, Patricia. "En busca del vino genuino: Origen y consecuencias de la Ley Nacional de Vinos de 1904." *Mundo agrario* 8, no. 15 (August/December 2007). http://www.scielo.org.ar.

Beezley, William H. "La senda del Malbec: La cepa emblemática de Argentina." *Universum* 20, no. 2 (2005): 288–297. http://www.scielo.cl.

Bianchi, Alejandro. "Un fondo de inversión compró las bodegas Santa Silvia y Graffigna." *La Nación*, June 11, 1999. http://www.lanacion.com.ar.

Bigongiari, Diego. *Viñas, bodegas y vinos de América del Sur*. Buenos Aires: Austral Spectator, 2005.

Bonné, Jon. "Uncorked: Argentine Vintners Make Wine a Family Affair." *San Francisco Chronicle*, January 4, 2008. http://www.sfgate.com.

Briley, Harold. "Book Review: Official History of Falklands Conflict." *Merco-Press*, June 29, 2005. http://en.mercopress.com.

Brown, Corie. "Putting Place in a Glass." *Los Angeles Times*, January 8, 2006. http://www.latimes.com.

Busaniche, José Luis. *San Martín visto por sus contemporáneos*. Buenos Aires: Instituto Nacional Sanmartiniano, 1995.

Bustos Herrera, Gabriel. "Caso Greco: De don Héctor a Felisa." *Los Andes*, March 25, 2007. http://www.losandes.com.ar.

Bustos Herrera, Gabriel. "El estigma de los feudos." *Los Andes*, December 13, 2009. http://www.losandes.com.ar.

Caddick-Adams, Peter. "Britain's 'Forgotten' Invasion of Argentina." *BBC News*, August 10, 2006. http://news.bbc.co.uk.

Campbell, Christy. *The Botanist and the Vintner: How Wine Was Saved for the World*. Chapel Hill, NC: Algonquin Books, 2005.

Campbell, Jodi. "Charles II (Spain) (1661–1700)." *Encyclopedia.com*, 2004. http://www.encyclopedia.com.

Castlereagh, Robert Stewart, and Charles Vane, ed. *Correspondence, Despatches, and Other Papers of Viscount Castlereagh, Second Marquess of Londonderry*, vol. 7. London: William Shoberl, 1851.

Catena, Laura. *Vino argentino: An Insider's Guide to the Wines and Wine Country of Argentina*. San Francisco: Chronicle Press, 2010.

"El CEMA, academia y política." *La Nación*, February 16, 1997. http://www.lanacion.com.ar.

Čermák, Vladimír, and Jan Kozák. *The Illustrated History of Natural Disasters*. New York: Springer, 2010.

Choren, Gustavo. *El gran libro del Malbec argentino*. Buenos Aires: Planeta, 2003.

Chrabolowsky, Enrique. "La Leyenda." *Cusine & Vins*, May 2008. http://www.cuisine.com.ar.

Collado, Patricia A. "Desarrollo vitivinícola en Mendoza—Argentina. Apuntes sobre su origen." *Trabajo y sociedad* 7, no. 8 (Fall 2006).

Colman, Tyler. "The Sales Potential of Argentine Wine." *Wine Business Monthly*, January 16, 2007. http://www.winebusiness.com.

Coria López, Luis Alberto, and Lidia Fortín de Iñones. *El boom vitivinícola Mendocino (1883–1912) y la acción del estado*. Jornadas de ciencias económicas. Mendoza: Universidad Nacional de Cuyo/Facultad de Ciencias Económicas, 1994, 328.

Correa, Rubén. "La anónima se endeuda con ON." *La Nación*, April 14, 1996. http://www.lanacion.com.ar.

Correas, Edmundo, Enrique Díaz Araujo, J. Draghi Lucero, and Dardo Olguín, eds. "La vitivinicultura Argentina." *Todo es historia* 51, suppl. no. 40 (July 1971): 4–31.

Correas, Jaime. *Historias de familias.* Mendoza: Diario UNO, 1997.

"Creció 68% el turismo en las bodegas de Mendoza." *Los Andes,* December 16, 2010. http://www.losandes.com.ar.

Criscenti, Joseph T., ed. *Sarmiento and His Argentina.* Boulder, Colo.: Lynne Rienner Publishers, 1993.

Crosariol, Beppi. "Run, Don't Walk, to Taste This under-$8 Treasure." *Globe and Mail,* August 9, 2008. http://www.theglobeandmail.com.

Cuculiansky, Sabrina. "El pionero." *La Nación,* June 3, 2007. http://www.lanacion.com.ar.

Darwin, Charles. *The Voyage of the Beagle.* The Five Foot Shelf of Classics, vol. 29. Edited by Charles W. Eliot. New York: Cosimo Classics, 2010.

Diaz Araujo, Edgardo. *La vitivinicultura Argentina I: Su evolución histórica y régimen jurídico desde la conquista a 1852.* Mendoza: Universidad de Mendoza/Editorial Idearium, 1989.

Diaz Araujo, Edgardo, and María José Iuvaro. *Vitivinicultura y derecho.* Buenos Aires: Editorial Dunken, 2006.

Draghi Lucero, Juan. *Los benefactores de Mendoza: Tejeda-Pouget.* Mendoza: Ediciones Culturales de Mendoza, 1991.

Echikson, William. *Noble Rot: A Bordeaux Wine Revolution.* New York: W. W. Norton, 2004.

Eloy Martínez, Tomás. *Santa Evita.* Buenos Aires: Punto de Lectura, 2007.

Eloy Martínez, Tomás. "The Woman behind the Fantasy." *Time,* January 20, 1997. http://www.time.com.

Falanga, Ángel Pedro. *Veinte años . . . un día: Grupo Greco, la otra parte de la verdad.* Mendoza: Zeta Editores, 2001.

Flynn Siler, Julia. *The House of Mondavi: The Rise and Fall of an American Wine Dynasty.* New York: Penguin, 2007.

Frank, Mitch, and Diana Macle. "Europe's Plan to Pull Up Vines Decried . . . Again." *Wine Spectator*, September 30, 2007. http://www.winespectator .com.

Frank, Robert. "Most Expensive Bottle of Wine Ever Sold at Auction." *Wall Street Journal*, October 29, 2010. http://blogs.wsj.com.

Gallardo, Darío. "Catena se expande con su cuarta bodega en Mendoza." *Los Andes*, April 2, 2001. http://www.losandes.com.ar.

"Gallo Named U.S. Importer for Catena's Alamos wines." *E&J Gallo Winery*, November 4, 2008. http://gallo.com.

Gargiulo, Julieta, and Agustín Borzi. *Il vino si fa cosi: Transferencias en la cienca de la enología y la vitivinicultura entre Italia y Mendoza*. Mendoza: Polo Rossi, 2004.

Gatti, Enrique, Pablo Lacoste, and Silvia Jardel, eds. *Resumen de "El vino del inmigrante" y "Antecedentes para la negociación en materia vitivinícola entre Argentina y la Comunidad Europea."* Mendoza: Consejo Empresario Mendocino, 2003.

Girini, Liliana. "Arquitectura e industria: La Bodega Giol hito funadmental de la vitivinicultura mendocina." Paper presented at X Seminario Iberoamericano de Vitivinicultura y Ciencias Sociales. Mendoza: Universidad Mendoza, 2007.

Godoy, María Verónica. *Los Huarpes y su cultura*. Mendoza: Tintar Editorial, 1999.

González, Roxana, et al. *La cultura de la vid y el vino*. Mendoza: Fondo Vitivinícola Mendoza, 2003. http://www.fondovitivinicola.com.ar/escuelas.

González, Soledad. "Argentina Exported More Than Chile and Had Great Impact." *WineSur*, February 1, 2011. http://www.winesur.com.

"González Videla: Añeja historia de la bodega más antigua." *Los Andes*, February 13, 2003. http://www.losandes.com.ar.

Goodman, Joshua. "Don't Cry for These Argentine Wines." *Businessweek*, October 14, 2002. http://www.businessweek.com.

Gott, Richard. "Bad Day for the Empire." *Guardian*, July 13, 2007. http:// www.guardian.co.uk.

Graham-Yooll, Andrew. *The Forgotten Colony*. Buenos Aires: LOLA [Literature of Latin America], 1999.

Grimshaw, Susie. "Malbec, the Resurrection of France's Forgotten Wine." *Guardian*, May 22, 2010. http://www.guardian.co.uk.

Harsanyi, Doina Pasca. "Reviewed Work: *The Man Who Had Been King: The American Exile of Napoleon's Brother Joseph* by Patricia Tyson Stroud." *Pennsylvania Magazine of History and Biography* 130, no. 4 (October 2006): 426–427.

Head, Francis Bond. *Rough Notes Taken during Some Rapid Journeys across the Pampas and among the Andes*. London: John Murray, 1826.

Hotz, Robert Lee. "Perhaps a Red, 4,100 B.C." *Wall Street Journal*, January 11, 2011. http://online.wsj.com.

Howe, Robert F. "The Fall of the House of Mondavi." *Business 2.0*, April 1, 2005. http://money.cnn.com.

Janofsky, Michael. "How to Be a Billionaire." *Entrepreneur Magazine*, March 2010. http://www.entrepreneur.com.

Kesmodel, Davis. "Wine Advocate Writers Spark Ethics Debate." *Wall Street Journal*, March 26, 2009. http://online.wsj.com.

Kingsbury, David. "Clos de los Siete: Michel Rolland Develops Argentine Winery." *Wine Business Monthly*, September 10, 2002. http://www.winebusiness.com.

Knap, Chris. "An O.C. Transplant's Argentine Lesson: Malbec, Yes; Mariposa, No." *Orange County Register*, September 1, 1999, early edition.

Koppel, Ken. "Country Competitive Analysis: Argentina—Malbec Exports to U.S. Rise 61 Percent in 2008." *Wine Business Monthly*, May 15, 2009. http://www.winebusiness.com.

Kramer, Matt. "The Master of Malbec." *Wine Spectator*, June 30, 2010. http://www.winespectator.com.

Kramer, Matt. "Two Worlds of Argentine Wines." *Wall Street Journal*, March 19, 2010. http://online.wsj.com.

Krauss, Clifford. "That Other Maker of Andean Wines." *New York Times*, March 10, 2001, late edition.

Labrador R., Alberto. *Desde nuestros Huarpes*. Mendoza: Editora del Este, 1999.

Lacoste, Pablo. "La cárcel y el carcelero de la mujer colonial." *Estudos Ibero-Americanos* 33, no.2 (December 2007): 7–34.

Lacoste, Pablo. *La generación del '80 en Mendoza*. Mendoza: EDIUNC (Editorial de la Universidad Nacional de Cuyo), 1995.

Lacoste, Pablo. *La Union Cívica Radical en Mendoza y en la Argentina (1890–1946)*. Mendoza: Ediciones Culturales de Mendoza, 1994.

Lacoste, Pablo. *El vino del inmigrante*. Mendoza: Consejo Empresario Mendocino, 2003.

Lacoste, Pablo. "Los 'vinos de Dios' (alegato contra la pena de muerte). Mendoza, Reino de Chile, siglo XVII." *Atenea* no. 494 (2006): 83–109.

Langewiesche, William. "The Million-Dollar Nose." *Atlantic*, July 2000. http://www.theatlantic.com.

Lechmere, Adam. "Nicolas Catena Honoured as Decanter Man of the Year." *Decanter*, September 18, 2009. http://www.decanter.com.

Llorens, Marc. "Septeto multimillonario, de Francia a los Andes argentinos." *ElMundoVino.com*, July 21, 2002. http://elmundovino.elmundo.es.

Lubow, Arthur. "A Higher Purpose." *Departures*, November/December 2007. http://www.departures.com.

Luna, Félix. *Breve historia de los argentines*. Buenos Aires: Planeta, 2005.

Luxner, Larry. "No End in Sight to Chile's Wine Export Boom." *Wines & Vines*, November 2000.

Madigan, Anthony. "Jacques Lurton: French Connection." *WBM: Australia's Wine Business Magazine*, August 2010, 16–20.

Malizia, Gabriela. "Malbec: A Risky Supply and Demand Game." *WineSur*, April 14, 2010. http://www.winesur.com.

Malizia, Gabriela. "Small Wineries Negotiate with US Importers." *WineSur*, August 11, 2010. http://www.winesur.com.

Mariani, John. "'Satan' of Grape Consulting Blends Own High-Alcohol Red Wine." *Bloomberg News*, August 31, 2010. http://www.bloomberg.com.

Mateu, Ana María, and Steve Stein, eds. *El vino y sus revoluciones: Una antología sobre el desarrollo de la industria vitivinícola argentina*. Mendoza: EDIUNC, 2008.

Matthews, Thomas. "The 1855 Bordeaux Classification." *Wine Spectator*, March 29, 2007. http://www.winespectator.com.

McInerney, Jay. "Pioneering Wine in Patagonia." *Wall Street Journal*, December 8, 2010. http://blogs.wsj.com.

McIntyre, Dave. "The Recession Claims Billington." *Dave McIntyre's Wine-Line*, May 26, 2009. http://dmwineline.typepad.com.

McIntyre, Dave. "Wine: What Is It about Argentina?" *Washington Post*, September 8, 2010. http://voices.washingtonpost.com.

McWhirter, Kathryn. "Grapevine: Kathryn McWhirter Savours This Week's Best Buys." *Independent*, November 7, 1993. http://www.independent.co.uk.

Micale, Adriana, and Jaime Correas. *Mendoza, de pura cepa*. Buenos Aires: Caviar Bleu, 2001.

"Modern Living: Judgment of Paris." *Time*, July 7, 1976. http://www.time.com.

Molesworth, James. "Argentina's Hit or Miss Year." *Wine Spectator*, December 15, 2010. http://www.winespectator.com.

Molesworth, James. "More Malbec Please." *Wine Spectator*, December 15, 2008. http://www.winespectator.com.

Molesworth, James. "Winemaker Talk: Paul Hobbs." *Wine Spectator*, November 8, 2006. http://www.winespectator.com.

*Mondovino*, directed by Jonathan Nossiter (ThinkFilm, 2004).

Montes de Oca, Aldo. "El Caso Greco." *Todo es historia* 348 (July 1996): 8–20.

Morales Guiñazu, Fernando. *Primitivos habitantes de Mendoza*. Mendoza: Best Hermanos, 1938.

Morán, Rafael. "Condenaron a ocho años a José Greco." *Clarín*, September 27, 1997. http://edant.clarin.com.

Morelli, Liliana. "Vinificar sigue siendo un arte." *Noticias* no. 1580, April 5, 2007. http://www.revista-noticias.com.ar.

Mount, Ian. "Money on the Vine." *Wall Street Journal*, March 29, 2008. http://online.wsj.com.

Mount, Ian. "U.S. Wine-Makers Flock to Argentina." *Fortune Small Business*, September 7, 2007. http://money.cnn.com.

Mustacich, Suzanne. "Amid Wine Boom, Chinese Buy Up Bordeaux Chateaux." *Agence France-Presse*, March 2, 2011. http://www.france24.com.

"The Myth of the Family Winery." *Marin Institute*, December 2009. http://www.marininstitute.org.

"La nieta de Giol que descubrió Mendoza." *Diario UNO*, November 17, 2009. http://www.diariouno.com.ar.

Nimo, Mercedes. *Análisis de la cadena de vinos*. Buenos Aires: Secretaria de Agricultura, Ganaderia, Pesca y Alimentacion, 2003. http://www.alimentosargentinos.gov.ar.

O'Neill, Molly. "Maynard Amerine, 87, California Wine Expert." *New York Times*, March 13, 1998. http://www.nytimes.com.

P. "Charles III (Spain) (1716–1788; Ruled 1759–1788)." *Encyclopedia.com*, 2004. http://www.encyclopedia.com.

Pachner, Joanna. "The Man Who Sparked the Fuzion Explosion." *Globe and Mail*, April 26, 2010. http://www.theglobeandmail.com.

Parker, Robert, Jr. "Parker Predicts the Future." *Food & Wine*, October 2004. http://www.foodandwine.com.

Parker, Robert, Jr. "Wine Personalities of the Year 2005: Alfredo Bartholo-maus, Importer, Billington Imports." *Wine Spectator*, December 26, 2005.

Pérez Ferrando, Gladys, and Jorge Tartarini. *El estilo López*. Buenos Aires: Bodegas López, 2005.

"Phylloxera Ravages Italy." *New York Times*, November 8, 1895. http://www.nytimes.com.

Pigna, Felipe. "José de San Martín." *El historiador*, accessed March 31, 2011. http://www.elhistoriador.com.ar.

Pigna, Felipe. *Los mitos de la historia Argentina 2*. Buenos Aires: Planeta, 2004.

Pigna, Felipe. *Los mitos de la historia Argentina 3*. Buenos Aires: Planeta, 2006.

Ponte, Jorge Ricardo. *Mendoza, aquella ciudad de barro. Historia de una ciudad andina desde el siglo XVI hasta nuestros días*. Mendoza: Municipalidad de la Ciudad de Mendoza, 1987.

Precilla, Maricel E. "Mendoza Mountain High." *Saveur*, October 2005, 92–104.

Pregler, Bill. "2006 Barrel and Oak Report." *Wine Business Monthly*, December 15, 2006. http://www.winebusiness.com.

Prial, Frank. "Bordeaux Family Values." *New York Times*, November 6, 2005. http://www.nytimes.com.

Queyrat, Enrique. *Los buenos vinos argentinos*. Buenos Aires: Librería Hachette, 1974.

Quiroga, Annabella. "Vinos nacidos en Mendoza, pero con un toque francés." *Clarín*, March 19, 2002. http://edant.clarin.com.

"Record High 2010 Wine Shipments Make U.S. the World's Largest Wine-Consuming Nation." *Wine Institute*, March 15, 2011. http://www .wineinstitute.org.

Reina Rutini, Rodolfo. *Conferencia pronunciada por el Dr. Rodolfo Reina Rutini en ocasión de ser incorporado como Miembro de Número de la Junta de Estudios Históricos de Mendoza*. Mendoza: Junta de Estudios Históricos de Mendoza, 1985.

Richard-Jorba, Rodolfo. "¿Echar raíces o hacer la América? Un panorama de la inmigración europea hacia la región vitivinícola argentina y algunos itinerarios económicos en la provincia de Mendoza, 1850–1914." *Amérique Latine Histoire et Mémoire. Les Cahiers ALHIM*, March 4, 2005. http:// alhim.revues.org.

Richard Jorba, Rodolfo. "Los empresarios y la construcción de la vitivinicultura capitalista en la provincia de Mendoza (Argentina), 18502006." *Scripta Nova* 9, no. 271 (August 15, 2008). http://www.ub.edu.

Richard-Jorba, Rodolfo. *Formación, crisis y reorientaciones de la vitivinicultura en Mendoza y San Juan, 1870–2000. Aportes para el estudio del sector en la Argentina*. Boletín Geográfico, no. 28. Neuquén, Argentina: Departamento de Geografía, Facultad de Humanidades, Universidad Nacional de Comahue, 2006.

Richard Jorba, Rodolfo. "Hacia el desarrollo capitalista en la provincia de Mendoza. Evolución de los sistemas explotación del viñedo entre 1870–1900," *Anales de la Sociedad Científica Argentina* 224, no. 2 (1994): 1–34.

Richard-Jorba, Rodolfo. "El mundo del trabajo vitivinícola en Mendoza (Argentina) durante la modernización capitalista, 1880–1914." *Mundo agrario* 9, no. 18 (2009). http://www.scielo.org.ar.

Richard Jorba, Rodolfo. *Poder, economía y espacio en Mendoza 1850–1900. Del comercio ganadero a la industria vitivinícola*. Mendoza: Editorial de la Facultad de Filosofía y Letras de la Universidad Nacional de Cuyo, 1998.

Robinson, Jancis. "Donald Hess—the Man Who Beat Allied-Domecq." *JancisRobinson.com*, November 7, 2003. http://www.jancisrobinson.com.

Robinson, Jancis, ed. *The Oxford Companion to Wine*. New York: Oxford University Press, 2006.

Romano, Aníbal Mario. "Mendoza y el terremoto de 1861." *Los Andes*, March 25, 2010. http://www.losandes.com.ar.

Rose, Anthony. "Interview with Nicolas Catena, Decanter Man of the Year 2009." *Decanter*, March 27, 2009. http://www.decanter.com.

Rosen, Maggie. "Decanter Man of the Year 2009: Nicolás Catena." *Decanter*, February 24, 2009. http://www.decanter.com.

Saieg, Laura. "El top 10 de las marcas más vendidas." *Area del vino*, December 29, 2010. http://www.areadelvino.com.

Sainz, Alfredo. "Alertan sobre la pérdida de competitividad de las bodegas." *La Nación*, April 13, 2011. http://www.lanacion.com.ar.

Santos Martínez, Pedro. *Historia de Mendoza*. Buenos Aires: Editorial Plus Ultra, 1979.

Santos Martínez, Pedro, ed. *Homenaje al Dr. Edmundo Correas*. Mendoza: Ediciones Culturales de Mendoza, Junta de Estudios Históricos de Mendoza, 1994.

Sarmiento, Domingo Faustino. *Recollections of a Provincial Past* [*Recuerdos de provincia*]. Translated by Elizabeth Garrels and Asa Zatz. New York: Oxford University Press, 2005.

Sax, David. "Kendall-Jackson Pulls Out of Argentina." *Wine Spectator*, December 2, 2003. http://static.winespectator.com.

Scalvini, Jorge M. *Historia de Mendoza*. Mendoza: Editorial Spadoni, 1965.

Schachner, Michael. "Argentina Surpasses Chile in U.S. Exports." *Wine Enthusiast Magazine*, July 28, 2010. http://www.winemag.com.

Schávelzon, Daniel. *Historia de un terremoto: Mendoza, 1861*. Buenos Aires: De Los Cuatro Vientos Editorial, 2007.

Schumacher, Edward. "Wine Industry Flourishes in Argentina." *New York Times*, February 15, 1984. http://www.nytimes.com.

Shapin, Steven. "Hedonistic Fruit Bombs." *London Review of Books*, February 3, 2005. http://www.lrb.co.uk.

Shriver, Jerry. "Argentina Grows Famous through the Grapevine: The World's Oenophiles Develop a Taste for Wines from Way South." *USA Today*, March 24, 2000, final edition.

Shriver, Jerry. "Heady Times at Argentina's High-Altitude Vineyards." *USA Today*, March 28, 2008. http://www.usatoday.com.

Silanes, Raúl, Sergio Terrera, and Gustavo Vitale. *Cesar Cipolletti 1843–1908*. Mendoza: Irrigación Edita, 2007.

Smith, Jeremy. "Winemakers Pour Cold Water on EU 'Wine Lake' Plan." *Reuters*, July 4, 2007. http://www.reuters.com.

"Socma Sells Shares in Galicia Advent." *SABI (South American Business Information)*, November 28, 2001.

Stein, Steve. *Our Saviors May Not Speak Spanish: Changing Markets and Strategies in Argentina's Wine Revolution, 1990–2008*. AAWE Working Paper, no. 21. New York: American Association of Wine Economists, 2008.

Steinberger, Mike. "The Tastemaker." *Slate*, July 30, 2004. http://www.slate.com.

Stimmell, Gord. "Fuzion Frenzy Uncorked." *Toronto Star*, January 24, 2009. http://www.thestar.com.

Stockley, Tom. "Wines from Around the World." *Seattle Times*, January 13, 1993. http://www.seattletimes.com.

Stockley, Tom. "Hot For '97: The Full Flavors of Argentina." *Seattle Times*, December 25, 1996. http://www.seattletimes.com.

Suárez, Julio, ed. "El terremoto de Mendoza." *Revista de la Junta de Estudios Históricos* 10 (1938): 121–161.

Taber, George M. *Judgment of Paris: California vs. France and the Historic 1976 Paris Tasting That Revolutionized Wine*. New York: Scribner, 2006.

Tasker, Fred. "Woman Winemaker Warms to Argentina." *Miami Herald*, September 3, 1998.

*La viti-vinicultura Argentina en 1910*. Buenos Aires: Centro Viti-Vinícola Nacional, 1910.

Wade, Nicholas. "Lack of Sex among Grapes Tangles a Family Vine." *New York Times*, January 24, 2011. http://www.nytimes.com.

Walker, Larry. "Argentine Wines Are Showing a New Look." *Wines & Vines*, June 2004. http://findarticles.com.

Walker, Larry. "Enologist Lynda Hanson's Vineyards in Argentina." *Wines & Vines* 80 (September 1, 1999): 46.

Wesley, Nathan. "Stolichnaya Owner Buys Majority Share in Achával-Ferrer." *Wine Spectator*, April 15, 2011. http://www.winespectator.com.

Whitley, Robert. "Spunky Winemaker Looks Forward to Argentine Task." *San Diego Union-Tribune*, July 2, 1997.

Winn, Peter. *Americas: The Changing Face of Latin America and the Caribbean*. Berkeley: University of California Press, 2006.

Zlotogwiazda, Marcelo. "Qué es el caso Greco." *Pagina/12*, March 4, 2007. http://www.pagina12.com.ar.

# INDEX

Page numbers in *italics* refer to illustrations.

Index

Index

Index

2